THE KENYAN CUT FLOWER INDUSTRY AND GLOBAL MARKET DYNAMICS

FUTURE RURAL AFRICA

Series Editors
Michael Bollig and Detlef Müller-Mahn

In recent years, there has been a social-ecological transformation in land use in Africa, brought about by climate change and the globalisation of natural resource management and rural landscapes, such that rural Africa has become a laboratory of global future-making. This new series offers a rich and valuable perspective on the processes and practices that produce and critically reflect upon visions of the future on the continent. Volumes within the series will address social-ecological, cultural, and economic development in sub-Saharan Africa, and their relation to climate change, sustainability, and migration. Showcasing cutting-edge research into societal change and the reverberations of global dynamics playing out in sub-Saharan Africa, the series will provide an essential resource for an interdisciplinary scholarly audience in areas such as geography, anthropology, history, political science, natural science, and African studies as well as political planners, governmental and non-governmental organisations.

Published in association with the University of Bonn and Cologne's Collaborative Research Centre 'Future Rural Africa', funded by the German Research Council (DFG), the series will be mainly monographs, but we also welcome occasional edited volumes that enable a continent-wide, multi-disciplinary approach – see https://boydellandbrewer.com/future-rural-africa.

Please contact the Series Editors with an outline or download the proposal form at www.jamescurrey.com.

Prof. Dr. Michael Bollig, University of Cologne:
michael.bollig@uni-koeln.de

Prof. Dr. Detlef Müller-Mahn, University of Bonn:
mueller-mahn@uni-bonn.de

The Kenyan Cut Flower Industry and Global Market Dynamics

Andreas Gemählich

JAMES CURREY

Published in association with
Future Rural Africa

First published 2022
James Currey

ISBN 978 1 84701 295 1

James Currey is an imprint of Boydell & Brewer Ltd
PO Box 9, Woodbridge, Suffolk IP12 3DF, UK
and of Boydell & Brewer Inc.
668 Mt Hope Avenue, Rochester, NY 14620-2731 (US)
website: www.boydellandbrewer.com

A CIP catalogue record for this book is available
from the British Library

The publisher has no responsibility for the continued existence or accuracy
of URLs for external or third-party internet websites referred to in this book,
and does not guarantee that any content on such websites is, or will remain,
accurate or appropriate

This publication is printed on acid-free paper

CONTENTS

ILLUSTRATIONS

Map

Figures

Tables

Full credit details are provided in the captions to the illustrations in the text. The author and publisher are grateful to all the institutions and individuals for permission to reproduce the materials to which they hold copyright. Every effort has been made to trace the copyright holders; apologies are offered for any omission, and the publisher will be pleased to add any necessary acknowledgement in subsequent editions.

ABBREVIATIONS

ANT	Actor-Network Theory
AR	Archival Report
b2b	business-to-business
b2c	business-to-customer
CBA	Collective Bargaining Agreement
CSR	Corporate Social Responsibility
EAC	East African Community
EPA	Economic Partnership Agreement
EU	European Union
FBP	Flower Business Park
GCC	global commodity chain
GMO	genetically modified organism
GPN	global production network
GVC	global value chain
IV	Interview
KEPHIS	Kenya Plant Health Inspectorate Service
KFC	Kenya Flower Council
KNBS	Kenya National Bureau of Statistics
LaNaWRUA	Lake Naivasha Water Resource Users Association
LDC	Least Developed Country
LNRA	Lake Naivasha Riparian Association
LNGG	Lake Naivasha Growers Group
m.a.s.l.	Meters above sea level
MPS	Milieu Project Sierteelt
NGO	non-governmental organisation
OB	Observation

SES	social-ecological system
STA	sociotechnical agencement
WAP	Water Allocation Plan
WRMA	Water Resource Management Authority
WRUA	Water Resource Users Associations

ACKNOWLEDGEMENTS

I would like to thank the CRC 'Future Rural Africa' and the Deutsche Forschungsgemeinschaft (DFG) for the funding that supported the empirical fieldwork and the publication of this book. I would like to thank the former and current members of the Development Geography Group and especially Detlef Müller-Mahn for creating a stimulating environment during the writing of this book.

Moreover, I want to express my gratitude to all the people involved in my research in Kenya and the Netherlands. Thanks to my research assistants Evans, Erick and Bob, to all flower farm workers and managers, to all the stakeholders and other people around Lake Naivasha who generously shared their time with me.

I would like to thank all my friends and colleagues who have helped me with developing the argumentation of this book, especially Gerda Kuiper and Florian Weisser. I would like to thank my family for their lifelong support that has led me to where I am now. And finally, I thank Nina Knops, for her tremendous support during the finalisation of this project.

ROSE TERMINOLOGY

Flower Bud
Cut stage refers to
opening of flower
bud (inter alia)

Head
size

*Single cut flowers
are referred to as
stems*

Stem length
Small   <35   cm
Medium =35-50 cm
Large   >50   cm

1

Introduction

Roses, you dazzling ones,
Balsam you're sending us,
Floating and trembling,
Secretly quickening,
Branches inspiring us,
Buds sweetly firing us,
Hasten to bloom!
Crimson and green, here
Springtime assume!
Carry the sleeper
To Paradise' room.

Johann Wolfgang von Goethe
Faust, Part II (1832), Act V, Scene VI, 'Choir of Angels'

Roses are extolled by the choir of angels in Goethe's *Faust*. One hundred seventy years later, they are said to be the reason for apocalypse in Mark Seal's biography on environmentalist Joan Root. He depicts their production at Lake Naivasha as 'resulting in slums, squalor, crime' (Seal 2010, iv). Roses elicit controversial accounts not only in prose and documentaries. These accounts also represent the two faces of roses in their biographies and geographies. In Europe, every day millions of them are bought for cheap prices as a gift or as decoration. In Kenya, every day millions of them are produced under disputed social and environmental conditions. Over the last 40 years, cut flowers have become one of the many agricultural commodities whose production has shifted from the Global North to the Global South. In the countries of the Global South, roses have brought foreign currencies and created employment. At the same time, low wages and the exploitation of nature are the backbones of this upswing. Lake Naivasha,[1] just 80 km

---

[1]   In this book, the term 'Lake Naivasha' refers to the lake itself and the surrounding area, if not stated otherwise. The delineation of this area will be discussed later (see Chapter 8).

north-west of the Kenyan capital Nairobi, is one of the new centres of cut flower production. Since its beginnings in the 1970s, flower farms have spread along its shores and created one of the most productive agro-industrial clusters in Eastern Africa. Over the last 20 years, flowers have also become one of the many agricultural commodities that are sold by corporate retail chains in Europe. Many supermarkets offer ready-made bouquets of roses for less than five Euros in their entrance areas.

This book aims to show how these two processes – the shift of cut flower production to equatorial countries and the shift of cut flower sales to supermarkets – relate to each other. It will explore how the entry of European retail chains into the market links to both its expansion and the creation of new dynamics within it, as well as to ensuing crises and conflicts in the cut flower industry at Lake Naivasha. It will present the Kenyan cut flower industry as a sometimes typical and sometimes extraordinary case of the globalisation of agricultural production and trade, and the centralisation of global retail. Finally, its purpose is to scrutinise linear and unidirectional representations of the relation between global cut flower market dynamics and local consequences in Naivasha.

Lake Naivasha's contested cut flower industry

The ongoing expansion of the capitalist 'world system' (Wallerstein 1974) results in a sharp rise in global economic entanglements. Between 1990 and 2020, the volume of global trade flows grew from US $ 3.5 trillion to over US $ 17 trillion.[2] New linkages have not only been forged between countries of the Global North but also incorporate more and more countries of the Global South. Developing countries and former 'peripheries' of global capitalism (Hopkins, Wallerstein 1977) have become integrated into commodity and capital circuits. To a large extent, this integration is based on agricultural export products. The new global agriculture of the 21st century is dominated by corporate actors. The centralisation of capital in the retail sector and the merging of production, trade, and retail in transnational conglomerates have led to an oligopolisation of control over production and consumption (Lawrence, Burch 2007, 6), or, as McMichael calls it, a 'corporate food regime' (McMichael 2009). Although not a food commodity, the globalisation of cut flower production and trade can be situated within these debates. Aimed at European export markets and previously unknown to domestic culture and agriculture, cut flowers were introduced to Kenya in the 1960s.

---

[2]   According to the World Trade Organisation data portal, see https://data.wto.org.

Lake Naivasha has been the centre of production since the first days of the Kenyan cut flower industry. The introduction of export-oriented, large-scale floriculture has had enormous consequences for the social-ecological system around the lake. In 1985, only a few farms at South Lake had been established. Karagita, today the main workers' settlement, consisted only of a few houses and Naivasha Town was a rather small rural town. Today, the South Lake farms cover almost all of the Lake's vicinity. More farms have been established at North Lake. A third flower farm cluster, the Flower Business Park, is growing north of Naivasha Town. Almost 40,000 people are living in Karagita. Within just 40 years, Lake Naivasha has turned from a scarcely populated rural area into a convergence zone for labour migrants, foreign agribusiness investors, and government institutions, which compete with wildlife conservancies, tourist operators, and indigenous Masai pastoralists.

These dynamics have already been earning attention in scientific literature for more than two decades. The research foci ranged from employment and workers' rights (Hale, Opondo 2005; Gibbon, Riisgaard 2014), and the implementation and efficiency of standards (Opondo 2006; Riisgaard 2007, 2009a, 2009b, 2010, 2011), to coordination and governance in the value chain between Kenya and the United Kingdom (UK) (Hughes 2000; Hughes 2001; Tallontire et al. 2011) and the moral dimensions of Fairtrade flower production and consumption (Dolan 2007). These studies drew attention especially to three topics. Firstly, the social and environmental effects of cut flower production in Kenya were problematised (Becht 2007; Kimani et al. 2012; Mekonnen et al. 2012). In the late 1990s and early 2000s, the flower farms at Lake Naivasha were linked closely to the pollution of lake water, its demise caused by water abstraction through irrigation pumps, and the excessive use of pesticides. The spraying of these pesticides without the necessary protective gear put exploitive labour relations into the spotlight, along with accounts of poverty wages, sexual harassment, and unpaid extra hours (Hale, Opondo 2005). Secondly, new governance patterns within the cut flower value chain were observed. With the entry of retail chains into the market in the 1990s, the cut flower industry shifted towards a buyer-driven value chain, dominated by big European supermarkets (Hughes 2000; Tallontire et al. 2011). And thirdly, certification schemes and standards were discussed as means to regulate the cut flower industry, to diminish harmful social and environmental effects, and also as a tool to exert control over producers (Hughes 2001; Riisgaard 2007, 2009a).

Most recently, two anthropological accounts of the cut flower industry at Lake Naivasha have been published. In some detail, Kuiper (2019) investigates labour relations on the flower farms and their interdependence with social life around the lake. I conducted my research together with her, so this book will complement her study from a global and more economic perspective.

In another study, Styles (2019) explores the situation of Lake Naivasha both during and right after the post-election violence of 2008. Her analysis puts actors in the spotlight who are part of the cut flower industry or linked to it. From a predominantly local point of view, she discusses farm managers', civil servants', or labour advocates' perspectives on Lake Naivasha and the floriculture's influence on its development. Yet, the book says little about the internal reorganisation of the cut flower industry or its linkages to global markets, and therefore only sparsely explores the interrelation between global and local dynamics. These lacunae have rather been met by studies investigating the links between the South and North American cut flower industry (see e.g., Ziegler 2007). However, the differences between the American and the European-African case are fundamental. Today, the Ecuadorian and Colombian cut flower industries are focused on mid- to high-value cut flowers, and the industrialised conditions on display in those regions are far removed from those to be found among Kenyan (and also Ethiopian) flower growers.

This book therefore focuses on the interrelation between global and local dynamics in the European-African cut flower industry. It aims to contribute to the wider question of the ways in which local social-ecological systems relate to the development of global (agro-)industries and to the rise of corporate retailers. In previous accounts, the role of Lake Naivasha as a *place* of the cut flower industry has not been scrutinised. The Lake Naivasha cut flower industry has mainly been examined as a part of the national agro-industry. So, the focus has rarely been put on the local or even the farm level (see Hughes 2000; Hughes 2001; Gibbon, Riisgaard 2014). This book takes social-ecological systems (SES), defined as complex systems of multiple integrated ecological, social, and cultural subsystems with reciprocal feedback, interdependence, and self-organisation (Anderies et al. 2004, 3) as a starting point to analyse interdependencies between global linkages and local conditions. The lack of regard for the notion of place in the global cut flower industry also concerns the biggest flower trade hub: despite its importance in the global flower trade, the role of the Dutch cut flower trade hub remains largely unexplored in previous studies.

Recent dynamics in the cut flower industry call for a new assessment of the Lake Naivasha cut flower industry that explicitly takes into account the role of places of production and trade. These new dynamics can be traced back to the recent development that supermarkets have become the most important outlet for Kenyan cut flowers. New patterns of production, trade, and consumption have emerged over the past 20 years, but their effects have only become fully visible since 2010.

Recent dynamics in the cut flower industry

To understand the dynamic processes at play in the Lake Naivasha area, a short look at the basic structures and newly emerging dynamics within the cut flower industry over the last few years is helpful.

After roses became a mass product in Europe and the US in the second half of the 20th century, their production was shifted to equatorial countries. Today, Colombia, Kenya, Ecuador, and Ethiopia dominate the global cut flower export statistics together with the Netherlands. As a result, the amount of global flower exports has leaped from one billion to US $ 8.5 billion within 30 years between 1988 and 2020.[3] Even the global Covid-19 pandemic starting in 2020 did not significantly reduce flower exports. Yet, it is not only cut flower production that has shifted, but also patterns of consumption. The cut flower market channels can be divided into specialised retailers – mostly traditional florists – and unspecialised retailers composed of supermarkets, fuel stations, kiosks, etc. In the US, supermarkets started to establish floral departments in their stores in the 1970s (Ziegler 2007, 145). In Europe, British supermarkets were the first to start selling cut flowers from Kenya in the 1980s and rapidly increased their share in the UK cut flower market from 4% to 30% from 1986 to 1995 (Hughes 2000, 183). Since then, unspecialised retail chains from all over Europe have joined the cut flower market. The tendencies are identical all across the EU: supermarkets have increased their share substantially, while florists' sales have dropped. These dynamics have also shifted the importance of the supplying nations. South American flowers, famous among European buyers mainly for their quality, have lost significant market share to East African growers, who mainly target customers at large retail chains.

This trend has been fuelled massively by the Covid-19 pandemic. While florist shops were partially and temporarily closed during lockdowns all over Europe, supermarkets were open throughout. Thus, they expanded their sales significantly all over Europe. For instance, retail chains and discounters increased their market share from 38% to 43% within just one year from 2019 to 2020 in Germany (Quetsch 2021, 10) – which has long been considered a stronghold of traditional florists. So called 'one-stop' shopping became more and more popular among consumers, who got used to buying goods other than food in supermarkets.

---

[3] According to data from the International Trade Centre (www.intracen.org) and UN-Comtrade (https://comtrade.un.org).

The market channels differ greatly in how they sell what cut flowers to whom and at what prices, as well as how they source those flowers. Retail chains offer standardised bouquets of small to medium sized flowers that are predominantly roses of uniform quality. A large portion of these flowers are certified with a sustainability or fair-trade label, although the prices in this market segment are very low, especially in comparison to the specialised retail chain.

Most retailers in the specialised channel rely on wholesalers and their links to the traditional Dutch flower auctions. Corporate retail chains prefer to source flowers directly from wholesalers or even growers on a contractual basis, bypassing the auctions. These developments are also mirrored in the dynamics at play in the global centre of the flower trade: the Dutch trade hub. For almost a century, flower auctions had been the most important trade platforms within the Netherlands. Yet, since 2015, 'direct sales' have outnumbered auction sales (FloraHolland 2015a).

These dynamics are highly relevant for the Kenyan agro-industry, as it is largely dependent on the European cut flower market. Since their first days, Kenyan flower farms have exclusively grown their products for export markets. Europe is and has always been the most important destination for these exports, and today 70% of cut flowers from Kenya are sold to the EU. The biggest import country is the Netherlands with a share of over 60%.[4] As such, dynamics in the global cut flower market are, to a great extent, mediated to the entire EU region through the Dutch trade networks. The Dutch flower hub and its dynamics, therefore, require close attention when investigating the reorganisation of the Lake Naivasha cut flower industry.

Similarly, the situation at Lake Naivasha cannot be fully grasped without considering the role of its cut flower industry for Kenya's national economy. Agricultural export products, such as coffee, tea, and sugar, are one of the backbones of Kenya's economy. Even among those, cut flowers stand out: in 2017, they accounted for 13.8% of Kenya's exports, nearly 1% of its gross domestic product, and they are the second biggest export product after tea (KNBS 2018). The Kenyan economy relies on these exports to generate income in foreign currencies, such as the US-Dollar (US $) and the Euro (€). This prominent role influences policy measures and public discourse in Kenya, which often revolves around narratives of the industry as an economic powerhouse and a creator of employment and wealth. The importance of the floriculture industry has been steadily growing for the last 20 years, since cut flower exports have increased almost twentyfold from € 45 million in 1997

---

[4]   According to export data from the Kenya Flower Council shared with the author (unpublished).

to € 845 million in 2020.[5] This raises the question of how this increase is linked to market dynamics and how this translates to everyday operations in the production areas across Kenya. At Lake Naivasha, the ongoing boom of cut flower exports is mirrored in a rise in the number of farms, the cultivated area, and employees. Today, a fluctuating number of 50 to 60 farms grow cut flowers with the help of 40,000 employees on 2,000 hectare (ha) and account for 70% of Kenya's produce. But according to environmentalists, and both Kenyan and international media, this expansion came at a price: they claim that due to the residue of pesticides, land sealing by greenhouses, and the water abstraction by irrigation systems, 'Lake Naivasha is dying' (Riungu 2009). Competition over scarce resources has been fuelled by the ongoing expansion of flower farms. Together with employment numbers, the general population has also grown massively over the past decades. In 2009, the Lake Naivasha basin was home to approximately 380,000 people, almost four times as many as 20 years before (KNBS 2010). Migrants from other Kenyan provinces seeking jobs in the cut flower industry and their families account for most of the population growth. The numerous informal settlements around the lake have absorbed this growth without sufficient adjustments to their sanitary, educational, or transport infrastructure.

Given the knock-on effects the entry of supermarkets into the flower market has had, the constantly growing export of cut flowers in general, and an increasingly unstable social-ecological system growing up around it, Lake Naivasha seems to be a setting prone to conflict, collapse, and reorganisation.

Objectives of the book

In this book I want to get to the core of this contested setting. I will examine the relationship between the global cut flower market and the Lake Naivasha cut flower industry and its surrounding social-ecological system. Heterogeneous consumer behaviour, new market channels, and a globally spread production and trade system show that *the* cut flower market is actually far from being a single homogenous driving force in the flower industry. Due to its heterogeneity, the market itself needs to be addressed conceptually and its various dynamics have to be considered as part of the inquiry and within the associated research questions. The link between markets and producers has been conceptualised as Global Commodity Chains (GCCs) and Global Value Chains (GVCs). Yet, these chain-approaches often imply a relationship between global markets and local producers based on what Hart has called the

---

[5] According to export data from the Kenya Flower Council shared with the author (unpublished).

'impact model' (2004, 91). Here 'inexorable forces of global capitalism bear down, albeit unevenly, on passive "locals"' (Hart 2004, 91). As Hart remarks, and as 'the various different dynamics at play within the European market' and its dependency on imports from equatorial countries demonstrates, an investigation of a global agro-industry should rather 'focus on processes of interconnection and mutual constitution, … encouraging attention … to interrelations, constitutive processes, and forms of power – as well as to slippages, openings and contradictions' (Hart 2004, 97). A focus on marketisation, inspired by Actor-Network Theory, brings the market itself into question and thus seems to be more adequate for this task.

Based on these ideas and any and all potentially relevant dynamics, this book is an attempt to answer the question: how do dynamics in the Lake Naivasha cut flower industry and its surrounding social-ecological system relate to the entry and growing dominance of European retail chains in cut flower sales? On the one hand, this implies the broader questioning of the ways in which retail chains are driving dynamics in the Lake Naivasha cut flower industry and its surrounding social-ecological system. On the other, it also embraces an investigation in the opposite direction, inquiring to what extent the retailers' rising importance is based on Lake Naivasha's cut flower industry and its social-ecological system?

In this book, I argue that the market entry of big European retail chains has led to a reorganisation of the way cut flowers are consumed, traded, and produced. On the one hand, this reorganisation is based on the social-ecological environment of the cut flower industry at Lake Naivasha and, on the other hand, it is profoundly changing that environment.

By doing so, I hope to contribute conceptually to debates on the usefulness of Global Commodity Chain (GCC), Global Value Chain (GVC), and Global Production Network (GPN) approaches. I critically engage with these approaches and show the extent to which they provide helpful insights but are insufficient in themselves to explain the complex dynamics of the cut flower industry. By also applying a marketisation perspective, I show how the role of place in economic globalisation can be framed beyond the top-down, linear logic of chain-approaches. In order to do so, I cross epistemological boundaries between economy, ecology, and politics, and show that current dynamics in the cut flower industry are not limited to companies or people directly involved in it, but that they exceed the epistemological boundary of 'the economic'. Thus, I argue that the social-ecological system of Lake Naivasha is not only an 'add-on' to economic relations, but rather a crucial part of them.

Using this case study of cut flowers also allows me to show how the global rise of corporate retailers affects (agro-)industries. Until now, the growing importance of international supermarket chains has mainly been described with regard to the production, trade, and consumption of food as a part of the food regime debate (Bernstein 2016). However, the 'branching out' (Lawrence, Burch 2007, 5) of supermarkets into diverse product lines suggests that the political economy of the global production, trade, and consumption of agri-goods exceeds that of food commodities. In this sense, central features of the 'corporate food regime', as formulated by McMichael (2005, 2009), also seem to pertain to the cut flower industry. McMichael describes this regime as a consequence of neoliberal globalisation in agriculture: 'The "corporate food regime" is yet another moment, ... an unprecedented conversion of agriculture across the world to supply a relatively affluent global consumer class. ... The distinguishing mark of the corporate food regime as a new moment in world capitalism lies in the politics of neo-liberalism. ... [F]irms relocated manufacturing to Third World export processing zones' (McMichael 2005, 273). I show not only that this concept of a corporate regime is applicable and has become dominant in the cut flower industry, but also scrutinise why and how corporate retailers have gained control over flower production, trade, and consumption.

Empirically, I explore the entanglements between global economic dynamics and the Lake Naivasha cut flower industry. Most previous accounts of the Kenyan cut flower industry have been told from a local point of view (e.g., Styles 2019). Here I take on a different perspective to show how the market entry of retail chains and the reorganisation of the Lake Naivasha cut flower industry are mutually dependent. Furthermore, I scrutinise the complex and multi-scalar linkages of actors at Lake Naivasha, both inside and outside of the cut flower industry, and how these linkages drive the reorganisation of the agro-industry as well as the social-ecological system. The focus of my analysis is on roses.

Roses are by far the most important product in the flower trade between Lake Naivasha and Europe. By using them for a case study of the cut flower industry, I am able to examine the role agro-industries in the Global South played in the reorganisation of global trade and retail of agricultural commodities, and vice versa, as well as the many and partly contradictory consequences that this reorganisation has had for agriculture and sustaining social-ecological systems.

Following roses: Methodology and methods

The following account is based on multi-sited empirical fieldwork. At the beginning, the project that led to this book was geared towards a classical GCC or GVC study. The main objective of this study was to 'follow' roses (see Cook 2004) from production to consumption and explain how the external influences of these linkages impact social-ecological systems. This way, the study aimed to show why a conceptualisation of resilience in spatially confined systems is insufficient. But while conducting the research, I became more and more dissatisfied with the shortcomings of the chain-approaches, especially regarding the role of place in GCC and GVC. The empirical and methodo-logical basis of this research was a constant struggle with these concepts that were eventually complemented by a marketisation perspective. In what follows, I do not intend to present the study as being completely realigned to a marketisation framework. Instead, in accordance with Crang and Cook's critique on the 'read-*then*-do-*then*-write model for academic research' (2007, 2), I will analyse the empirical material alongside the frictions of chain and marketisation perspectives. Conceptually as well as methodologically, these frictions tend to surface when considering the tracing of economic linkages and the role of places in these linkages.

GCC and GVC theory entails a specific methodology focused on the vertical linkages between different nodes, distinct steps of production, and trade. These connections are 'mapped' and contain the flow of services, people, and added value (Kaplinsky, Morris 2001, 53). Horizontal dimensions play a minor role and are considered as a territorial dimension or institutional framework (Gereffi 1994, 96–7; McCormick 2001, 106; Sturgeon 2001, 10–11; Sturgeon 2009, 123). The marketisation perspective of this book is inspired by Actor-Network Theory (ANT). Similar to the chain-approaches, tracing linkages is a key strategy of ANT. According to ANT, actors constitute their own realities, their own contexts, and even their own ontologies (Latour 2010, 253). Therefore, ANT itself can be understood 'as a method to learn from actors themselves without imposing on them an *a priori* definition of their world-building capacities' (Ruming 2009, 453). The key task for scientists is then to follow actors and simultaneously describe them as well as the networks into which they are enrolled (Latour 2010, 59, 293). This is best done by tracing associations of materials and relations that constitute Actor-Networks (Ruming 2009, 454). Although similar at first sight, ANT's methodological premise of tracing associations differs substantially from the mapping of chains: since Actor-Networks constitute their own ontology, they are neither vertical nor horizontal (see Chapter 2). This also implies that the task of scholars is not to categorise Actor-Networks in predefined scales but to leave questions of scales to the actors themselves (Latour 2010, 327).

What do these methodologies and their criticism mean for the study of economic linkages in the global cut flower industry? Since this project started out as a GVC study, its methodological approach to global economic linkages is inspired by several of the discussed perspectives. Initially, I aimed to trace global economic linkages as suggested by the chain methodologies. Yet, in the interviews with flower farm managers, it became clear that the myriad relations of the flower farms can hardly be reduced to a simple chain logic. The interactions between the farms and their surroundings can neither be captured as an 'institutional framework' (Raikes et al. 2000, 393), nor can producer-buyer linkages be reduced to a single value chain. In what follows, although still mainly based on interviews, the methodological approach is geared more towards an understanding of micro-processes, which eventually create global linkages. In this way, I tried to open the 'black box' (Coe et al. 2008, 277) of the value chain and of the firm (i.e. the flower farm). This entailed an analysis not only of verbally represented data but also of media discourses, materiality, and documents, as all of these are dimensions of global economic linkages. In accordance with Latour's call for ANT (see above), but also with many previous chain studies, I traced networks by following the associations of actors. This methodology resembles both the fluidity and the multitude of interconnections and linkages more than any single predetermined route. By following these linkages, the methodology also became multi-sited (see Marcus 1995): it led me from the place of production at Lake Naivasha to Nairobi, the place of flower handling, exporting, and political representation of the cut flower industry, and finally, it brought me to Aalsmeer, the place of trade, capital, and knowledge creation.

Beside the investigation of economic linkages, the second methodological challenge for this study was the following: how can Lake Naivasha's role in the global cut flower industry be approached methodologically? Therefore, we have to take one step back and look at the processes that constitute places: 'A processual and relational understanding refuses to take as given discrete objects, identities, places and events; instead it attends to *how* they are produced and changed in practice in relation to one another' (Hart 2004, 98). Thus, a methodological approach to places in global economic entanglements has to avoid the impact model's narrow focus on local consequences of global processes. Instead, ANT's topological understanding of space is helpful. Regions or places are here addressed as 'the intertwining of networks and ... based on pragmatist, constructionist and ethnographic approaches' (Ruming 2009, 457). Localities can be conceived as unique configurations that are 'part of a larger network environment, one that is not separate from global, transnational, national or local influences' (Ruming 2009, 457). This understanding requires the researcher to trace all kinds of relations that make local configurations unique, whether economic, ecological, or social, and whether physically close to or far from Naivasha.

Following these methodological considerations, I chose a qualitative approach inspired by multi-sited ethnographies. I conducted the empirical fieldwork for this project between 2014 and 2017. This included four field trips of one to four months to Kenya, a trip to the Netherlands, and interviews and workshops in Germany and Austria. The fieldwork can be divided into four categories.

First, flower farms. At the beginning of my fieldwork, the flower farms at Lake Naivasha seemed fenced off from me and their surroundings, both in a literal as well as a metaphorical sense. Limited access to company offices, greenhouses, and warehouses is a common problem in studies of agro-industries (Freidberg 2001, 363), and the Kenyan cut flower industry is a particularly critical case. The flower farms at Lake Naivasha have had many frustrating experiences with interviewers from Europe (or North America). They have faced regular media coverage and NGO campaigns depicting the flower farms as exploiters of Kenyan labourers or polluters of the lake's ecosystem (see e.g., Food & Water Watch 2008). Moreover, as many farm managers told me, they had previously cooperated with European and American researchers before without ever getting any feedback on the results or benefitting from these studies. Nonetheless, my strategy of establishing contact with the flower farms was based on two main reasons. Firstly, my research assistants had direct contact with the managers. One of them had worked as a general worker on a flower farm, and another as a driver for various farm managers. Both had their own networks within the industry. The second reason was based on a snowball system: the sampling of interlocutors mainly guided by relations of previously contacted actors (see Ruming 2009, 459). Latour's advice (2010) to follow actors and trace Actor-Networks is therefore not only a theoretical premise but in this regard also a practical strategy. Although the area around Lake Naivasha is home to over 50 flower farms with roughly 40,000 employees, the network of the upper farm management is quite small. Most farm managers know each other, and foreign managers especially have close ties and consider themselves as friends. It took almost the entirety of my first stay in early 2014 to establish contact with some farm managers. Eventually, some of them gave me access to their networks by sharing phone numbers or even introducing me to their friends in the industry. Overall, the portion of the study on flower farms is based on 43 interviews and observations. It includes 17 farms and the full spectrum of the Lake Naivasha cut flower industry. Out of the 17 farms, 13 are represented by more than one encounter in the sample, five because of a farm tour after an interview, eight because of several visits. Serial interviews and observations are appropriate methods to gain in-depth insights and observe dynamics over time (Crang, Cook 2007, 73–4). Therefore, I visited one farm six times and another one nine times. These two farms in particular served as typical case studies, which is a useful method in qualitative research and in chain-studies to gain deep insights into causal mechanisms (Coe 2011; Gerring 2017).

The second category of the fieldwork is the flower industry beside the Lake Naivasha farms itself. Studies of economic globalisation not only require us to take into account regional industries but also their external linkages. In my methodological approach I have followed the advice of GCC and GVC studies to trace the linkages of flower farms up and down (see Gereffi et al. 1994; Sturgeon 2001). By interviewing the suppliers, service providers, traders, and buyers of the farms, the Actor-Networks of the cut flower industry were tracked beyond the boundaries of the Lake Naivasha region. This tracking made the study multi-sited. Freight forwarders, service providers, and suppliers of the Kenyan cut flower industry are mainly based in Nairobi. The Kenyan capital also hosts the annual IFTEX,[6] one of the largest floriculture trade fairs, which I visited twice. Finally, the critical link for Kenyan flowers to European buyers is the flower trade hub in the Netherlands with its main centre in Aalsmeer south of Amsterdam. There, I visited the mother company of a Lake Naivasha farm, the auction, and various trade companies. In addition to their material connections, the farms also have strong relations to social and political floriculture organisations. These include local and national interest groups of the cut flower industry, unions, and certifiers.[7] In total, the non-farm sample of the floriculture study consists of 27 interviews and observations. The main purpose of these inquiries was to investigate which role actors at Lake Naivasha play in the global cut flower Actor-Network; thus, they were focused on the nature of relations, hierarchies, market access, and distributional issues.

The third category is stakeholders. In order to assess Lake Naivasha's role in the global cut flower industry, I tried to trace Actor-Networks that constitute it as a place. I mainly approached this task by talking to stakeholders. 'Stakeholder' in its most basic understanding refers to an actor 'with an interest or concern in something' (Oxford Dictionary 2018). These actors are numerous and heterogeneous at Lake Naivasha. They consist of governmental organisations, NGOs, environmental activists, tourist operators, pastoralists, small-scale farmers, etc. As it is impossible to include all stakeholders (since potentially every inhabitant is one) in the sample, I chose to approach stakeholder groups that claim to represent communities and interview their members or representatives. A stakeholder conference held by Imarisha Naivasha, a parastatal coordination organisation for stakeholders

---

6   See https://hppexhibitions.com/iftex.

7   It is hard to categorise certifiers, as they can be both industry groups (e.g., KFC) and NGOs (e.g., Fairtrade).

around the lake, provided an entry point.[8] In total, this sample contains 24 interviews and observations.

The fourth and final category is discourses. Studies of marketisation as well as GCC, GVC, and GPN studies have stressed that economic globalisation takes place on different levels: socially, materially, discursively, etc. (see e.g., Levy 2008, 944; Ouma 2015, 13). Therefore, a methodological approach to Lake Naivasha's role in the cut flower industry cannot solely rely on its representation in interviews, it must also take into account other artefacts. These artefacts can be distinguished into the three spheres of media, science, and organisations. This distinction is inspired by Joffe's (1999) categorisation of influencers on common-sense thinking into the three spheres of journalists, experts, and lay thinkers. Media outputs have an important role in the shaping of discourses about places. On the one hand, they represent images; on the other hand, they create and influence them (Cloke et al. 2004, 71). Therefore, I analysed media outputs on two levels. In Kenya, the Nations Archives provided a useful source of information. The digital archive is owned by the Nations Media Group and contains articles of their print media, such as *The EastAfrican*, *Daily Nation*, *Business Daily Africa*, and *Daily Monitor*. These cover an important part of the Kenyan media landscape and provide a good insight into medial representations (Ogola 2011). Artefacts by organisations are sometimes hard to distinguish from those by media or scientists, as the lines in both directions are blurred. All kinds of organisations actively take part in the debates about Naivasha and push their concerns in various publications. NGO publications and governmental publications are not 'neutral' (Cloke et al. 2004, 54). All publications have to be 'demystified' (Cloke et al. 2004, 61) and the ideas or concerns that led to the construction of the information scrutinised. Hence, I not only use these publications as sources, but I will compare them to the results of primary data analysis and categorise claims and arguments in relation to the background of the editors or authors. This is also valid for scientific publications. Lake Naivasha has for a long time been a research hub with plenty of output, mainly in ecology and natural sciences. In my analysis, I do not treat these as neutral, objective sources, but rather use the knowledge that these papers produce to contextualize my study. Scientific knowledge – as all knowledge – has to be situated, since it 'is produced in specific circumstances and those circumstances shape it in some way' (Rose 1997, 305). The scientific knowledge produced about Lake Naivasha is especially rife with various concepts of sustainability, stability, or resilience of the (social-) ecological system (Everard, Harper 2002; Tarafdar, Harper 2008; Njogu et al. 2010; Otiang'a-Owiti, Oswe 2010; Harper et al. 2011; Oyugi et al. 2014).

---

[8]   For a detailed account of the conference, see Chapter 7.

Yet, concepts like resilience or sustainability have to be situated in regard to their political dimensions (Cote, Nightingale 2012), especially because they often put forward rationalistic logics that disregard power inequalities derived from ecosystem approaches (Cannon, Müller-Mahn 2010).

In total, the primary data that makes up this study consists of 93 interviews and observations that were conducted between 2014 and 2017. As this data was sampled by following specific Actor-Networks within the Lake Naivasha cut flower industries, it has particular emphases and some limitations. The core Actor-Networks I traced were the ones around foreign, mainly Dutch, managers or shareholders. This book analyses the linkages of these networks to primarily European markets via the Dutch flower hub. Although this focus is the result of a non-representative sample, it portrays the most important part of the Lake Naivasha cut flower industry and its market linkages. This book prioritises production in comparison with trade and especially retail. From a marketisation perspective, economic globalisation is not necessarily a story about what markets or retailers do, but how this is articulated in the spaces of production and trade.

Although the principal empirical fieldwork was conducted some years ago, I would argue that the conclusions reached have proven to be more relevant than ever since 2020. The Covid-19 pandemic has accelerated many of the market dynamics in the cut flower industry; for instance, supermarkets have increased their market share significantly (see above). From this perspective, the years around 2015 seem to have laid the foundations for a new era in the cut flower industry. This book will scrutinise these foundations and their coming-into-being. Finally, in the conclusion, I return to the recent acceleration of market dynamics in the cut flower industry and their implications.

Structure of the book

The structure of the book is as follows. Chapter 2 discusses the merits and limits of GCC, GVC, and GPN as the most common approaches to the analysis of global economic linkages. I then introduce studies of economisation and marketisation to enhance these approaches and outline the conceptual framework that I used for the research investigation. In Chapter 3, I examine how the Dutch trade hub remained pivotal to the cut flower industry and analyse its role in Lake Naivasha's linkage to the markets. The following three chapters scrutinise the role of Lake Naivasha's agro-industry in the global cut flower market. Chapter 4 provides an overview of the historical development of Lake Naivasha into an agro-industrial centre, and goes on to show how Lake Naivasha is a different type of cluster by tracing its current Actor-Network. Chapter 5 addresses the linkages of local flower farms to buyers. I argue that, in contrast to simplifying representations of cut flower value chains, these linkages form a complex network, mainly regulated by certifications restricting market access. Chapter 6 is concerned with how flower production has been reorganised in reaction to these market dynamics. I examine how producers have coped with growing financial precariousness and how corporate retailers have influenced the creation of new types of cut flowers for their own interests. Finally, Chapter 7 reflects on how the local cut flower industry, but also the global cut flower market, is entangled in Lake Naivasha's social-ecological system. Thus, I will argue that a global sense of place, as shaped in this book, is necessary to capture the manifold cross-scalar dynamics shaping Lake Naivasha and similar agri-businesses in Africa.

2

Place, Chains, and Actor-Networks:
Conceptualising Economic Linkages

This book seeks to explore entanglements between global economic dynamics and the Lake Naivasha cut flower industry. The general question of how dynamics in the Lake Naivasha cut flower industry and its surrounding social-ecological system relate to the entry and growing dominance of European retail chains in the global cut flower market can be further subdivided into three main research questions that this book's conceptual framework looks to address.

1. *How are global economic linkages organised? How are dynamics in these linkages brought about? And how do these processes influence the actors and regions that are part of these settings?*

These are fundamental questions of economic globalisation and have been addressed across many disciplines, and by many different theories and empirical studies. The common approach of these theories is to trace connections between globally dispersed places of production, trade, and consumption of a single commodity. The multi-scalar nature of these linkages makes the tracing of products like cut flowers a complex yet worthwhile task to understand globalisation, as David Harvey points out in his famous example of tracing a meal's inputs:

> Tracing back all the items used in the production of that meal reveals a relation of dependence upon a whole world of social labor conducted in many different places under very different social relations and conditions of production. That dependency expands even further when we consider the materials and goods used in the production of the goods we directly consume. (Harvey 1990, 422)

The various concepts dedicated to this task can be divided into vertical perspectives – mostly based on a chain heuristic – and a combination of vertical and horizontal approaches, based on a network heuristic. Previous studies on the Kenyan cut flower industries made use of these approaches: for instance, Hale and Opondo (2005) conducted a study on Global Commodity Chains,

Riisgaard (2009a) examined Global Value Chains, and Hughes (2001) applied a Global Commodity Networks framework. These concepts offer methodological tools to analyse translocal relations in the cut flower industry. Moreover, they assist in theoretically interpreting interdependencies between local and global dynamics in the cut flower industry. Chain approaches continue to be popular not only in studies of the cut flower industry, but also in the analysis of economic globalisation in general, as well as in development practice. The contribution of chain and network approaches to this book and their ongoing popularity renders a close examination of these concepts, their merits, and limits necessary. Therefore, in the following pages, the most important ones will be introduced and discussed regarding their applicability to the cut flower industry. I intend to critically engage with these approaches and show why they provide useful insights on a macro-level, but also why they are insufficient to explain the complex and sometimes contradictory reorganisational dynamics at play in the cut flower industry. Their limitations especially concern the role of 'place' in globalisation and how dynamics in economic relations unfold. Hence, the remaining questions for the conceptual framework of this book:

2. *What role do specific local settings or places, and more generally non-economic factors, such as social or ecological matters, play in global economic linkages?*

Cut flower production, trade, and consumption are not only economic processes, but especially in Naivasha they strongly relate to social and ecological matters, materially as well as discursively. As such, these dimensions have to be considered in the framing of places within global entanglements. This is an intricate task, since it goes beyond the vertical logic most chain-approaches are based upon. It also triggers more general questions about what is included in 'economic' linkages or in the respective analyses of these.

3. *How can reorganisation in global economic linkages be explained?*

This question exceeds the analysis of the status quo of the global cut flower industry, the actors involved, and their mutual relations. Rather, reorgani-sation implies dynamic processes of inclusion *and* exclusion, the breaking *and* forging of links, and the complex positive and negative outcomes of these processes.

These two questions require a theoretical perspective that goes beyond conventional chain and network concepts. A marketisation perspective on the reorganisation of the cut flower industry can provide these insights. It enables us to query the cut flower market itself and to overcome the impact model of the relation between global dynamics and local producers.

In this chapter, I will first discuss the aforementioned chain and network approaches before directly responding to the three questions. In order to understand their popularity and to critically engage with these theories in the following analysis, a close inquiry of their origins, their main ideas, their benefits, and their shortfalls will be necessary. Afterwards, in order to overcome these deficiencies, I will introduce the background and central thoughts of geographies of marketisation. Building on this critical reflection, I will develop a conceptual framework for the analysis of the reorganisation of the cut flower industry along four main lines: networks versus chains; power and governance; places and regions in global linkages; and reorganisation in global economic linkages.

Global economic linkages as chains and networks

A shift in agricultural production to equatorial countries, lengthened transport and trade relations, and large corporate retailers as lead firms: the developments in the global cut flower industry over the past 40 years reflect the accelerated dynamics of economic globalisation since the second half of the 20th century. These dynamics have been critically reflected by economics, sociology, and geography since as early as the 1970s. Tracing back commodities and revealing their relations of production has emerged as a popular approach across these disciplines. Therefore, there is a rich body of empirical studies and theories of the organisation of economic production and distribution processes. These studies and theories share the objective of describing the process of production, handling, marketing, distribution, and consumption and its spatial contexts. Moreover, they are based on a diagrammatic account (chain, network, circle) of the organisation process, which serves as a graphic heuristic. The cut flower industry seems to be a model case for these theories and has often been portrayed as such (see Introduction). Therefore, the three most important ones – (Global) Commodity Chains, Global Value Chains, and Global Production Networks – have to be examined closely to show why they alone are insufficient to analyse current dynamics in the flower market.

(Global) commodity chains

In order to understand the underlying objectives of chain and network theories, a brief reflection on their common intellectual origins is necessary. The first attempt to conceptualise multi-scalar linkages in a globalised economy arose within World-System Theory in the late 1970s. This dependency theory was principally developed by Immanuel Wallerstein as a response to predominant modernisation theories. According to Wallerstein, since the development of the capitalist 'world-economy' (Wallerstein 1974, 15) in the 16th century and its subsequent global expansion, economic factors came to transgress political boundaries such as national borders and render the nation state an inappropriate analytical scale. Therefore, the 'world-system' is the adequate methodological unit to analyse the global political economy (Wallerstein 1974, 1980, 2001). A world-system describes a coherent social system whose development is driven by internal dynamics. On the one hand, these internal dynamics lead to a spatial expansion; and, on the other hand, they result in a 'stratification' of the world-system into core and periphery with regard to their economic productivity (Hopkins, Wallerstein 1977, 127). This stratification is mainly caused by a functional and spatial division of labour (Wallerstein 1974, 349). In order to investigate this division of labour in a world-economy, Wallerstein and Hopkins for the first time introduced the term 'commodity chain':

> Let us conceive of something we shall call ... 'commodity chains': what we mean by such chains is the following: take an ultimate consumable item and trace back the set of inputs that culminated in this item – the prior transformations, the raw materials, the transportation mechanisms, the labor input into each of the material processes, the food inputs into the labor. This linked set of processes we call a commodity chain. (Hopkins, Wallerstein 1977, 128)

Hence, in its original sense, commodity chains are a tool in neo-Marxist analysis to describe the historical development of a capitalist world-economy. Commodity chain analysis seeks to reconstruct the path a specific good passes along from its production to the consumer. This chain consists of 'nodes' that are recorded with regard to the flows in between, the relations of production, the organisation of production, and their geographical location (Hopkins, Wallerstein 1986, 158–62). Although rarely used in its original sense, this analytical structure laid the foundation for most of the following chain-based approaches to a globalised economy.

Building upon this groundwork, the first comprehensive collection with conceptual, analytical, and empirical contributions to commodity chains was edited by Gereffi and Koreniewicz (1994). These contributions were inspired by Wallerstein's intellectual edifice but differ in some crucial ways, starting with the renaming of commodity chains as Global Commodity Chains (GCCs). This emphasis on the global was derived from the observation that the international division of labour was increasing due to mass production and flexible specialisation (Piore, Sabel 1984). Moreover, the influence of network theory in sociology (e.g., Alba 1982) had led to the definition of GCCs as 'interorganizational networks' (Gereffi et al. 1994, 2) that structure the world-economy. The new framework also shifted the focus of analyses from the (historical) development of the capitalistic world-economy to firms and their networks.

Nevertheless, GCCs still preserved the neo-Marxist demand for a politically engaged science, for example by critically reviewing different development strategies from a GCC perspective (Gereffi 1994).

A 'classic' GCC analysis investigates the input-output structure, the territorial dimension, and most prominently the chain's power structures by distinguishing between producer- and buyer-driven commodity chains (Gereffi 1994, 96–7). The analysis is carried out along 'boxes' whose boundaries are socially defined and into which the production process is divided (Hopkins, Wallerstein 1994a, 18). The GCC approach has been used widely for empirical research. This had already started with the wide range of case studies in the original volume, which covered topics from shipbuilding (Özveren 1994), over footwear and garments (Appelbaum et al. 1994; Korzeniewicz 1994), to automobiles (Kim, Lee 1994; Lee, Cason 1994).

Even today, the dichotomic distinction between producer- and buyer-driven GCCs draws attention but also generates criticism. The categorical division of governance types provides a powerful terminology but has little explanatory significance (Hughes, Reimer 2004b; Bair 2009b). Moreover, the concept's approach to understanding the global economy by tracing back a single commodity leads to a superficial analysis in contrast to its holistic aspiration (Bair 2005). Therefore, the analysis is often highly descriptive as the reconstruction of GCCs is usually very complex (Starosta 2010, 435). Finally, GCC analyses often neglect scales other than the global, especially national and individual habits (Leslie, Reimer 1999, 404; Raikes et al. 2000, 395; Raghuram 2004, 120).

Constructive criticism on GCCs have sought to address these problems and propose conceptual, methodological, and empirical enhancements. The volume *Geographies of Commodity Chains* (Hughes, Reimer 2004a) follows the claim to spatialise commodity chains and tries to 'highlight the geographies of commodity flows' (Leslie, Reimer 1999, 411), for example by focusing on '*sites* of retailing (and to a limited extent consumption), import, export and production' (Barrett et al. 2004, 25, my own emphasis). Bair and her *Frontiers of Commodity Chain Research* (2009a) provide a similar approach. Here, GCCs are presented as a basic framework that brings together conceptually, methodologically, and empirically diverse research focused on producer-consumer linkages. Arguing against a narrow understanding of GCCs based on a purely vertical analysis (Topik 2009, 38), the advantage of the concept is seen in its social and political impact because of its potential to reconnect producers and consumers (Bair 2009b, 28).

Bair specified her criticism and further elaborated on the GCC concept in the following years. She is especially concerned about GCC's 'empirical and theoretical emphasis on incorporation' (Bair, Werner 2011, 989). Yet, dynamics in global production produce 'moments of inclusion *and* exclusion' (Bair, Werner 2011, 989) and cannot be fully grasped by exclusively focussing upon the actors within the production systems. To overcome this shortfall, a 'disarticulations' perspective has been suggested. This perspective draws attention to two basic questions (Bair, Werner 2011; Bair et al. 2013): how are linkages in GCCs forged and dissolved? And who is included and who is excluded in these linkages? In this way, a disarticulation perspective on GCCs goes beyond the description or analysis of a status quo. It allows for an explanation of the dynamic reorganisation of the cut flower industry, which for instance entailed new market access barriers potentially excluding producers from GCCs. Its objective to explain the uneven geographical development of global capitalism also fits into the widespread initiative to link GCC studies back to development theory in general and especially to dependency theory (Peters 2008; Selwyn 2012, 2015; Bair 2014; Dunaway 2014a). This trend back to GCC's neo-Marxist roots in World-System Theory enables an engagement of chain studies with recurring debates about global inequality. In this context a focus on capital-labour relations and on global class relations within GCCs was brought into the discussion to enhance the GCC concept (Selwyn 2012, 2015).

Finally, the GCC concept was criticised and broadened by feminist scholars (Dunaway 2014b). This is particularly of interest for the following empirical analysis, since the cut flower industry is often presented as a classic case of the exploitation of female labour in GCCs (see Hale, Opondo 2005). Yet, most of the contributions do not concentrate on gender issues in labour relations, but the hidden roles of the household, unpaid labour, and social reproduction (see Clelland 2014; Collins 2014; Dunaway 2014c). It is shown that GCCs and thus also global capitalism rely to a certain extent on productive factors besides core economic activities. In this way, the feminist enhancement of GCC theory also fits into the focus on exclusion of the disarticulation perspective.

Despite the shortfalls and the manifold criticisms, the GCC concept is an interesting approach to analyse the links between European markets and the Kenyan cut flower industry. The chain-metaphor offers a strong heuristic to analyse globalised economies by applying a vertical analysis. The consideration of its neo-Marxist roots in particular and the recurrent connection to recent debates about global inequality enable links to empirical case studies, such as the cut flower industries with the broader development of global capitalism: 'Why should we be interested in reconstructing commodity chains? The crucial element for us is that it is a chain, and allows us to get beyond the observation of particular production processes in particular times and places in themselves' (Hopkins, Wallerstein 1994b, 49). Although the producer- versus buyer-driven dichotomy of GCCs may be reductionist to a certain extent, it is appropriate for a basic description of the dynamics in the cut flower industry. A disarticulation perspective as well as enhancements of the GCC approach from a feminist perspective help in conceptually framing the cut flower industry's fundamental changes. They shift the focus towards the dissolving and forging of linkages and, as a result, to the inclusion and exclusion of actors, which is entailed by the reorganisation of the industry.

From commodities to value: Global value chains

In 2001, a second strand of research on chains emerged. While GCC studies continued to be empirically, methodologically, and conceptually diverse, Global Value Chains (GVCs) were designed right from the start as a consistent research project with a clear analytical framework. The agenda was first laid out in an *IDS-Bulletin* (Gereffi, Kaplinsky 2001), then methodologically specified in a handbook (Kaplinsky, Morris 2001), and related work was gathered by the Global Value Chains Initiative on a corresponding website.[1]

The new term was selected as 'the most inclusive' (Gereffi et al. 2001, 3). Ultimately, it designates the focus on value-adding sequences in the production of commodities. The choice was mainly inspired by Kogut's 'value-added chain' (1985) and Porter's 'value chains' (1998). Conceptualising his observation of an increasing international fragmentation of production, Kogut's concept defines value-added chains as 'the process by which technology is combined with material and labor inputs, and then processed inputs are assembled, marketed, and distributed' (Kogut 1985, 15). Porter's concept of value chains had already been established in international business literature. It was introduced to explain the comparative advantage of firms that are able to successfully coordinate and optimise their separated activities (Porter 1998, 40–4). According to Porter, value chains are a tool to analyse the origin of cost advantages in the organisational structures of firms (Porter 1998, 43). Although these two concepts inspired the terminology of GVCs, their conceptual contribution is limited, as they focus primarily on individual, vertically integrated firms and less on their institutional and territorial contexts and corporate power (Gereffi et al. 2001, 2; Henderson et al. 2002, 439). Rather than to Porter's understanding of value chains, GVCs are actually more similar to his 'value systems' (Porter 1998, 42) into which a firm's different value chains are integrated.

Transaction cost theory had the biggest intellectual impact on the shift from commodity to value chains. The GVC authors were looking for explanations of the increasing physical division of different production steps and found them in transaction cost theory (see Coase 1937; Williamson 1985).

---

[1] See www.globalvaluechains.org.

This influence was explained by the fact that firms outsource standardised processes whereas complex processes are internalised. This simplified rule can be refined by incorporating trust and interdependencies in the analysis of economic relations. According to network theory, these two dimensions diminish the influence of transaction costs and therefore were incorporated into the GVC framework (Gereffi et al. 2005, 81).

These inspirations influenced the shift of GVCs towards a focus on economic and organisational questions, diverging from the emphasis of GCCs on inequality, production, and labour. According to key publications (Gereffi, Kaplinsky 2001; Kaplinsky, Morris 2001; Global Value Chains Initiative 2016), GVCs are defined by three central aspects that also differentiate them from GCCs: they include the 'whole range of activities from design to marketing' (Gereffi et al. 2001, 2) and not only production; GVCs take into account physical transformation as well as services; and they concentrate on the productive, that is the value-adding sequences of production. This definition is useful in the case of the cut flower industry, as it points to the importance of productive processes besides actual growing. Designing new flowers and value-adding processes in handling or marketing, therefore, have to be investigated.

A GVC analysis is typically conducted at industry level and in two steps (Kaplinsky, Morris 2001; Sturgeon 2001, 10): first, the mapping of the GVC consists of a description of the production and distribution process. This step is similar to the 'input-output' description in GCC analysis and is sometimes also termed this way in GVC analysis (see e.g., McCormick 2001, 106). It contains the physical flow of commodities, but also the flow of services, people, and the value added to the commodity in each step (Kaplinsky, Morris 2001, 53). It also requires the investigation of the geographical dimension of the value chain, that is its physical and territorial fragmentation and the interdependencies of different scales within the GVC (McCormick 2001, 106; Sturgeon 2001, 10–11; Sturgeon 2009, 123). The second step consists of an analysis of upgrading and governance within the GVC. Upgrading refers to the improvement of an economic actor's link to a GVC in order to gain access to more profitable positions (Gereffi et al. 2001, 2–5). Governance describes power relations between firms within the value chain. It picks up the criticism on the narrowness of GCCs' producer-/buyer-driven dichotomy and expands the governance concept to a more nuanced categorisation. The categories are identified by the complexity of transactions, the ability to codify transactions, and the suppliers' capabilities (Gereffi et al. 2005). Different configurations of these indicators lead to five types of governance that differ with regard to their power asymmetry and their degree of explicit coordination (here listed from low to high): markets, modular GVCs, relational GVCs, captive GVCs, and hierarchy. This categorisation of governance is the central element of GVC analysis: 'It is important to trace the shifting patterns of global production and understand how GVCs work or are "governed", and determine the roles they play in rich and poor countries alike' (Global Value Chains Initiative 2016). Upgrading and governance from a GVC perspective enable a more precise description of the cut flower industry compared to the GCC framework: upgrading introduces an explicitly dynamic dimension to the analysis. This perspective leads to instructive questions for the empirical analysis, for example does packing bouquets for supermarkets result in a repositioning of flower growers? Also, a focus of the concept of governance on economic coordination adds a micro-perspective on power relations. It goes beyond the description of power relations in the cut flower industry as a whole and provides a tool for analysing the multitude of relationships between producers, traders, and buyers.

Yet, the shift from value to commodity also brought with it some problems. The evolution from GCC to GVC came along with a shift from an analysis of capitalist development to an economist assessment of the coordination of economic globalisation. The strong influence of transaction cost theory on the GVC approach entails a focus on inter-firm relations, competitiveness, and institutional arrangements; aspects that are more suitably analysed by the macro-perspective of the GCC concept slip out of sight. These aspects include the unevenly distributed power relations on a macro scale, inequality, gender and class, and labour relations (Barrientos et al. 2003; Ouma 2015, 46; Niebuhr 2016, 8; Selwyn 2016). Selwyn especially criticised the insufficient attention of the GVC concept to workers, their agency, and collective power, as labour is only seen as a commodity input into production (Selwyn 2013, 2016). Yet, these are key aspects in the cut flower industry. How can a macro-analytical perspective on these dimensions be combined with a micro-analytical focus on trade and production relations? The chain approaches cannot sufficiently respond to this question.

Despite these critical issues, the GVC framework has become popular in development practice: 'Over the last decade, value chains have literally exploded as a sub-field in development policy' (Werner et al. 2014, 1223). This 'success' was enabled by the conceptual turn from GCC to GVC and the influence of business and management theory. The scholars who drafted the initial framework in the *IDS-Bulletin* were open to collaborations with development agencies. The *Handbook for GVC* (Kaplinsky, Morris 2001) in particular provides a useful and pragmatic basis for applied science. Development agencies like the World Bank and many others developed strategies for 'Making Global Value Chains work for the Development' (Taglioni, Winkler 2016), frequently collaborating with the original creators of the framework (see e.g., Cattaneo et al. 2010; Gereffi 2014).[2] It is used both as an analytical framework and as a tool kit for economic development. This seemingly contradictory application mirrors the fuzzy understanding of the concept and of its potential to enable development. Broken down to its most basic understanding, and often mingling Porter's value chain concept with the GVC framework, participation in GVCs is promoted as a crucial factor for human development: 'GVCs are a powerful driver of productivity growth, job creation, and increased living standards' (World Bank 2018). By translating the importance of institutions reflected in the GVC approach into a 'business enabling environment', interpreting governance solely as inter-firm coordination that can be facilitated by governments, and focusing upgrading narrowly on industrial upgrading, an approach originally rooted in critical political economy has come to be used for a neoliberal development agenda promoting market liberalisation, private investment, privatisation, and a state whose main task is to facilitate market access for private actors (Neilson 2014; Werner et al. 2014; Ouma 2015, 4). In the cut flower industry, these developmental readings of the GVC framework especially surface in discourses on state regulations (see Chapter 5).

In sum, the GVC approach offers some helpful ideas for the analysis of the empirical case at hand. It points out that economic coordination is central for the reorganisation of global economic entanglements. Therefore, governance is not only a question of globally uneven distributed power but is also performed in the everyday relations between economic actors and has to be analysed on different scales.

(Global) production networks

Both of the previously discussed concepts are based on the chain-metaphor. This metaphor is often criticised for being too one-sided, linear, hierarchical, vertical, and simplistic (Dicken et al. 2001; Henderson et al. 2002; Jackson 2002; Hughes, Reimer 2004b; Levy 2008). As already pointed out, this results in a neglect of the geographical, social, cultural, and economic contexts within global linkages. To overcome this weakness, several scholars have proposed using the notion of networks instead of chains:

> In fact, such processes are better conceptualized as being highly complex network structures in which there are intricate links – horizontal, diagonal, as well as vertical – forming multi-dimensional, multi-layered lattices of economic activity. For that reason, an explicitly relational,

---

[2]   For a comprehensive review of the application of the GVC approach in development practice, see Neilson 2014.

network-focused approach promises to offer a better understanding of production systems. (Henderson et al. 2002, 442)

This claim has been followed most prominently in the concept of Global Production Networks (GPNs). The GPN concept was mainly developed by the Manchester School around Peter Dicken in the early 2000s. The concept follows ideas of new economic geography that aspired to less hierarchical and more open and relational conceptions of the economy and proposed networks as an appropriate topology (Thrift, Olds 1996, 321–3). On the one hand, the understanding of networks in the GPN approach is influenced by Actor-Network Theory (see Law 1999); and, on the other hand, it is influenced by an embeddedness perspective that stresses the interdependencies of economic objects with social relations (see Granovetter 1985; Grabher 1994). Thus, networks are defined as 'neither purely organizational forms nor structures. Networks are essentially relational processes' (Dicken et al. 2001, 91).

A GPN is relationally constituted by interactions of actors while these interactions are embedded in specific structures of power, hierarchy, and dependence. This relational perspective enables a complex and multi-dimensional analysis that takes into account factors other than purely economic ones (Hughes, Reimer 2004b). This way, it opens up space for the inclusion of the social-ecological system surrounding the Lake Naivasha cut flower industry into an investigation of global entanglements. The methodological consequences of this perspective are fundamental: the network analysis does not only include various geographical scales but is also conducted on an organisational scale (i.e. firms, industries, networks, and institutions) that is not defined *a priori* (Dicken et al. 2001, 91; Henderson et al. 2002, 445–6). It focuses on three categories (Henderson et al. 2002, 448–55): firstly, it has to be analysed how firms create, enhance, and capture value within networks. Secondly, power is seen as a practice that enables the creation, enhancement, and capture of value and not as a position in a network (Dicken et al. 2001). And thirdly, the embeddedness into the network of value creation and into territorial contexts is examined. On the basis of these three categories, the analysis is carried out with four dimensions in mind: firms, networks, institutions, and sectors.

The GPN framework allows the inclusion of factors external to the linear relations within the production and distribution process, such as territorial contexts, that is to say it facilitates a combination of horizontal and vertical perspectives (Henderson et al. 2002, 448–55). By introducing the notion of 'strategic coupling', GPN scholars include regional development in the conceptualisation of economic globalisation. Strategic coupling refers to the process of matching regional assets with the needs of translocal actors in GPNs and can be enhanced by appropriate institutional structures (Coe et al. 2004). However, this integration of horizontal factors also implies giving up the advantages of chain approaches: showing multi-scalar linkages in the global economy in a simplified, yet expressive way. Therefore, GPN studies tend to be diffuse and overly complex and eventually are similar to GCC or GVC studies (Ermann 2005, 107; Levy 2008, 951; Bathelt, Glückler 2012, 310).

In 2015, Coe and Yeung introduced 'GPN 2.0' (2015). Their proposition seeks to bring together existing studies of GPN and to develop a 'more dynamic theory of global production networks' (Yeung, Coe 2015, 32). GPN 2.0 argues that three competitive dynamics – cost-capability rations, market development, and financial discipline – are the main factors for the competitiveness between firms within GPNs. Its ambitions to highlight causal mechanisms and increase the explanatory ability of the GPN framework were appreciated (see e.g., Dörry 2017), although it fails to conceptualise how exactly GPNs are influenced by different varieties of capitalism (Scholvin et al. 2017).

The GPN framework conceptually enriches this investigation as it engages with sub-national spaces, especially regions. Furthermore, it picks up a 'deeply relational view of the world' (Coe et al. 2008, 273) that enables the incorporation of non-firm actors, which is crucial for the following analysis. Yet, similar to 'chain' studies, as Neil Coe observes, it fails to provide an explanation for the making and breaking of economic linkages, in his words, the 'ruptures and frictions', the 'dark side' (2011, 391) of strategic coupling. Also parallel to GVC studies, GPN analyses tend to be apolitical in the sense that they first and foremost are interested in economic development. This focus constricts the view on Lake Naivasha by undervaluing social and ecological matters. Thus, for the empirical case at hand, the GPN framework is rather complimentary to the chain concepts – as it has been for many other studies (see Bair 2008, 357). It introduces an important horizontal perspective but does not overcome the limitations of the chain approaches.

Reflecting GCCs, GVCs, and GPNs: Merits and limits of chain and network heuristics

The GCC, GVC, and GPN frameworks have been widely applied, transformed, and enhanced over the years. Many of the discussions about their usefulness dealt with the vertical-horizontal dichotomy and the associated incorporation of extra-chain or non-firm actors. GCC and GVC studies are vertical in their designs and almost exclusively focused on relations within the chain (Dannenberg 2012, 32). This impedes the analysis of the effect of the global cut flower market on the social-ecological system of Lake Naivasha. In this regard, the GPN framework is more progressive, as it explicitly takes extra-firm networks into account (Coe 2011, 390). Furthermore, it also applies the network heuristic to the firms themselves and therefore allows the analysis of intra-firm dynamics (Coe et al. 2008, 277). These aspects are crucial to understand the Lake Naivasha cut flower industry. Considering these differences and the diverse theoretical backgrounds, it is crucial to distinguish precisely between the concepts and their associated terminologies (see Table 1). The instrumentalisation of the GVC framework for development intervention due to its fuzzy understanding renders a definitional precision even more necessary. It also requires a reflection about the performativity of scientific theories: the cut flower industry can be analysed from a GVC perspective, yet, simultaneously, GVCs as a development tool also gain influence on discourses about market integration and access.

Although distinctive, the three concepts have common limitations. As mentioned above, all three frameworks are unable to theorise, in any profound way, on how linkages are forged, dissolved, or stabilised: 'the existing chain literature often tells us little about how global economic connections come into being, how they are assembled practically by different actors, and what such chains look like "from below" or even "from within"' (Ouma 2015, 7). These shortfalls are at least partly grounded in the use of chains and networks as heuristics impeding the merging of micro- and macro-perspectives on the reorganisation of the cut flower industry. The three theories provide important tools to analyse economic relations and their embeddedness in local contexts. Nevertheless, they need to be enhanced by further theoretical input in order

Table 1. Summary and comparison of chain and network approaches to global economic entanglements (Source: Author).

Approaches	Key texts and authors	Origins and Influences	Heuristic	Research Focus
CC	Hopkins, Wallerstein 1977, 1986	Sociology, Political Economy; World-System Theory, Dependency Theory	Chain	(Historical) development of the capitalist world-economy
GCC	Gereffi, Korzeniewicz 1994	World-System Theory, Network Theory	Chain	Inter-firm relations as basis of the world-economy, especially regarding the producer-driven/ buyer-driven chain categorisation
GVC	Gereffi, Kaplinsky 2001; Gereffi et al. 2005	Economics: Institutional Economics, Transaction Cost Theory	Chain	Sectoral analysis of inter-firm coordination, especially regarding governance and upgrading
GPN	Dicken et al. 2001; Coe, Yeung 2015; Henderson et al. 2002	New Economic Geography, Network Theory, Actor-Network Theory	Network	Value, power, and embeddedness in firm networks

to explain the reorganisation of the internal functionalities within the floriculture industry under the consideration of the role and importance of the Lake Naivasha SES. In the next chapter, this problem will be addressed by introducing a theoretical framework that uses networks not as heuristic but conceives Actor-Networks as ontology.

Global linkages as actor networks: Geographies of marketisation

The GCC, GVC, and GPN frameworks offer valuable ideas for the study of global economic linkages and their reorganisation under the condition of market dynamics. At the same time, they lack an explanation of how this reorganisation is realised, who and what is incorporated and excluded in new linkages, and how non-economic factors can be included in the analysis (see Bair, Werner 2011, 989; Ouma 2015, 7). These lacunae indicate a wider problem of economics in general and studies of economic globalisation in particular: the essentialisation of the economy, of markets, of market relations, or even of networks. These entities are often taken for granted instead of being questioned with regard to what they are: networks of humans, things, etc. that need to be stabilised time and again. Although adopting a relational network perspective, even the GPN concept does not consistently reflect the construction or performative character of economic linkages and especially actors within these linkages. It fails to do so as it does not radically enough follow its relational approach and does not apply it to its conceptualisation of actors: according to GPN scholars, actors exist *a priori* of networks and outside of them, instead of perceiving 'actors *through* networks' (Müller 2015, 72).

In the analysis of the reorganisation of the Lake Naivasha cut flower industry questions of what or who is an actor within the global floriculture network, how linkages are forged, stabilised, and broken, and what is seen as economic are crucial: for instance, stakeholders in Naivasha try to relate their concerns to the cut flower industry in order to get media attention or funding. If they are recognised as affected by flower farms, they become entangled in the global floriculture network; they are transformed into economically relevant actors. In this chapter, studies of marketisation will be introduced to capture these questions. Marketisation is rooted in an analysis of the economy by Actor-Network Theory (ANT). It criticises the aforementioned essentialisms and puts forward a radically relational and performative perspective on economic linkages. In this chapter, basic ideas of ANT and their application to economics will be explained to better understand the following discussion of studies of marketisation and their geographical dimensions.

Actor-Network Theory and economic relations

After discussing the applicability of chain and network approaches, some theoretical challenges that the reorganisation of the Kenyan cut flower industry poses remain unsolved: How do economic relations come into being? Who are economically relevant actors? In which way are economic networks embedded in the social-ecological system of Lake Naivasha and to what extent are dynamics in the social-ecological system part of economic entanglements? These questions go beyond the debate of chains versus networks. Instead, they require a more fundamental questioning of categories, such as the economy, nature, or society, and more generally of actors, networks, and agency. ANT provides some first responses in this regard. It emerged as an approach within the social study of science and technology (see Latour, Woolgar 1981; Latour 1987, 1993) and proposes a profoundly different approach to society. First, it disapproves of the modernistic 'purification' (Latour 2002) in the form of the dichotomy of nature and culture, local and global, economy and society, etc. These binaries are seen as analytical delineations and not as ontological categories (Zierhofer 1999). By essentialising these dichotomies, 'hybrids' that exist between these categories have slipped out of sight (Latour 2002). Contemporary hybrids out of control are, for instance, environmental problems that are caused by human culture but are analytically attributed to the sphere of nature. Instead, Latour proposed a 'parliament of things' (Latour 2001), in which human and non-human entities are viewed symmetrically as equally important. Second, ANT puts forward a new understanding of actors. Entities only become actors once they are enrolled in networks. Networks are neither structures nor constructions, as they do not exist *per se*, but only come into being when they are performatively produced by actors. In consequence, Actor-Networks also do not have a predetermined outside and inside (Law 1999, 7; Latour 2009). This is in stark contrast to GPNs' conceptualisation of networks; GPNs clearly do have a structural dimension and boundaries. According to ANT, the 'social' (and, as will be shown later, the 'economic') does not exist *a priori* determining actions; it only comes into being through translations, that is the arrangement of different entities into Actor-Networks (Latour 2009). Third, this has vast consequences for social science, as it implies a new methodology. According to Latour, the task of scientists is to describe Actor-Networks by tracing translations of entities into Actor-Networks (Latour 2010, 59); they have to simultaneously analyse the actors and the network they are enrolled in (Latour 2010, 293). In summary, ANT can be understood as a call for a relational perspective on everything (Bosco 2008, 141).

Apart from sociology and the social study of science and technology, ANT has been applied to challenge essentialist and dichotomic thinking in many fields, such as hazards and environmental crises (Hinchliffe, Woodward 2004; Hinchliffe 2007) or human-nature and human-animal relations in more-than human studies (Whatmore 2002, 2005). Accordingly, ANT has also been extended to the economic field (see Callon 1998c; Callon, Muniesa 2005; MacKenzie et al. 2007; Çalışkan, Callon 2009, 2010). Studies of economisation are concerned with the question of how activities, behaviours, spheres, or fields are established as 'economic' (Çalışkan, Callon 2009, 370). The empirical focus of these studies is mainly the performativity of economics and the relationship between economic theories and economic reality: 'The point of view ... is radically different. It consists in maintaining that economics, in the broad sense of the term, reforms, shapes and formats the economy rather than observing how it functions' (Callon 1998b, 2).

The question whether something is qualified to be called economic or to be part of the economy is crucial in the study of the reorganisation of the Lake Naivasha cut flower industry: conceptually, it reflects the criticism on the GCC, GVC, and GPN frameworks and their narrow focus on existing economic relations while theorising social or ecological matters as external influences. An alternative framework has to already incorporate these matters in the analysis of the coming-into-being of economic relations. And politically this perspective draws attention to questions of legitimisation. In public and political discourses, the economic is traded off for social and ecological concerns and often prioritised, for example by stressing the importance of employment opportunities or economic growth. This is especially problematic since it is rarely reflected in what is considered as economic and what is not. As these legitimisation processes are central to the reorganisation of the cut flower industry at Lake Naivasha, it is worthwhile to take a closer look at one particular form of economisation that will inform the theoretical framework of this book: marketisation.

Marketisation

The analysis of current dynamics in the cut flower industry and the role of specific places in these processes requires an investigation of the cut flower market itself, of its emergence and the underlying relations between producers, traders, and buyers. The GCC, GVC, and GPN approaches need to be enhanced in order to not only depict a shift towards buyer-driven power relations, but also examine how it comes into being and how it materialises in everyday relations. Here, a marketisation perspective is suitable, since it does not take the cut flower market's existence and status quo for granted, but asks how it is produced time and again. Marketisation is understood as a specific form of economisation and directly linked to it: 'If the dynamics of economic markets are to be understood, then they must be placed within the context of broader movements that bring the economic into being' (Çalışkan, Callon 2010, 22). Similar to the economy, markets are 'practical accomplishments' (Ouma 2015, 23), and the realisation of these accomplishments under specific circumstances are the object of inquiry. This perspective deviates from other approaches to markets. It does not examine the market as an abstract place of impersonal exchange as neoclassical economics does. Rather, it acknowledges the performative power of abstract market models and concomitant rationalities like the *homo oeconomicus* (Muniesa et al. 2007; Çalışkan, Callon 2009). It also criticises the view of markets as social institutions or as social constructions, as put forward by new economic sociology (Polanyi 1978; Granovetter 1985; see also White 2004) and also often by economic geography (see Berndt, Boeckler 2009, 536; Ouma 2015, 11). These perspectives conceive the market as an economic outcome of social processes, of networks, or as being embedded in them; within economic geography the GPN framework takes this stance. Here, the market exists outside of institutions and social relations; hence, this view is based on an arguable ontological dichotomy between the economic and the social.

The social studies of economisation and marketisation adopt a different stance and define markets as sociotechnical agencements (STAs) or assemblages[3] (Callon 2007b). Referring to Deleuze and Guattari's (1988) use of the term, Callon defines agencements as 'a combination of heterogeneous elements that have been adjusted to one another' (2007b, 319). 'Heterogeneous' refers to the composition of agencements (and accordingly assemblages) of human and non-human, technical and natural, discursive and material elements (Muniesa et al. 2007, 2; Çalışkan, Callon 2010, 9; Anderson, McFarlane 2011, 124). Agency does not exist *a priori* and is neither individual nor collective, but it is distributed in many different ways within agencements (Muniesa et al. 2007, 2). From this perspective, markets are not purely social constructions, but sociotechnical agencements, in other words 'arrangements of people, things and socio-technical devices that format products, prices, competition, places of exchange and mechanisms of control'

---

[3] Callon prefers the term agencements, as assemblage implies a passive status, in which things have been put together (assembled) by (human) agents, and therefore reifies the human non-human divide (Callon 2007b, 320).

(Berndt, Boeckler 2012, 206). What distinguishes markets from other STAs is that they involve specific calculative agencies, such as the valuation of goods intended for exchange (Callon, Muniesa 2005, 1229; Çalışkan, Callon 2010, 11). Many different actors can have calculative agency, such as economic models, financial algorithms, accounting techniques, but also consumption practices, farming techniques, etc. In social sciences, price-making mechanisms are usually interpreted either as processes of quantitative (or numeric) calculation (mainly in economics) or as qualitative judgement (mainly in anthropology). By situating the process of price making in STAs that entail calculative agencies with both quantitative and qualitative abilities, this dichotomy is blurred (Callon, Muniesa 2005, 1230–2). Marketisation emphasises the performativity of market arrangements and refers to the constant process of (re)producing, designing, implementing, and maintaining them (Muniesa et al. 2007, 4; Berndt, Boeckler 2010, 560). These market-making processes have a strong impact on social and economic relations, as they 'include anonymization, the cutting of social ties, and rational, calculative and efficient post-social coordination' (Berndt, Boeckler 2012, 200). Marketisation can be related to either newly emerging market relations or the reconfiguration of existing market relations (Ouma 2015, 9).

Studies of marketisation are mainly concerned with the description and the analysis of the processes bringing market STAs about. Five basic dimensions for this description and analysis have been identified (Callon, Muniesa 2005; Çalışkan, Callon 2010): first, goods need to be pacified or objectified, that is they have to be transformed from entangled beings ('goods') into passive objects with predictable qualities ('commodities'). This usually involves processes of singularisation, standardisation, and certification. Second, calculating agencies have to be deployed to value the pacified good. Third, in order for these valuations to take place, meetings between pacified goods and calculating agencies, so-called market encounters, have to be realised. These encounters are often framed by encountering devices, which are mediators organising the meetings between goods and agencies. Fourth, in these meetings, the goods are valued in the form of prices; therefore, struggles and power asymmetries in the process of price-setting need to be taken into account. Fifth, the dynamics of market sociotechnical agencements, their design and maintenance, are crucial factors; in other words: how are these agencements arranged, and how are they stabilised? These processes can be controlled by deploying all kinds of knowledge about markets and their performativity; therefore, knowledge is key in the analysis of market dynamics, design, and maintenance. These five dimensions point to some central categories of analysis: for instance, the process of producing and trading (new) cut flower varieties, the different forms of encounters between producers and buyers, and the role of the knowledge of retail chains on consumer preferences in price negotiations.

Furthermore, they are essential for the framing of markets. Here, Callon refers to Goffman (1976) and understands framing in general as 'establish[ing] a boundary within which interactions ... take place more or less independently of their surrounding context' (Callon 1998a, 249). Framing thus creates an inside and an outside, although relationships in-between are omnipresent. In the process of market-making, it needs to be established what is included within market relations and what is excluded. For instance, 'green' certification schemes and standards often lead to an inclusion of certain environmental factors into market relations, while social factors are excluded. Market framing thus 'constitutes powerful mechanisms of exclusion, for to frame means to select, to sever links and finally to make some trajectories (at least temporarily) irreversible' (Callon 2007a, 140). The framing of markets is costly, hard to control, and never complete, as unexpected outcomes may occur quite frequently in the marketisation process. These instabilities are called overflows (Callon 1998a, 255). In economic theories overflows are often referred to as externalities, that is indirect and non-economic effects of economic activities within markets. A good example of this process is environmental damage caused by industrial activity. For instance, as the degradation of soil or water is not included within industrial markets, it is not integrated within its market frame; therefore, it becomes an overflow, or an unexpected (in this case negative) consequence.

Geographies of marketisation

ANT, performativity, assemblages, and agencements have fallen on fertile ground in geography (see Barnes 2008; Bosco 2008; Robbins, Marks 2010; Anderson, McFarlane 2011). Yet, it took some time before Callon's and others' ideas on economisation and marketisation were adopted by economic geography.[4] The GPN framework takes the topological nature of networks as proposed by ANT (see Law, Mol 2001) (at least partly) into account. Topology refers to a relational understanding of spatiality: '[I]n a network, elements retain their spatial integrity by virtue of their position in a set of links or relations' (Law 1999, 6). Depending on the form of these relations, different spatialities are possible as 'spatiality is an aspect of network stability' (Law,

---

[4] In the process of marketisation, economic geography is an observer, but also plays a performative role, for example by spatialising economic models in location theory (Barnes 2008).

Mol 2001, 611). For instance, if a flower bouquet is shipped from Kenya to Amsterdam, it remains stable in network space, since its composition is not changed, but it clearly moves through Euclidean space.

More recently, Callon's work has inspired an approach that is central to this book: geographies of marketisation (Berndt, Boeckler 2012). Market-making processes bring along specific spatialities. On the one hand, they are based on specific geographical settings; on the other hand, they actively transform them. Lake Naivasha itself is a good example: its integration of the region into the global cut flower market was based on its location and its historical development (see Chapter 4). Three decades later, its position in the global cut flower network has turned Lake Naivasha into an agro-industrial centre. Geographies of marketisation investigate the emergence of market orders, their expansion, and their interdependence with spatial configurations (Boeckler, Berndt 2013). So far, most geographical studies interpreted this expansion in a Euclidean sense, as they have scrutinised the world market integration of regions in the Global South (see Berndt, Boeckler 2011; Ouma et al. 2013; Niebuhr 2016). Yet, Lake Naivasha has already been part of the global cut flower market for more than 40 years. Therefore, I will instead investigate the expansion of a new market order into an existing market STA. It deals with questions of stability, fluidity, and maintenance of markets rather than focusing on the effects of the emergence of newly 'marketised' regions.

Studies (and geographies) of marketisation and economisation significantly broaden the conceptual framework of this book. A relational perspective enables the analytical inclusion of human and non-human actors, of discourses, techniques, sciences, standards, calculating instruments, metrology, and material infrastructure as part of market formation processes, all of which are critical in the cut flower industry. It furthermore draws attention to the constructivist nature of the divide between the economic, the social, and the ecological in global linkages. Thus, it helps bridge these divides and allows for the inclusion of non-economic factors in the analysis. And lastly, the fluidity, emergent stability, and the necessary maintenance of the global cut flower industry can best be captured by conceptualising it as an STA. It allows the analysis of the dissolving and forging of linkages: 'Actor-networks ... are often fluid and emergent: connections break and are transformed, elements slip out of networks and are enrolled in others and different configurations are counterposed' (Müller 2015, 79).

A framework for analysing the reorganisation of the cut flower industry

After introducing the main ideas, benefits, and shortfalls of the concepts that influence this book, the remaining question for this conceptual chapter is: in what way can these concepts be applied or combined to guide the analysis of the reorganisation of the cut flower industry? For this purpose, the three conceptual challenges that introduced this chapter have to be remembered:

1. *How are global economic linkages organised? How can dynamics in these linkages be explained? And do these processes influence the actors and regions that are part of the settings?*
2. *What role do specific local settings or places, and more generally speaking non-economic (i.e. social and ecological) factors play in global economic linkages?*
3. *What drives the reorganisation of global economic linkages?*

In the following pages, I will argue for a pragmatic and flexible, yet precise use of the different concepts, depending on which scale, place, actor, or sphere (economic, social, ecological) the particular part of the analysis is focused on. To illustrate the necessity of this approach, a quick look at the different empirical dimensions of the reorganisation of the cut flower industry is helpful. From a macro-perspective, the reorganisation seems to be a clear case of the shift towards a buyer-driven commodity chain, replacing market-based governance structures as formulated in the GVC approach; this is a typical and often described dynamic in agricultural markets that face the entry of big retailers (see Dannenberg, Kulke 2014). Yet, this only answers a part of the first question; it does not tell us much about what role Lake Naivasha as the major production site or the Netherlands as the central trade hub play in that process, nor does it tell us how this process was realised. A marketisation perspective on the micro-level of these dynamics can help to answer these questions. New market orders, such as the shift in governance structure in the cut flower industry, do not simply appear out of thin air, but rather are constantly produced and stabilised. Furthermore, they are not introduced by one active actor and imposed on another passive actor, but their emergence involves all actors. By looking closely at market-making processes, a marketisation perspective helps us to explain how market orders are realised and how new governance structures come into being and are consolidated. Nevertheless, the macro-analysis remains meaningful, worthwhile to explore, and not to be neglected over micro-analytical issues.

The remaining section of this chapter will synthesise the previously discussed concepts to outline the conceptual framework of this book along four key lines of analysis concerning the reorganisation of global linkages. Firstly, regarding the debate about networks versus chains, I will argue for a flat ontology that does not perceive actors and linkages *a priori* as neither vertical nor horizontal, nor as global or local. Secondly, I will perceive places, regions, and social-ecological systems in global economic linkages as specific settings produced by linkages of actors, no matter if economic, social, or ecological. Thirdly, I will define reorganisation in global economic linkages as a fluid and dynamic process that produces order as well as disorder in markets, and includes as well as excludes actors. And fourthly, I will analyse diverse forms of power in their uneven distribution amongst agencies.

Chains versus networks: A question of scale

'Before addressing particular dimensions of global linkages and local dynamics and the relation between these phenomena, it is important to set out the perspective from which they shall be analysed. Reconsidering the previously discussed concepts (GCC, GVC, GPN), at first, this seems to be a question of a vertical or a horizontal perspective and chains versus networks.

The chain-metaphor was explicitly introduced to establish a vertical perspective on the global economy (Hopkins, Wallerstein 1994b, 49), and continues to be a powerful tool to meet the principal claim of 'chain-geographies', that is to 'critically examine the spaces through which consumers are connected to producers' (Hughes, Reimer 2004b, 1). A vertical analysis follows the chosen commodity and focuses on linkages and not on the boxes, nodes, or particular places within the chain. The criticism of this perspective for being too linear, hierarchical, and simplistic promoted the introduction of network-based approaches to economic globalisation and thus the addition of a horizontal dimension. Networks are a central notion within economic geography and are used in various meanings and contexts. The understanding of networks as a form of governance or economic organi-sation and the relationship of social networks and economic organisations (as formulated in the embeddedness concepts) are prevailing (Grabher 2006). The GPN approach builds on both of these concepts, since firms are defined as 'a relational network embedded in wider networks of social actors and institution' (Coe et al. 2008, 272). This allows network approaches to include extra-firm actors in a multi-scalar analysis.

Although networks and chains in the GCC, GVC, and GPN concepts seem to be contrary concepts, they are based on a surprisingly similar ontology.

From the very beginning of GCC research to recent GVC studies,[5] chains are defined as a linked system of networks: 'a GCC consists of sets of interorganizational networks' (Gereffi et al. 1994, 2). Vice versa, the GPN concept acknowledges the importance of linearity and verticality in the structure of links and nodes (Coe et al. 2008, 274). As such, in regard to the GCC, GVC, and GPN concepts, the chain-network dichotomy is only an epistemological divide: chains and networks are deployed as analytical categories or perspectives and not seen as the underlying structure of social and economic reality. At best, this leads to the realisation that 'horizontal and vertical factors each have salience and can be analysed in isolation or in various combinations'; at worst to 'analytical confusion' (Leslie, Reimer 1999, 409) and a fuzzy and overcomplex analysis.

There are several ways to overcome this epistemological dichotomy. In this regard, it first has to be made clear that the chain and GPN's network approaches are both based at least partly on hierarchical concepts of scale. For GCCs and GVCs and their vertical perspective, this observation is obvious, but it is also applicable to GPNs or the use of networks in economic geography in general. These are often based on a 'hybrid' interpretation of scale that integrates vertical and horizontal understandings (Marston et al. 2005, 419). Here, a network is simply a combination of vertical and horizontal linkages between nodes or social actors (Grabher 2006, 177). This way, the vertical-horizontal divide cannot be overcome. Instead, a topological and non-hierarchical conception of ActorNetworks as proposed by ANT (see Law 1999) rooted in a 'flat ontology' is useful (Grabher 2006, 178; Müller 2015, 73). A flat ontology does not rely on any transcendent predetermination – whether the local-to-global continuum in vertical thought or the origin-to-edge imaginary in horizontal thought. In a flat (as opposed to horizontal) ontology, we discard the centring essentialism that infuses not only the up-down vertical imaginary but also the radiating (out from here) spatiality of horizontality (Marston et al. 2005, 422).

Taking these claims seriously, ANT suggests that Actor-Networks themselves are an ontology, and therefore perceives networks neither as global nor local, nor as hierarchical or vertical. Here, scale is a purely epistemological point of view and should therefore not be defined *a priori* but left open for definitions by actors (Latour 2010, 317).

---

[5]   Dannenberg and Revilla Diez (2016) provide a recent example of this definition as they conceive regions and their institutional settings that participate in GVCs as socio-economic networks.

What does this conception of Actor-Networks rooted in a flat ontology mean for the analysis of the cut flower industry? Firstly, it means that linkages between the flower farms and their environment, between workers and farm managers, or between producers and buyers are not local or global *per se*. Rather, they are what these actors make of it. For instance, local stakeholders at Lake Naivasha make their concerns global by linking them to cut flower market relations. The analysis is thus open to linkages on all levels between all actors. Of course, this should not end up in arbitrariness. Instead, the identification of central nodes and important actors results from empirically tracing Actor-Networks. And secondly, viewing the cut flower industry from the perspective of a flat ontology means that vertical and horizontal relations are not taken as an ontological premise. Rather, they arise from the actors' selective framings of the topology of these networks.

Beyond the economic and non-economic divide: Places and regions in global linkages

After breaking the vertical-horizontal divide and establishing a flat perspective on Actor-Networks and therefore also on global linkages, the question remains what role specific settings or places, and more generally speaking non-economic (i.e. social and ecological) factors play in these economic linkages. This question refers to one of the oldest and most frequently discussed problems in human geography – the debate about the relationship between the local and the global, and between place and space (see Amin 2002). In economic geography, this debate is often framed as regional development in economic globalisation. The GCC, GVC, and GPN concepts have developed different approaches to this problem.

In the GCC and GVC approach the various sites of production, trade, and consumption are framed as boxes or nodes that are linearly linked like pearls on a string (see Chapter 2). Additionally, in more recent conceptualisations, specific local settings were recognised as territorial dimensions or as institutional frameworks. These settings determine how local, national, and international conditions and policies shape the globalisation process at each stage of the chain, or rather how they 'shape the environment for the embedded companies and are key determinants for economic success' (Dannenberg, Revilla Diez 2016, 170). But since GCC and GVC studies are vertical and unidirectional in their design and almost exclusively focused on relations within the chain (Dannenberg 2012, 32), they hardly incorporate non-economic factors and effects of the linkages on these sites.

In this regard, the GPN concept is more instructive. With strategic coupling and its interpretation of embeddedness, it deploys two concepts that capture the relationship between local sites and global linkages.[6] Strategic coupling refers to the process of matching regional assets with the needs of translocal actors in GPNs (Coe 2011, 391) and is seen as the major driver of regional development. Region is understood here as a sub-national unit but also as 'a porous territorial formation whose notional boundaries are straddled by a broad range of network connections' (Coe et al. 2004, 469). Regional development is conceived as a relational and interdependent process that needs to be analysed beyond the purely economic sphere (Coe 2011, 391). Yet, often studies of strategic coupling tend to exclude social and historical context (Selwyn 2016, 1771). This context is framed by GPNs' interpretation of embeddedness, possibly *the* central concept in economic geography in the debate about the relationship between economic activity and space or place. First introduced by Karl Polanyi (1978), Granovetter (1985) scaled down the analytical focus and stressed the importance of the embeddedness of actors in institutional and social relations. Building on this, the GPN theorists developed a threefold, relational concept of embeddedness (Henderson et al. 2002; Hess 2004; Coe et al. 2008): societal embeddedness grasps the social background of actors; network embeddedness describes the relationships actors or organisations are involved in; and territorial embeddedness stresses the territorial configuration of places that actors are dependent on. By applying this scheme, the GPN framework tries to acknowledge that GPNs are not purely economic, but also social, political, cultural, and environmental phenomena, and that they are deeply influenced by spatial configurations (Coe et al. 2008). Although the GPN concept puts forward a relational and flexible interpretation of embeddedness and thus incorporates non-corporate actors, the two basic problems of embeddedness concepts persist. First, there is the risk to 'overterritorialise' embeddedness (Hess 2004, 174; Grabher 2006, 172; Bair 2008, 340): the focus on personal relationships often leads to a preference for local- or meso-level analysis (e.g., in cluster analysis) and the negligence of relational and respectively societal and network embeddedness. The second problem is – to put it in Latour's words (2002) – the purification of the economic from the social, the cultural, the political, and also the ecological. By analysing economic actors that are embedded *into* context, the context is made a pure 'background scenery' (Jones 2008, 72), it is ontologically separated from the sphere of the economic. Thus, the concept of embeddedness reinforces the

---

6 Apart from these two approaches, scholars of the GPN programme and the World City Network tried to forge a conceptual dialogue between their disciplines (Coe et al. 2010; see also Derudder, Witlox 2010; Sassen 2010); yet, without producing significantly new contributions to the debate about local sites in global networks.

binary logic of mainstream economics (Ettlinger 2008, 45) and the separation of the economic and the non-economic, which is the object of critical inquiry for studies of economisation. The embeddedness approach defines *a priori* what is economic, whereas the social, the political, and the ecological are only meaningful when it impacts on the static economic. The economic here is clearly privileged over other spheres, and therefore 'we must do away with the flawed distinction between "the economic" and "the social" that is so often perpetuated in economics, sociology and economic geography' (Ouma 2015, 29).

For the following analysis, I will apply a relational approach to the analysis of local-global linkages and differentiations; an approach that is similar to what Massey has described as 'a global sense of place' (1991) or Amin as a 'topological interpretation of contemporary globalisation' (2002, 395). Massey answered the question how to think about locality in the age of time-space compression progressively with an extroverted and dynamic understanding of place:

> ... a sense of place which is extroverted, which includes a consciousness of its links with the wider world, which integrates in a positive way the global and the local. ... [T]he point is that there are real relations with real content – economic, political, cultural – between any local place and the wider world in which it is set. (Massey 1991, 28)

Building on Massey's ideas, Amin (2002) argues for an ontological (in contrast to a scalar) interpretation of globalisation. In these interpretations, spatialities as well as territories and scales are conceived as produced. In non-territorial terms, places can then be thought of as nodes in relational networks. From this perspective Lake Naivasha is not simply a physical location that is transformed by market dynamics, but the centre of relations between a large variety of actors such as flower growers, buyers, local stakeholders, wildlife, material infrastructure, etc. Both Amin's and Massey's arguments can be linked to ANT's topological interpretation of spatiality. This interpretation indicates that Actor-Networks constitute their own distinct spatialities. Actions and relations are always grounded within these networks and thus do not simply shift or jump scales, but rather they define scales and also places by themselves (Murdoch 1998, 361; Law, Mol 2001; Bosco 2008). This perspective turns the logic of embeddedness upside down: it is not the surrounding places or regions that influence networks and linkages; rather, these places and regions are produced by linkages and networks (see Berndt, Boeckler 2011, 1061–2).

What implications does this have for the analysis of the Kenyan cut flower industry? It means that one has to trace linkages and networks to reconstruct places. These linkages are not constrained to the economic sphere, but they are social, political, cultural, and ecological, because, as explained above, 'it is impossible fully to separate economic action from the wider realm of social action. ... All economic action is always and everywhere entangled in social influences' (Jones 2008, 76). The economic is then perceived as an outcome of these relations, and not as a prerequisite. Applied to the analysis of the relation between market dynamics and the Lake Naivasha cut flower industry, this means that Lake Naivasha only becomes a production site of the cut flower industry – and thus economic – by a myriad of linkages between all kinds of actors (human and non-human) on different scales.

Reorganisation: Dynamics in global economic linkages

In economic geography, the conceptualisations of place and region are often closely linked to their development. Dynamics within places or regions play a crucial role not only in economic but also in development geography. This also applies to the global cut flower industry: after being established in the 1960s and 1970s, cut flower production at Lake Naivasha has been a seemingly consolidated and stable industry for decades. Yet, the recent reorganisation is conceived as a dynamic process that forges new and breaks with old ties. The question is: how can these dynamics and, therefore, also the reorganisational processes in global economic linkages be explained?

Apart from strategic coupling, the GCC, GVC, and GPN concepts offer a second explanation for the development of regions or actors within global linkages: upgrading. Upgrading refers to the improvement of an economic actor's link to a GVC in order to gain access to more profitable positions (Gereffi et al. 2001, 2, 5). It describes the process of development as well as a higher competitiveness as its aim and can be applied to firms, industries, and regions (Gereffi 1999; Humphrey, Schmitz 2000; Fleury, Fleury 2001). Although already used within the GCC framework (see Lee, Cason 1994; Korzeniewicz 1994), it was mainly developed within the GVC concept (see e.g., Dolan, Tewari 2001; Humphrey, Schmitz 2002). Since in this conceptualisation upgrading is also applicable to regions, it has been used as a policy instrument; especially in developmental contexts (see Chapter 2).

Upgrading was criticised for its focus on industrial upgrading and the concomitant negligence of social outcomes (Bair 2005, 166–7). As a result, it was later complemented by the concept of social upgrading (Barrientos et al. 2011). Yet, some key problems remain: the distinction between industrial (or economic) and social upgrading once again reifies the economic-social dichotomy and externalises social and ecological matters. Furthermore, upgrading is criticised for its unidirectional, top-down conceptualisation that neglects for instance the agency of labour (Goger 2013; Selwyn 2013). But the main problem of upgrading is its narrow focus on positive outcomes and inclusion. Especially when taking into account social and ecological factors, (economic) upgrading may not be the best alternative and can have unexpected negative outcomes (Coe 2011, 396). Also, upgrading dynamics can lead to the exclusion of actors, which is hardly recognised within the concept. This reflects the concentration of GCC, GVC, and GPN studies on inclusion in general. But it is not only this 'inclusionary bias' (Bair et al. 2013, 2544) of the chain approaches that hinders a profound consideration of dynamics within global economic linkages. In GVC studies particularly parts of the setting of a value chain are taken for granted, for example the buyer-driven structure, codes of conduct, or lead firms are just there; their coming-into-being is hardly questioned or made the object of inquiry. A good example of this thinking is given by Barrientos et al. in their study about codes of conduct in African horticulture: 'Powerful lead firms (supermarkets) govern supply networks that span several African countries, defining not only what is to be produced but also how and under what conditions it is to be produced' (2003, 1513). Lead firms simply 'govern' and 'define'; these pivotal processes are not scrutinised.

If upgrading and the GCC and GVC approach in general do not consider profound dynamics sufficiently, how else can they be conceptualised? First, it has to be clarified what is meant by dynamics or specifically by reorganisation in economic linkages. Reorganisation includes the forging and breaking of linkages, exclusion and inclusion of actors, winners and losers, and economic and non-economic outcomes. A disarticulations perspective as proposed by Bair and others can help to include these aspects in the analysis (see Chapter 2). Borrowing the notion from Stuart Hall (1996), Bair and Werner define articulation as 'the forging of a unity out of difference' (2011, 992). Articulation and disarticulation draw attention to the dialectical processes of inclusion and exclusion that constitute commodity chains (Bair, Werner 2011; Goger 2013). Although reorganisation is at least to a certain extent a process of ordering, it is also always a chaotic process that causes disorder. Networks (and hence, also GCC or GVC) are:

> ... often temporary and shifting; links and nodes drop out, leading to separations and failures. Feedback loops, either positive or negative, can produce chaos or noise, and can potentially remove the system from homeostasis (if such equilibrium ever existed). Every change is potentially unbalancing; every stability is also potentially unbalancing when other connected processes change. Networks can bring people together into states of enmity, fear and incoherence as easily as they can bring them into cooperation. Networks break, and distribute disorder as quickly as order. ... Looking primarily for order and regularity leads us to marginalize those aspects of society that we consider disordered when they may be central to social dynamics. (Marshall, Goodman 2013, 283)

This perspective of (dis)articulation and (dis)order gives important hints for the empirical analysis. It serves as a reminder to pay attention to both processes of inclusion and exclusion that are mainly brought about in the breaking and forging of linkages. These processes can best be traced on a micro-scale, for example in 'everyday practices and struggles over value' (Bair, Werner 2011, 990). Furthermore, it reminds us not to be analytically biased towards networks as a form of ordering or to perceive disorder as inherently negative (Marshall, Goodman 2013). And lastly, it highlights the fact that global economic linkages are fluid. Although the idea that markets need work to be maintained and stabilised is central in studies of marketisation, so far economic geography in particular has not given sufficient attention to fluidity (Müller 2015, 79). Yet, in the case of the cut flower industry, fluidity is pivotal, since it does not represent a case of market integration or the making of a new market, but rather one of maintenance and of reorganisation.

Power and governance

Reorganisation or market-making in general are not egalitarian processes, but they are directly linked to questions of power and/or governance. In GCC and GVC literature, power and governance are often used synonymously and in general refer to the 'capacity to exercise' (Dicken et al. 2001, 92). Since the beginning of chain-studies in the 1990s, three perspectives on governance in global economic linkages have evolved (Gibbon et al. 2008): the first perspective was put forward by GCC scholars and defines governance as driving power. In this context, governance is used as a macro-perspective to describe the structure of the whole chain and its dependency on lead firms. The famous producer-/buyer-driven dichotomy that stems from this concept explains global power asymmetries in economic linkages in accordance with World-System Theory. The GVC concept redefined governance as coordination. This approach narrowed governance down to inter-firm coordination between lead firms and their suppliers and distinguishes between five different organisational types of these relations (see Chapter 2). Governance as normalisation of practices complements this list. It was developed based on convention theory and focuses on the process of 'realigning a given practice so that it mirrors or materializes a standard or norm' (Gibbon et al. 2008, 324). From this perspective, powerful actors' attempts to shift institutional frameworks in their own interest can be captured (Ouma 2010).

While the dualistic GCC approach to governance was mainly criticised for being too simplistic, the conceptualisation of governance as coordination is based on functionalist reasoning that does not investigate the coming-into-being of power asymmetries within coordination processes or the underlying market logics (Ouma 2015, 45–6). A focus on economisation and marketisation turns the logic of GCCs' and especially GVCs' perspective on governance upside down: instead of just asking what consequences governance structures have, it also asks how power asymmetries are created and how they materialise in market STAs. Thus, similar to the GPN concept's approach to governance (see Chapter 2), power is conceived 'as being diffused in a Foucauldian (capillary-like) sense whereby it is always present in all social interactions' (Dicken et al. 2001, 93). Yet, in contrast to GPN's 'economistic approach to power relations' (Levy 2008, 945), a marketisation approach includes non-economic actors. Power asymmetries in the process of market-making are predominantly based on the unequal distribution of knowledge and material equipment between calculating agencies. Powerful agencies are able to impose their qualification and valuation of goods on others (Callon, Muniesa 2005, 1238; Çalışkan, Callon 2010, 13; Ouma 2015, 39–40). In these valuation processes, standards are an important device to enforce specific modes of qualification and calculation. From a marketisation perspective, standards can therefore be defined as sociotechnical devices within the calculation process of goods, they are 'socially constructed and enforced conventions that not only aim to achieve specific corporate targets but also emerge from and reinscribe specific power asymmetries in terms of the ability to define what counts as quality and as legitimate behaviour in the marketplace' (Ouma 2010, 204).

If power is first and foremost analysed in its uneven distribution amongst agencies and their interactions, there are numerous different forms of power and governance that can be described. Thus, the different definitions of governance as a driving power or as a coordinating force are helpful in the analysis of the reorganisation of the cut flower industry; less as an ontology of power, but rather as a description of variations in Actor-Networks. They can then be complemented by other definitions of governance, such as the distinction between public (state-based) and private (industry-based) governance or hybrid types between these two forms (Bair 2017), or between corporate, institutional, and collective power (Henderson et al. 2002). Governance and power are contingent parts of all relations, between lead firms and their suppliers, between producers and workers, between traders and retailers, or between governments and firms. Thus, a flexible approach to governance should be able to capture how dynamics in these relations create order and structure, but also how they are created by order and structure: 'asymmetries and power relations are produced *in* and *through* markets' (Ouma 2015, 41).

Conclusion

In this chapter, I have discussed conceptual approaches to the questions of how global economic linkages are organised, what role place plays in global economic linkages, and how reorganisation in global economic linkages can be explained. I first discussed the GCC, GVC, and GPN frameworks, which offer valuable approaches for the empirical analysis. The chain-metaphor continues to be a strong heuristic. On the one hand, its verticality enables engagement with recurring debates about global inequality and the linking of the empirical case of the cut flower industry with the broader development of global capitalism. On the other hand, the use of chains and networks impedes the merging of micro- and macro-perspectives on the reorganisation of the cut flower industry. Furthermore, the chain-approaches entail an inclusionary bias and an ontological distinction between categories such as the economy, society, and nature. Therefore, these concepts lack a theoretical explanation for the emergence, stabilisation, and breaking of economic linkages. Also, the question of what role sites like Lake Naivasha or the Dutch trade hub play in these entanglements remains open. Framing the reorganisation of the cut flower industry as a process of marketisation enables us to overcome these obstructive binaries and include non-economic factors in the analysis. A marketisation perspective helps to explain how new market orders are realised, and how new governance structures come into being and are consolidated in an already existing market.

Considering the diverse merits and limits of chain and network concepts, as well as their ongoing popularity in research and in developmental policies, the examination of these approaches cannot be limited to the conceptual dimension. As such, I will continue this discussion throughout the empirical analysis. A pragmatic and flexible, yet precise use of the different concepts allows for a juxtaposition of the GCC, GVC, and GPN frameworks and a marketisation perspective on the cut flower industry.

Nevertheless, some basic conceptual specifications have to be established: firstly, the analysis is focused on linkages in myriad forms. I understand these connections as neither vertical nor horizontal, neither as global nor local *a priori*. Secondly, I conceive place in a 'global sense' (Massey 1991) and as unique nodes of economic, social, political, cultural, and ecological linkages of Actor-Networks. Thirdly, power in economic linkages is analysed in its uneven distribution amongst agencies and their interactions. Thus, there are numerous different forms of power and governance that can be described. Fourthly, I frame reorganisation in global economic linkages as a fluid and dynamic process that produces order as well as disorder in markets, and includes as well as excludes actors.

Finally, I approach the cut flower industry as a STA and thus as being composed of 'heterogeneous elements' (Callon 2007b, 319). This means that its reorganisation takes place on different levels all at once: socially, technically, materially, and discursively. Therefore, I include all these levels in the analysis. The economic is conceived as an outcome of relations on all of these levels. To trace economic outcomes, I focus the analysis on the breaking and forging of linkages within the cut flower industry and the inclusion and exclusion of (human and non-human) actors. These linkages are best traced in a micro-analysis of Actor-Networks, by exploring how specific linkages are brought about, organised, or ordered. After tracing these Actor-Networks and the cut flower STA, it will be possible then to categorise the reorganisational processes by applying the different concepts discussed in this chapter, depending on which scale, place, actor, or sphere (economic, social, ecological) on which the particular part of the analysis is focused.

3

Trading Roses: Reorganising Producer-Buyer Relations in the Dutch Cut Flower Network

'For me, flowers, it's about talking Dutch'.[1]

The Netherlands is the most important link between Kenya's cut flower industry and European retailers and consumers. In 2015, the country was the destination of over 60% of Kenya's exports. Consequently, the question of how the Dutch floriculture network gained and managed to retain its pivotal role in the cut flower industry is central in the analysis of Lake Naivasha's relation to European floricultural actors. The Dutch cut flower hub becomes even more interesting when one considers the dynamics of cut flower trade, retail, and consumption. The shift of flower production to equatorial countries, the increasing flower sales of retail chains, and the growing importance of standards in retail are fundamental changes that challenge the established linkages and roles within the flower network.

Nevertheless, much like markets, firms, and the forging of trade relations in chain-studies, the Dutch cut flower network has not been made the object of inquiry in any previous studies of the Kenyan cut flower industry (see e.g., Hale, Opondo 2005; Gibbon, Riisgaard 2014). In this chapter, I want to open this 'black box' (Latour 1987, 1) and address the questions of how the cut flower industry developed into a global network, how the Dutch flower industry, as a main hub of trade and production, was reorganised by current dynamics in this network, and how it managed to sustain its pivotal role despite shifting relations in the cut flower industry.

In the following pages, I want to give four main answers to these questions: firstly, I will show that the changing role of the Dutch flower industry can be related to general tendencies in agricultural trade and current dynamics in the sales and consumption of flowers. Secondly, the Dutch flower industry plays a crucial role in reframing the cut flower market, although it has undergone fundamental changes. Key market encounters are tightly bound to Dutch flower networks including traditional auction sales, but also recently

---

[1]   IV 84, Sales and Marketing, Flower Company.

established direct sales and virtual encounters between producers and sellers. Thirdly, the definition of what is actually traded is closely related to these market encounters in the Netherlands. Objectifications of flowers, that is the determination of what is a tradeable commodity, became more diverse with a new focus on bouquets and mass products. And fourthly, the Dutch flower network controls the valuation of cut flowers and the price-making process. It has kept its pivotal role by a reconfiguration of its strong Actor-Network: business strategies were adapted, linkages to new actors were built and reorganised, knowledge about the breeding, production, and trade of flowers was deployed, and Dutch governmental policies backed the reorganisation of its cut flower industry.

From a conceptual perspective, I will also evaluate in this chapter the ways in which the concepts of the GCC and GVC frameworks can assist in outlining basic changes in the Dutch cut flower Actor-Network. On the one hand, they can explain the shift towards more buyer-driven relations and captive coordination mechanisms. Yet, on the other hand, they are not capable of explaining the way these dynamics influenced the establishment of new trade channels, the introduction of new commodities, and the making of prices.

Selling roses: A brief history of the global cut flower market

In order to assess the role of the Dutch trade hub in the global flower network, a quick look at the historic development of this network and current dynamics in the sales and consumption of cut flowers is necessary.

From local to global: The historical development of the cut flower industry

The 'culture of flowers' (Goody 1993) as known today emerged in the early 19th century. Before this, flowers were reserved for the lives of kings and nobles (Ziegler 2007, 16). The rise of cut flower production and consumption started with the industrial revolution. The industrialisation of Europe and North America brought along with it the formation of a new upper and middle class based on industrial wealth, urbanisation, and the adjacent alienation from 'nature'. Leisure practices such as domestic flower gardening and plant collecting as well as innovations like greenhouse gardening and the breeding and propagation of hybrid tea roses from Chinese roses in France led to a sharp rise in fresh flower sales at the end of the 19th century (Ziegler 2007, 20–3). During this time, the contemporary cultural meaning of flowers emerged. Fresh flowers became part of the identity and distinctive practices of the new upper-middle class in their suburban homes and for social events like weddings (Ziegler 2007, 24). By that time, most florists were retailers and small growers with two or three greenhouses just outside the urban areas (Ziegler 2007, 33). This changed with the emergence of wholesale florists that initiated a differentiation of retail florists and growers and enabled the expansion of flower growing into (domestic) areas distant from the cities. The agricultural restructuring process in countries of the Global North after the Second World War also applied to flower farming: farm numbers decreased, productivity rose, costs and prices dropped. Eventually, most local flower farmers gave up in favour of bigger farms (Ziegler 2007, 35–8). Since the emergence of a culture of flowers in the 19th century, the demand for cut flowers has always been especially high in winter. Therefore, seasonal constraints were a major problem for North American and European flower growers. In the 1960s, the cut flower industry was finally able to 'solve' this problem – by outsourcing production to equatorial countries. This outsourcing was part of a larger development: the integration of former 'peripheries' of global capitalism (Hopkins, Wallerstein 1977) into commodity and capital circuits through the production and trade of non-traditional agricultural export products. The integration of African, Latin American, and Asian countries into global commodity flows came along with a fundamental change in agricultural production, trade, and consumption – based on 'post-fordist models of agricultural production' (Raynolds 1994). Following Piore and Sabel's work on flexible production systems (1984), Raynolds (1994) shows that the globalised production and trade of fresh fruit and vegetables requires flexible, specialised, and efficiently organised agricultural supply chains. Innovations in communication and transportation technology enabled the outsourcing of fresh produce growing from their core destinations in North America and Europe. Fuelled by the developmental model of export-led growth and structural adjustment programmes, Latin American and African countries supported the introduction of non-traditional agricultural export products like wine, grapes, or cut flowers (Selwyn 2016, 1776). These products became a major source of foreign exchange for Colombia, Kenya, and other equatorial countries by making use of favourable climate conditions, cheap labour, and reduced freight charges (Robinson 2008; Selwyn 2016). Hence, since the 1970s, cut flower production, like many other agro-industries, has been globalising. The preconditions for this development were revolutions in cooling, packaging, hybridisation, propagation, transportation, and the migration of cut flowers 'from fields to greenhouses' (Ziegler 2007, 55). Fresh flowers were turned into a controllable, easy-to-handle mass product. This development attracted financial capital that facilitated the expansion of flower growing in equatorial countries.

At the same time, the number of domestic producers in North America and Europe dwindled. The majority were not able to meet the demand of year-round supply nor to produce as cheaply as the new growers did. Resistance against imports by tariffs could not be kept up, as nearly all other industry actors except flower growers (middlemen, wholesalers, and florists) profited from year-round, inexpensive supply (Ziegler 2007, 44). As a result, the amount of global flower exports leaped from US $ 1 billion to US $ 9.3 billion within 30 years between 1988 and 2018.

Higher imports, more labels, lower prices: Recent dynamics in the global cut flower industry

The contemporary global cut flower market is highly concentrated in terms of the main product, the country of origin, and the country of destination. The most important product by far are roses, the main importers are the European Union (EU) and the United States. Five countries dominate the export statistics with a total share of over 85%: after the establishment of equatorial countries as producers of cut flowers in the second half of the 20th century, Colombia, Kenya, Ecuador, and Ethiopia accounted for 35% of global cut flower exports in 2020.[2] The top producers of cut flowers are India (total production area 31,000 ha) and China (15,000 ha). Yet, these countries almost exclusively produce for the domestic market. For the first time, these developing countries outnumbered the Netherlands, which is still by far the most important single exporter with a share of 49%. After huge increases in the 1990s and early 2000s, the growth of overall trade volume has slowed down in the last five years. Therefore, current dynamics in the global cut flower market are not caused by a general market expansion or fundamental shifts in regional market shares (Rikken 2012; van Horen 2017c). The global Covid-19 pandemic has even led to a small decline in flower exports in 2020, mainly caused by the disturbance of air freight logistics.

The global cut flower trade is roughly channelled longitudinally: the main destination for South American flowers is North America, whereas the EU is the main importer of East African cut flowers. However, this categorisation predominantly concerns flowers sold in supermarkets. The European

---

[2]   Unless otherwise stated, the figures and statistics in this chapter refer to data provided by UN Comtrade and International Trade Centre (ITC). All data refers to HS Code 0603, which includes cut flowers and flower buds of a kind suitable for bouquets or for ornamental purposes, fresh, dried, dyed, bleached, impregnated, or otherwise prepared. Figures from UN Comtrade and ITC partly deviate from data by the Kenya Flower Council (KFC) and other Kenyan outlets, such as the Kenya National Bureau of Statistics (KNBS). Interviews with officials from the KFC, and my own data collection, suggest that KFC data is more valid for Kenya. Therefore, in the following sections, I will base my analysis of Kenya on KFC data. Nevertheless, I will also refer to UN Comtrade and ITC data, as only they provide data on global cut flower trade flows and the trends and general assumptions are identical.

specialised value chain for high quality cut flowers still relies heavily on South American suppliers, especially Ecuadorian roses. In the unspecialised value chain supplying European supermarkets, South American growers are not able to compete with East African growers on a larger scale. This is mainly due to high air freight costs, but also because of the less industrialised production standards and higher costs in the South American flower industry. Therefore, large Andean producers focus on the American market. Colombia especially has been the principal supplier of flowers for US-American retail chains, such as Wal-Mart and Costco, since the 1980s (Robinson 2008, 65).

In return, the Kenyan agro-industry is highly dependent on the European cut flower market and its dynamics: 70% of Kenya's exports are sold to the EU. But vice versa, Kenya also became a significant player in the European cut flower market, as it accounts for around 40% of EU flower imports. The EU cut flower market volume is estimated at € 20–25 billion, comprising almost half of the world's cut flower sales (CBI 2016). Regarding revenues (and not the number of sold stems), the European market is to a large extent saturated. Fluctuations in sales mainly depend on the consumer climate and currency exchange rates. This became evident during the economic crisis of 2008 as well as during the Covid-19 pandemic when sales numbers dropped. Overall, analysts expect European flower sales to increase only moderately in the coming years, whereas the global growth markets are mainly located in Asia (Altmann 2016; van Horen 2017b). Thus, dynamics in the European cut flower market are mainly related to shifting trade flows, volatile prices, new market channels, and changing consumer behaviours.

European cut flower trade flows can be divided into two categories: imports from non-EU countries and intra-EU trade. The former have gained significant importance over the last few years, amounting to over € 1 billion worth of imports in 2020. This development relates to the establishment of cut flower production in developing countries, as these account for over € 1 billion and therefore the vast majority of imports (see Figure 1). The rising importance of Kenya, Colombia, and Ethiopia has compensated for the slight decrease in domestic cut flower production, especially in the case of roses. Rose production areas have diminished drastically: in the Netherlands, from 932 ha in 2000 to 280 ha in 2015 (CBI 2017a); today, roses in Germany are grown on only 323 ha (Destatis 2017), roughly a tenth of Kenya's production areas and only 50% more than at Lake Naivasha.

But still, the majority of cut flowers are traded within the EU: at € 3.1 billion in 2020, imports from EU-countries are almost three times as high as other imports. Yet, these statistics serve to conceal producer-to-retailer and producer-to-consumer relations to a certain extent, since they do not unveil the 'black box' of the Dutch trade hub, i.e. they fail to reveal much about its

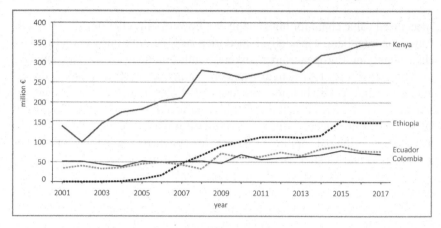

Figure 1. Flower exports to four selected EU markets, 2001–17: Netherlands, Germany, UK, France (Author, ITC).

internal functions and mechanisms. The Netherlands is an important producer, the leading exporter, and a trading centre for imported cut flowers all at once. A large portion of these imported flowers are later forwarded abroad and, therefore, appear in the Dutch import as well as the Dutch export statistics. This is why Kenya's relationship to end markets, especially in Europe, are hardly traceable by trade balances. Statistically, for all European countries, the Netherlands is the largest source of imports, whereas shares of developing countries are much lower. For instance, the direct trade flow between the UK and Kenya that was central to many previous analyses (Hughes 2000; Hale, Opondo 2005; Dolan 2007) equals only 15% of Kenya's exports and 7% of the UK's imports; in comparison: in 2017, 82% of UK flower imports came from the Netherlands. Consequently, the question of how the Dutch floriculture industry managed to retain its pivotal role is central to the analysis of the Kenyan cut flower industry's relationship to European markets; not only to unveil trade flows from producers to consumers but also to understand what implications this has for Kenyan producers.

Besides the Netherlands as the main European importer, developments in consumer markets are influential for the Kenyan flower industry. Germany (€ 4.3 billion), France (€ 3.1 billion), and the UK (€ 2.9 billion) are the most important consumers of cut flowers in Europe (CBI 2016). They are the main importers of Dutch flowers, of re-exported flowers from developing countries, and, apart from the Netherlands, of flowers directly exported from East-African countries. Although heterogeneous in certain aspects, such as consumption per capita or market channels, some similarities between these consumer markets can be observed. Roses are the most important cut flowers for all European countries with a total import of over 5 billion stems from non-EU countries in 2014, which equates to 65% of cut flower imports from developing countries (CBI 2016).

In all of these markets, prices are highly volatile and show huge seasonal deviations with peaks at Valentine's Day and Mother's Day and lows in European summer. Furthermore, they depend on political and economic stability in Europe: this was shown by the drop in flower sales during the economic crises in 2008 and 2013 and following the European sanctions against Russia in 2014 – an important export destination for flowers produced or traded in the EU. In the long term, prices seem to be stable as the average price for flowers traded at Royal FloraHolland indicates (see Figure 2). Yet, considering inflation rates, the decennial stagnation in prices from 2008 to 2017 actually equates to a drop in revenue per unit for producers of about 9% in the same period (see Figure 2).

The 9% decrease in real prices is closely related to a shift in market channels. These can be divided into specialised retailers – mostly traditional florists – and unspecialised retailers including supermarkets, fuel stations, kiosks, etc. Prices in the unspecialised retail channel are much lower than in the specialised channel. This development started with the market entry of supermarkets. The entry of supermarkets into the cut flower market is a consequence of the 'global retail revolution' (Selwyn 2016, 1776) which has been ongoing since the 1970s. The saturation of domestic markets for staple food and the liberalisation of retail led to a 'mega concentration and centralisation of retail capital' (Selwyn 2016, 1777) in many countries of the Global North. Making use of new transport and cooling technologies, new retail corporations

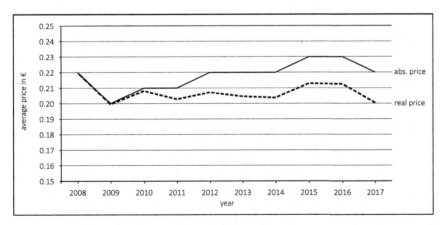

Figure 2. Average flower prices at Royal FloraHolland (absolute and real prices) (Author, FloraHolland 2008, 2011, 2015a, 2016, 2017, Statista).

were able to satisfy the demands of a high-income and high-consumption middle class by supplying niche markets with specialised and fresh import products year-round (Robinson 2008, 59; Aufhauser, Reiner 2010). McMichael describes this 'centralisation of agri-food relations' (McMichael 2005, 291) as a 'corporate food regime' that is the main reason for the 'reorganization of food supply chains' (McMichael 2005, 291). The size and capital of these new actors in the global food system enabled them to extend their influence from simply retail to consumption, trade, and production (Lawrence and Burch 2007). These powerful new corporate actors then proceeded to diversify their product portfolio and 'branch out' into non-food commodity chains (Lawrence, Burch 2007, 5). In this way, the introduction of cut flowers onto supermarket shelves was part of the formation of 'global supermarkets' (Robinson 2008, 59). These supermarkets are transnational corporations with commodity portfolios composed of products from all over the world. The market entry of retail chains ended traditional florists' centennial monopoly on cut flower sales (Ziegler 2007, 134). Today, the share of market channels varies significantly in Europe (see Figure 3).

Yet, the tendencies are identical all across the EU: supermarkets increase their share, while florists' sales drop. Moreover, online sales are still small, but have risen significantly in recent years. The global pandemic in 2020 accelerated both these trends tremendously. While in large parts of Europe,

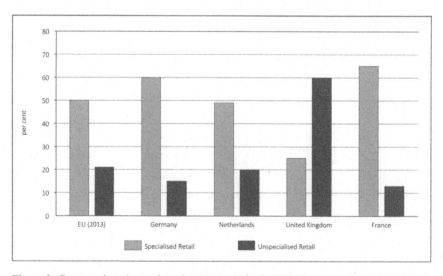

Figure 3. Comparative share of market channels in the EU, Germany, Netherlands, UK, France, 2016 (Author, CBI 2016b, Rabobank 2016).

florist shops were closed, consumers continued to buy flowers in supermarkets. In Germany, the share in the value of supermarket sales increased from 33% to 37% just from 2019 to 2020 (Quetsch 2021). In the UK especially online sales skyrocketed during lockdown. Market analysts expect equal market shares between unspecialised retail, specialised retail, and online sales within the next ten years (van Horen 2017a). The market channels differ greatly in terms of how they sell which cut flowers to whom and at what prices. Cut flowers in the specialised channel are often sold because of product quality, arrangement, and assortment. Traditional florists usually offer a broad range of flowers, including specialties, new and innovative varieties, and expensive high-quality flowers. In Eastern Europe, these are frequently sold as single stem, whereas in other European countries the focus lies on handmade and individual bouquets (CBI 2017c). Floral services play a crucial role, especially for special occasions such as weddings and funerals for which freelance floral designers are increasingly hired (Ziegler 2007, 132). On the other hand, retailers in the unspecialised market channel usually offer a narrow product range, since flowers are a secondary and supplementary product in their portfolio. Ziegler calls the supermarket channel an 'abundant chain' (2007, 132), since retail chains offer standardised bouquets of small to medium sized flowers which are predominantly roses in uniform quality. Many of these flowers are certified with a sustainability or fairness label, although the prices in this market segment are very low, especially in comparison to the specialised retail chain. For instance, the average price of supermarket bouquets was € 2.35 in Germany in 2020 (Quetsch 2021).

Finally, consumer behaviour is a driving force in the cut flower industry. Consumers buy cut flowers as a gift, for special occasions, or for personal and home use as decoration (FloraHolland 2015b). In contrast to those first two reasons, cut flowers purchased for personal use are usually bought on impulse. The unspecialised channel is mainly targeted at this group of consumers. Thus, it is not surprising that consumers buy cut flowers at supermarkets due to convenience and low prices, while florists rely on expertise, quality, and service (FloraHolland 2015b, 10). At first sight, certifications seem to be an important purchase incentive as well. Hence, the majority of market analysts (e.g., CBI 2017a; van Horen 2017c) and social scientists (e.g., Riisgaard 2009a) attribute the reason why more than half of the flowers sold in Europe are certified (Riisgaard 2011, 442) to a growing consumer demand for 'sustainable' and 'fair' products. Yet, consumer studies (FloraHolland 2015b) point out that, particularly in unspecialised retail channels, the main reasons for cut flower purchases are the price, the appearance, and the quality of cut flowers: 'Price is the only aspect that truly requires attention in order to increase satisfaction with the rose in the Netherlands, Germany and France'

(FloraHolland 2015b, 9). Meanwhile, the story behind the rose, its sustainability, or its country of origin are far less important. In fact, consumers are often not aware that the majority of cut flowers sold in supermarkets are imported from Eastern Africa (see FloraHolland 2015b). Therefore, the demand for labelled flowers does not sufficiently explain the spread of certification schemes in the cut flower industry.

The culture of flowers has undergone significant changes since its emergence. The shift of rose production to equatorial countries and the increase of trade flows have turned the cut flower industry into a global network. Within this global network, the Netherlands is the main centre for trade. Yet, recent dynamics such as the increasing flower sales of retail chains, the growing importance of standards in retail, and the decline of flower prices challenge established linkages and roles within the flower network. Before examining how these current dynamics relate to the Dutch flower network, I will show how this network gained importance in the global flower industry and how it developed from a production centre into a trade centre.

From growers to traders:
The shifting role of the Dutch flower industry

Market-making processes are based on specific geographical settings. At the same time, they serve to transform these settings. This becomes clear when looking at the shift of the role of the Dutch flower network within the cut flower industry. Historically, cut flower production evolved around the biggest population centres in the Netherlands. Dutch flower growers became the main suppliers for other European countries because of the well-developed Dutch agricultural infrastructure and the Netherlands' long colonial tradition of trading (Ziegler 2007, 74–5). Until the 1990s, the Dutch flower industry strengthened its leading position and became 'virtually unrivalled in world markets' (Patel-Campillo 2011, 90). This success was facilitated by governmental support and the establishment of grower cooperatives. The Dutch government set up the necessary transport infrastructure, agricultural research institutions, and *Productshappen* (Product Boards), vertical oversight organisations that spurred agricultural networks and ensured the quality of production (Ziegler 2007, 77). Furthermore, the Dutch government made the use of cooperative auctions mandatory in the early 20th century. After their initial establishment in 1912, these cooperatives centralised the production of small flower growers and created trading platforms. The pooling of supply enabled the standardisation and innovation of flower handling (Patel-Campillo 2011, 87–9). It also mitigated risks for growers by formalising transactions and introducing down payments. The broad and reliable supply ensured by these cooperatives, as well as the quicker trading and handling process compared to other flower hotspots, favoured the Dutch growers and enabled them to gain control over the European cut flower market. Today, cooperative auctions are the core of the Netherlands' flower industry.

After reaching a peak of over 5,000 growers in the 1980s (Patel-Campillo 2011, 90), Dutch flower growers have faced serious competition from equatorial countries over the past 30 years. High energy costs for the heating of greenhouses, higher labour costs compared to Kenya or Ecuador despite the increasing share of migrant workers from Eastern Europe and Turkey, and an increasing demand for standardised cheap flowers instead of specialties and high-value roses challenged the pivotal position of the Dutch flower industry. Initially, in 1994, the Dutch grower cooperatives tried to fight imports by restricting access to their auctions. Yet, after equatorial growers had established new links to European buyers in the 1990s, the Dutch flower industry changed its strategy. It shifted its focus from mere production to a combination of specialising its production on high-value varieties and the trade of imported flowers. The fact that the Netherlands kept its central role within the cut flower networks because of this profound shift from a production to a trade hub in the 1990s indicates that Actor-Networks may persist despite changes to the fundamental dynamics in its configuration (see Müller 2015, 79).

The linkages between flower firms, state actors, infrastructure, and many more human and non-human actors within the Dutch flower network proved to be flexible and steady for three reasons. Firstly, the tight entanglement between infrastructure, government support, and the cut flower industry facilitated the rapid distribution of billions of flowers in the Netherlands every day. For most Kenyan flower farms, Schiphol Airport south of Amsterdam is the most important physical entry port to European and even to Russian buyers. The expansion of Schiphol Airport into a logistics hub was supported by the Dutch government's 'mainport' strategy. The mainport strategy describes the Dutch policy to turn the Netherlands as a whole into a transportation hub for international trade, mainly by expanding the port of Rotterdam and Schiphol Airport (Levelt 2010, 84). This policy included the construction of a fifth runway, of new service areas, of freight handling facilities, an increase in customs efficiency, and better road connections to the flower industry's main location around Aalsmeer (Levelt 2010, 84–8). Linkages between these material infrastructures and other actors, such as governments, firms, and trade technologies, are strong in the Dutch flower network due to its historical development. Therefore, Schiphol's position as a major link for perishables to Europe is nearly unrivalled. The Perishable Center at Frankfurt Airport and its shareholder Lufthansa Cargo try to challenge this position and compete for flower freights. Despite lower prices, more modern facilities, and the relative closeness to Eastern European and German retailers, the number of flights from Kenya to Frankfurt was reduced in 2015 (IV 53, Product Manager, Cargo Airline) and some flower growers even haul their exports from Amsterdam to Russia by lorry (IV 22, Head of Production, Grower). '[O]nly if something extraordinary happens, they use ... Frankfurt' (IV 84, Sales and Marketing, Flower Company).

Secondly, the Dutch flower industry made good use of its knowledge with regard to both breeding and trading. As marketisation literature reminds us, power asymmetries arise mainly from the unequal distribution of knowledge (Çalışkan, Callon 2010, 13; Ouma 2015, 39–40). In the cut flower industry, knowledge is key in the process of flower handling, price-making, and in breeding new varieties (see Chapter 6). Flower handling was revolutionised in and around the auction halls in Aalsmeer, Dutch traders have significant advantages in the process of price-making (see 0), and Dutch companies – with the exception of one German breeder – dominate the flower breeding business. Although the top breeding companies are present at Lake Naivasha, with showrooms and farms, their activity there is limited to testing and the marketing of new varieties to local producers (see Chapter 6). The knowledge-intensive parts of the breeding process remain with the Dutch mother companies: 'the [Dutch] holding is owner of all genetics' (IV 37, Managing Director, Breeder), or, as one managing director put it, 'The knowledge is in Holland' (IV 34, Managing Director, Breeder).

Thirdly, the Dutch flower industry was not only able to maintain its valuable share of knowledge; it even spread its activities and expanded its network: Dutch flower companies outsourced their production and became global. A large part of the Kenyan cut flower industry consists of companies that have Dutch shareholders, a Dutch mother company, or at least Dutch managers. Since the 1990s, many of them gave up flower growing in the Netherlands, at least partly, and moved to equatorial locations. Though very local in their origins and in their internal interpersonal relations, Dutch flower companies went 'global' – or more precisely, they dispersed their locations while still considering themselves as 'family compan[ies]' (IV 37, Managing Director, Breeder). Often, the Dutch mother companies are responsible for the handling and marketing of flowers. From a GVC perspective, this process could be described as a governance process of vertical integration of functions into one company. Yet, these globalising strategies do not only occur among flower companies, but also among individuals: in the past, a major part of any career in the cut flower industry was either spent in or just a few kilometres around the auction halls. Today, farm managers in particular have become labour migrants, often going to equatorial countries. Therefore, this process can better be captured from a (dis)articulations perspective. Individuals as well as companies have been subject to processes of exclusion – mainly from production – as well as inclusion – mainly in trade, investment, and management. They have put in 'work to link up relations of production and complexly structured social formations' (Bair, Werner 2011, 992), for example by investing capital, learning Kiswahili, or moving to Kenya. In this regard, it becomes obvious that the forging and breaking of linkages is both social and spatial. Also, it illustrates that firms themselves are dynamic relational networks and not only nodes or actors within networks (Coe et al. 2008, 277). As networks, flower firms do not move up and down the GVC, but forge heterogeneous linkages at different locations in order to sustain their business.

The case of Flower Company A[3] demonstrates the shift the Dutch cut flower industry has undergone since the beginning of flower production in equatorial countries. In 1961, Flower Company A was founded near Aalsmeer by two families who turned an old carnation farm into a rose farm. After it became more and more difficult to profitably grow roses in the Netherlands, due to rising energy and labour costs, the shareholders started Flower Farm A' at Lake Naivasha in 2001. Since then it has been managed by members of the shareholder families. For tax reasons, there are no legal ties between these two farms except for the common shareholders. Yet, Flower Company A imports all flowers from Flower Farm A', and handles and markets them under the name of Flower Company A. For 13 years, roses were produced simultaneously in Kenya and in the Netherlands. In 2014, Flower Company A terminated its rose production in the Netherlands, whereas Flower Farm A' in Kenya was expanded by eight hectares the following year. Flower Company A and Flower Farm A' form a complex Actor-Network whose internal as well as external linkages have changed dynamically over the last 50 years. Actors have been excluded, such as (migrant) production workers in the Netherlands, whereas others have been included, such as (migrant) production workers in Kenya. The organisational linkage between Flower Company A and Flower Farm A' is worth considering more closely: legally, there is no vertical integration, but transactions are executed as if it was all one firm. The GVC governance model has difficulties in capturing these linkages characterised by strong personal ties that are not part of contracts or fixed transaction but performed on a daily basis.

These firm networks of (former) Dutch and foreign growers form the basis of the Dutch trade centre. They are complemented by other foreign producers, Dutch growers, and a few flower growing corporations. The network of these heterogeneous actors is the backbone of the Dutch cut flower industry as a trade hub. The core of its distributional role is precisely these linkages between

---

3 The names of the companies have been anonymised for reasons of confidentiality.

actors, not its territorial embeddedness. National infrastructure, state regulation, and formerly local networks undoubtedly played a role in the structural change, but it was the ability to link these assets to new actors and new places, and to break national boundaries that sustained the cut flower industry.

As I have shown, the Dutch flower network successfully shifted its focus from production to trade as a reaction to the rising production of equatorial countries. Yet, since the early 2000s, its position as the global trade hub has once again came into question given recent dynamics in the cut flower industry: the differentiation of consumer markets into unspecialised and specialised retail channels, the growing importance of corporate retail chains, and an increased demand for certified flowers.

Market encounters: Buyers, producers, and traders

Dynamics in cut flower trade become most visible in its core moments: market encounters. The Dutch trade hub with its centre around the world's biggest flower auction at Aalsmeer, 20 kilometres south-west of Amsterdam, is the central place for these encounters in the cut flower industry. In these encounters, calculating agencies meet goods in order to value and exchange them (Çalışkan, Callon 2010, 14). Referring to the different sociotechnical devices that organise and facilitate the valuing and exchanging of flowers (see Muniesa et al. 2007), I distinguish between three different types of market encounters: auctions, direct sales, and virtual sales. The establishment and rising importance of the latter two made cut flower trading more complex and dynamic. This created new agencies in cut flower trading, especially sales and marketing services and departments: 'the job is growing; ten years ago this job was not existing. [...] Ten years ago all flowers, cut roses – make a bunch and send it to the auction ... And now most flowers are selling by clock [i.e. by auction] *and* selling directly' (IV 84, Sales and Marketing, Flower Company, my own emphasis). As this sales manager describes, the establishment of direct sales made it possible to market flowers flexibly via different sales channels. Hence, traders are required to make use of these possibilities. Some flower growers integrate sales and marketing into their companies, or similarly export flowers to their Dutch mother companies. Others work with contracted service providers. Sales and marketing services are offered by individual freelance agents, but also by big corporate actors in the cut flower industry. These companies often provide different levels of sales services. Sometimes they act as intermediaries and only establish contacts between growers and buyers. In other cases, they are mediators that buy flowers, rearrange bouquets, export them themselves, or even market them through their own wholesale departments. These big companies have the advantage of offering the full range of flower handling and sales services to their members or customers: from transport, over unpacking to direct sales and auction deliveries. Service providers are rewarded for higher sales numbers, since growers usually pay for these services with a share of their turnover.

Sales and marketing departments, Dutch mother companies of equatorial growers, or contracted brokers ensure the engagement of cut flowers with buyers in market encounters. Buyers can be summarised in three groups. Firstly, small, specialised wholesalers aim for specific national flower markets, niche products, or express delivery. Secondly, corporative wholesalers try to offer a broad range of products to their customers, which include retail chains and florist shops. In order to optimise this system, a group of 30 wholesalers founded the Dutch Flower Group (DFG) in 2000. The DFG ensures stable supply for its members and links them to flower growers. The third group are retailers, such as supermarkets, florist chains, cash and carry stores, and independent florists. Yet, most of these buyers do not take part in primary market encounters themselves but cooperate with wholesalers or service providers: 'Supermarkets can't approach farms, they need someone to do the supply chain management for them, to take out all the hassle, and in the end the product is delivered to the door of retailers' (IV 61, General Manager, Service Provider).

Auctions

Grower cooperatives are the foundation of the Dutch flower industry's success, both in historical and contemporary terms (see also Levelt 2010; Patel-Campillo 2011). The cooperatives' main market devices are 'Dutch auctions', a clock-based selling system. This system was developed in the 17th century in the Netherlands to rapidly sell large volumes of flowers (Rockoff, Groves 1995, 11). The main device of Dutch auctions is a clock displaying the current offer price. These clocks run down at fixed rates until a buyer is willing to pay the price shown. Buyers can then buy the whole lot of offered goods or only a fraction. If they purchase only parts of the lot, the rest is auctioned in the following round. When there is only a small amount of goods left, these are usually offered as a fixed amount in the last round of the auction. All this happens in very short time, with up to 15 auction rounds and transactions per minute (van Heck, Ribbers 1997, 30). As large amounts are handled at minimal intervals, the clock cannot do any more than provide general information. Thus, the auction clock displays the attributes for the whole lot. To minimise the risk of the purchase that is executed, the buyers depend upon the goods to be homogeneous in size, quality, and appearance. In other words, the auction clock and the traded goods are not independent of each other, but form a crucial arrangement of the auction and the Dutch flower industry. This arrangement of actors is even broader: the transactions do not only include the interaction of buyers with a technical device, but also involve an auction master who sets a starting price and receives the bids and the prospective portion of the lot from buyers.

These auction systems operated by grower cooperatives have been the dominant form of market encounters in the cut flower industry for almost 100 years: for a long time, buyers have been more or less forced to participate in cooperative auctions, since growers pooled their produce in them, and at the beginning of the 20th century their use was mandatory in the Netherlands. Yet, auctions also offer buyers the advantage of a centralised trading place where a broad range of goods is constantly available. For growers, they are attractive as they mitigate the exposure to large buyers by pooling their supply. Moreover, auction sales are – as intended by the grower cooperatives – 'producer-driven' (Levelt 2010, 167) since the auction mainly acts in their interest. For instance, the main task of auction masters is perceived to be achieving high prices and high turnover rates (OB 85, Flower Auction).

In the last few years, direct sales have emerged as an alternative sales channel and the share of the market they command has continuously increased. Nonetheless, I argue that auctions have kept their pivotal role in linking (Kenyan) producers and (European) buyers. Because of its distinct role as a sociotechnical device within the Dutch cut flower industry, it does not only create linkages through actual transactions, but is also closely entangled in processes of valuation and price-making. I intend to explain this by focusing on the most important grower cooperative: FloraHolland (see Figure 4).

FloraHolland organises the most important Dutch flower auctions. The company is the result of a 2008 merger between FloraHolland and its biggest rival Bloemenveilingen Aalsmeer. Today, it consists of over 3,700 members and generated a turnover of € 4.7 billion in 2020. The cooperative operates 38 auction clocks through which almost 100,000 transactions are conducted per day (FloraHolland 2020). These auction clocks are spread over four branches in the Netherlands and one facility in Germany. FloraHolland's biggest trade centre is located in Aalsmeer, less than ten kilometres away from Schiphol Airport near Amsterdam, and therefore in relative proximity both to production sites (via air freight) and European consumer markets (via road freight). The auction facilities are not only home to the auctions themselves but also the centre of the Dutch cut flower cluster with businesses that cover the full spectrum of suppliers, flower growers, handlers, traders, and wholesalers. 720 of them even have facilities within the auction building in Aalsmeer (FloraHolland 2017) and hundreds more in its vicinity. Additionally, FloraHolland also offers flower handling and transport services. Both members

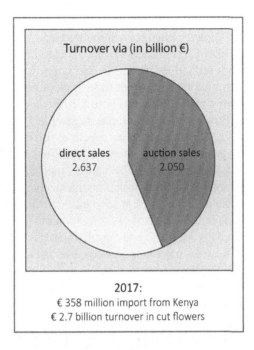

Figure 4. Key sales figures of FloraHolland, 2017
(Author, FloraHolland 2017).

and external customers have access to these services, with higher fees for non-members. Since the share of direct and virtual sales is increasing, the important role of flower auctions, as being the place where main market encounters happen, and therefore also FloraHolland's business model itself appears to be under threat. Yet, though the cooperative does face a necessary shift from regular auction sales to direct sales, flowers worth over € 2 billion were traded via the auctions in 2017. This turnover contained 6.3 billion cut flowers and the revenue of imported flowers at the biggest auction in Aalsmeer even grew by 2% to € 298 million (FloraHolland 2017).

One reason for this ongoing importance are the terms of FloraHolland's auction sales and membership. Firstly, growers highly appreciate the instant cash flows for sales ensured by the auction organisers: 'The benefits of the auction are [that] you get your money straight away. So, sold in the morning and straight away the money is in your account' (IV 45, General Manager, Grower). And secondly, FloraHolland actively binds members to its accounting system: they have to invoice all their transactions via FloraHolland's accounting system, no matter if direct, virtual, or via the auction.

The ongoing popularity of the auction is also rooted in the distinct relations of the Actor-Network around its clocks, in and beyond transactions. Market encounters between suppliers, flowers, and buyers are ephemeral on the auction; they last only for a few seconds until the next auction cycle is started. Selling and buying flowers on the auction is a 'gamble' (IV 21, CEO, LNGG) for all actors involved. From a GVC perspective, these transactions can be described as coordinated by market relations. Yet, linkages involving market devices are maintained and stabilised by various mechanisms that cannot be grasped by solely looking at the transactions themselves. Personal relations play an important role in flower market encounters. I want to stress that these personal relations do not lie outside of economic transactions. Rather, personal relations between buyers, brokers, and suppliers are an essential part of the process of valuing flowers, calculating prices, and deciding which goods to buy. As a look into the flower auction shows, it is impossible to separate personal from economic relations in the cut flower industry:

> [The] relationships seem to be very personal. [The Flower Trader] greeted almost everybody and seemed to know most of the people, even some of the 'normal' workers who were for example driving the electronic lorries. Everywhere we entered, we just went in without knocking or asking permission and nobody seemed to care. [The Flower Trader] helped himself (and me) [to] coffee both at the auction masters' room and at the premises of a wholesaler. The people we talked to appeared to be less business partners and more friends. … [T]hey were mixing private things (like [talking about] the Champions League football match yesterday) and business all the time. Though everybody is really busy, nobody was disturbed by [the Flower Trader] nor by me. One made a joke about me not being allowed to take pictures, which apparently was far from realistic to him. Most of the people we spoke to (especially the 'brokers') were men between 30 and 50 … [The Flower Trader] told me that most of the flower people grow up with the business, slip into its work and grow within a company. … Almost everybody talks in Dutch (though they speak decent English) and once [the Flower Trader] said that he prefers to talk Dutch while selling. Everybody is having coffee all the time and a small chat … It is important to stay in contact with the buyers, that's why he usually visits the auction and buyers after the clock time is over; then they have time for 'eye-to-eye contact' and a chat. (OB 85, Flower Auction)

Personal networks and economic networks cannot be distinguished *a priori*; only the outcomes of interactions in networks can *ex post* be described as economic, for instance when it is the exchange of flowers. These tight network relations have stabilising effects on the ephemeral auction market encounters. Two of these effects are visible in price-making mechanisms and the valuation of flowers: on the auction tribune, peer pressure leads to a homogenisation of prices around a medium if enough buyers are present (see Figure 5). And in order to value flowers, buyers need to be knowledgeable about the growers' reputation and their product qualifications. This information is not standardised nor written down in codes but rather circles as tacit knowledge among the cut flower network, as this observation from the auction shows:

> When [the Flower Trader] was talking to brokers they were without hesitation talking about which variety is being grown by which grower, who the breeder is, and how it is performing; this is really impressive regarding the countless different flowers being traded each day. (OB 85, Flower Auction)

Based on these relations and this knowledge, the auction continues to be an important market encounter. Yet, its function has changed: until the 1990s, it was basically the only relevant global trading place for cut flowers. Today, its importance in terms of the share and the total numbers of flower purchases is declining. Nevertheless, the auction is still the main reference point for price-making processes in the cut flower industry. For instance, when negotiations about an Economic Partnership Agreement between the EU and East African Countries failed in 2014 (see Chapter 7), levy taxes were introduced for flowers. Rates for these levies were calculated based on auction prices (Omondi 2014). For buyers, traders, and growers, the details of more than 100,000 transactions per day are made visible and transparent,[4] enabling them to instantly react to volatilities in the market. Furthermore, growers use the auction to present their produce and to test new varieties:

> ... in Holland we call it a 'vitrine'. Then you are on the clock and they buy [from] you on the clock, and [when] they are missing some flowers ... then they call you. But ... [it's] on the auctions [where] there are [the] most buyers. They are your eyes for the rest of the world. First, it is important to be there. We see some flowers they are not on the clock anymore and they have to hire extra people to sell all the flowers. When you have a standing position on the clock then you are in the connection, they see you, they hear you, they talk about you. (IV 84 Sales and Marketing, Flower Company)

---

[4] All auction participants can simply observe prices and deals on the clock. Yet, this transparency does not include general price statistics, which is much more sensitive information and not accessible to all auction participants.

The auction is thus a sociotechnical market device linking suppliers and buyers, although the actual transactions are not always conducted through it. Therefore, even buyers that prefer direct sales present a basic stock of their portfolio on the auction: 'We always have about 1,500 stems, each variety, each length on the clock' (IV 84 Sales and Marketing, Flower Company). Buyers still use the auction because of its broad supply. They trade via the auction to fill up their supply, especially on peak days, when their regular supply through direct sales is not sufficient, and on specialties that are still preferably traded via the auction: 'Some varieties need to sell through the auction, because it is high quality, bigger head size, it's a small niche market' (IV 45, General Manager, Grower).

This way, the auction managed to stay a pivotal actor within the Dutch cut flower network despite some disadvantages. The auction entails technical limitations that deter retail chains and some wholesalers. Due to the ephemerality and multitude of sales relations, supply chains are hardly traceable from producer to customer. Traceability is, however, a prerequisite for some business-to-customers (b2c) labels such as Fairtrade that are in high demand by retail chains. The auction clock only displays the MPS label, a business-to-business (b2b) standard which is a minimum requirement. Thus, social standards do not play a role on the auction (see also Riisgaard 2011). Lastly, transaction tariffs (€ 1.15 charge per transaction and a levy of 0.19% of the purchase revenue in 2018) and handling tariffs (€ 1.50 per transaction in 2018) at the auction are regarded as expensive compared to direct sales.

Direct sales

Since the 1990s, parallel to the auction, a second market encounter has emerged in the cut flower industry: direct sales. The growing importance of direct sales and direct sourcing is linked to the expansion of retail chains' activities from distribution to production and handling (Aufhauser, Reiner 2010; Burch et al. 2013). In the late 20th century, the creation of large, transnational corporate retailers resulted from the liberalisation of (food) retail markets in Europe and North America and the centralisation of retail capital. In order to generate profits all along their supply chains, these corporations aimed for control over production and trading processes. Instead of vertically integrating upstream activities, supermarket chains followed Wal-Mart's example and began to set up a network of distribution centres that enabled the direct sourcing of (fresh) agricultural products from independent and contracted producers (Lawrence, Burch 2007, 8; Aufhauser, Reiner 2010, 262–4).

Accordingly, in the cut flower industry, direct sales gained importance with the market entry of European retail chains. In 2014, direct sales outnumbered auction turnover at FloraHolland for the first time (FloraHolland 2015a). These direct sales provide several advantages when compared to the auction: trans-action costs are lower since auction fees and intermediaries can be avoided; they enable the traceability that consumers, retailers, and standard setting organisations ask for; direct sales ensure the efficiency and rapidity of transport and logistics necessary for perishables; prices are less volatile and more predictable; and lastly, the risks of a shortage of supply for buyers or of demand for suppliers is lower, since supply amounts are usually fixed for a certain period: '[S]upermarkets ... can't rely on the auction, because they need a specific number of stems every week. You can't buy that on the clock because one day it's not there and the other day it's there, so, you need regularity (IV 76, Sourcing Manager, Auction Services).

The term 'direct sales' implies a close relationships between large corporate buyers and comparatively small flower producers. This leads to a shift in coordination mechanisms and power relations, which have been described in previous studies as buyer-driven (Hughes 2000, 179; Hale, Opondo 2005, 302; Riisgaard 2009a, 328). The leading role of UK supermarkets in particular has been stressed: 'UK retailers are having a massive impact on the dynamics of the cut flower trade, both influencing patterns of consumption in their favour and re-ordering the supply channels that serve them' (Hughes 2000, 183). Making use of the dualistic, governance-as-driver conceptualisation of the GCC approach (see Gereffi et al. 1994), the idea that a shift towards buyer-driven agricultural value chains has been facilitated by direct sales or sourcing is very common among scholars (see e.g., Barrientos et al. 2003). It usually follows this line of argument (see Lawrence, Burch 2007, 6): due to company mergers, the purchase volumes of corporate retailers are growing. This increases their buying power and their economies of scale, which in the end leads to favourable sale terms for buyers that are forced upstream onto tightly controlled producers.

When looking at the cut flower industry as a whole from a macro-perspective, this argument is valid. Big buyers are performing the functions of lead firms that control producers. For instance, most Kenyan flower growers hold retail chains accountable for a decline in real prices over the last years: 'supermarkets ... just drive the prices down, down, and down. I have never seen the price go up in a supermarket' (IV 22, Head of Production, Grower). Yet, a closer look reveals that these power relations cannot be solely explained by the emergence of direct sales. In order to explain how buyers are 'defining not only what is to be produced but also how and under what conditions it is to be produced' (Barrientos et al. 2003, 1513), we first need to understand 'the processes that engender the forging and breaking of links between circuits of commodity production, people and places' (Bair,

Werner 2011, 992) and to scrutinise how direct sales come into being, and how they are stabilised and maintained.

Firstly, it is important to understand that direct sales not only involve growers and retailers, but a multitude of other actors, such as the sourcing companies for retail chains, wholesalers, exporters, and sales agents marketing products for growers. The term direct sales incorporates many different configurations of these actors. For instance, retailers source from wholesalers who have direct connections to a Kenyan farm's sales agent in the Netherlands. The configurations often depend on product specification, such as the flower's head size: 'We concentrate on exporters now because of the head size. Shortly, we had [a rose variety], it's small, it's for the retail but now we have a bit more bigger heads and small for the cash & carry and the wholesale' (IV 84, Sales and Marketing, Flower Company). Similar to auction sales, personal relations, reputation, and knowledge about products, prices, possible buyers, and suppliers are necessary to enrol oneself into the Actor-Networks of direct sales. The forging of these relations is often done via auction sales or based on personal contacts via phone calls or mails. This sales agent describes how he connects to direct buyers as follows:

> By the clock, the vitrine, and our name is on the sleeve and our name (...), our email, and [our] website is on the sleeve and they will find you. ... Yeah, sometimes it happens that [a wholesaler] is buying my roses, and he's buying more than 30,000 a week and he's calling directly, it happens. (IV 84, Sales and Marketing, Flower Company)

Only a few of the direct sales resulting from these encounters are based on formal written contracts. The quantity of supply and prices are usually fixed by oral agreements and handshakes: 'It is a fluid arrangement. There are not some sort of contracts with the supplier. No contracts, it's more about establishing a working relationship and the retailers prefer working with certain suppliers ... So it is a tricky relationship to maintain' (IV 43, Managing Director, Grower). As this manager describes, the stability of these linkages requires serious maintenance work, especially from suppliers; it is performative as it is the result of the daily relations and contacts between supplier and buyer. These 'fluid arrangements' also vary in regard to the time period and frequency of transactions. Some of them are just single purchases; others are fixed for a whole year.

The process of forging, stabilising, and maintaining these dynamic relations in direct sales is tightly enmeshed in the Dutch cut flower network: the forging of linkages is based on personal contact or the traditional market device of the auction itself; and knowledge about products, prices, and actors is the foundation of the valuation of linkages. These factors, combined with the obligation for

FloraHolland's members to invoice all transactions via its accounting system, has secured the Netherlands a pivotal role in the newly established market encounter of direct sales, which on first sight does not appear to be bound to any specific place.

The multitude, diversity, and informality of direct sales create producer-buyer relations in the cut flower industry very similar to what Harvey has observed for agro-food industries: '[The] pattern is very different from the stereotype of a linear supply chain. It is also quite contrary to the conception of any simple domination of the upstream economic agents by all-powerful, concentrated, oligopolistic, retailers' (Harvey 2007, 63). Power relations are to a large extent dependent on the actors involved in transactions, in other words they are relational. Therefore, the definition of direct sales, or even of the cut flower industry as a whole, as buyer-driven is too simplistic. In order to classify transactions, the governance terminology of the GVC approach is more applicable. In part, the market-based relations of the auctions have been replaced by more hierarchical relations. Yet, the hierarchy of these relations does not originate in exploitive contracts, as these barely exist. As I will show later in this chapter, they are more related to the ability of buyers to define which goods are suitable for retailers and customers and to their control over price-making mechanisms.

Virtual market encounters: Digital auctions and online sales platforms

Market encounters do not necessarily only entail personal contact between suppliers and buyers, an increasing number are conducted virtually. With the spread of information and communication technology throughout the cut flower industry, virtual market devices have become increasingly enmeshed in other market encounters or even form new encounters themselves. Three forms of virtual market devices have gained prominence in the cut flower trade.

First, consumer online shops have created new actors that source flowers directly from the Dutch cut flower network. Internet sales have been increasing, with the UK taking the lead role with 14% of all online flower purchases in 2015, and are expected to have an equal market share to supermarkets and florists by 2027 (van Horen 2017b). This trend has been accelerated by the various lockdowns that occurred during the global pandemic in 2020, when many consumers preferred online shopping over visiting retail shops – even when it came to buying flowers.

Second, auctions have been digitalised. In 1994, foreign producers set up The Tele Flower Auction, a digital alternative to the auctions of the Dutch grower cooperatives after the ban on their imports from other Dutch auctions. The success of these digital auctions, due mainly to their rapidness and efficiency, brought about a critical reassessment of the grower cooperative auctions. In the early 1990s, these were almost at maximum capacity with little opportunities to increase efficiency (van Heck, Ribbers 1997), as they relied fully on physical interaction: buyers had to be present at the auction tribune and the flowers for sale were displayed on trolleys on a rail track under the mechanical clock. As a consequence, the auctions were also digitalised at FloraHolland (Levelt 2010, 182). This included the digitalisation of the auction clock and subsequently the option to purchase remotely. Later in the 2000s, the act of physically displaying the flowers in the auction halls themselves was also abolished. Today, buyers can be situated anywhere in the world and, as a result, the auction tribunes are much less crowded (see Figure 5).

In 2017, over 70% of the turnover at FloraHolland's auctions were via remote purchases (FloraHolland 2017, 30). Following the impact of the Covid-19 pandemic and the restrictions on social contact since 2020, it is now even FloraHolland's official strategy to transform from a 'physical market place into [a] digital platform' (FloraHolland 2020, 10). Although, buyers do still have to interact verbally with the auction masters in order to make their offers.

Third, various online sales platforms have been established as new forms of market encounters. In part, these platforms are services offered by newly founded companies. Other platforms, such as FloraMondo, belong to established agencies like FloraHolland. FloraMondo combines two types of market encounters by offering so called 'clock pre-sales' and direct sales. The total turnover on these platforms grew to over € 150 million in 2017 (FloraHolland 2017). This development coincides with FloraHolland's vision to digitalise its

Figure 5. Auction tribunes at FloraHolland Aalsmeer. Only a few buyers are present on the auction tribune, where buyers sit to bid for flowers. Also note the tracks in the front below the auction clocks: until a few years ago, flowers were driven on these in front of the auction tribune (Author).

market encounters: '[We] are transforming from a physical marketplace to a digital platform at a rapid pace. This represents not only the digitalisation of our own services, but especially the digitalisation of the entire sector as well' (FloraHolland 2017, 13).

The emergence of virtual market devices and the digitalisation of traditional sales platforms changed market encounters in several ways. It put forward processes that are associated with marketisation, such as 'anonymization, the cutting of social ties, and rational, calculative and efficient post-social coordination' (Berndt, Boeckler 2012, 199). Prior to the digitalisation, all buyers had to be physically present at the auction tribune. This proximity led to a homogenisation of prices as deviating purchases were often commented upon or even laughed at. Since the digital auction can be accessed online from anywhere, this peer pressure among those present at the auction has diminished, resulting in higher uncertainty regarding prices. In the early stages of the digitalisation process, the 'cutting of social ties' through screen-based trading led to criticism and even boycotts by buyers and the first trials for digital auctions were terminated in the early 1990s (van Heck, Ribbers 1997, 30). Even today, more than ten years after the introduction, buyers partly refuse digitalised auctions: '[With] the online system, they destroyed it' (IV 87, Sales Manager, Import/ Export). Nowadays, the auction tribunes are only busy during peak days. To a large extent, the flower trade is now a digital business and resembles stock market trading. Digitalisation processes also affect the valuation of flowers through buyers. Since the abolishment of the physical display of flowers in the auction halls, product information is solely transmitted digitally by pictures, which are often stock images or only updated on a weekly basis, by the name of the buyer, and by the attributes of the flower (size, head size, variety). In this way, the digitalisation of auction clocks had some contradictory effects on flower trading: remote purchases anonymised auction sales, but the buyers' physical distance to the commodities on offer rendered certain social factors like trust and reputation more valuable. Additionally, digital market encounters brought along new price-making mechanisms: on digital platforms, prices are set by the suppliers during the upload process, 'it's a bit [like] gambling' (IV 84, Sales and Marketing, Flower Company). Virtual market encounters further complexified the cut flower trade. They were either enmeshed in existing systems or created new trade channels. Remote buying enabled the spatial dispersion of cut flower buyers; yet, as 'remote' implies, this only meant buying at a distance from a central trading place, it did not dissolve this centre itself. Virtual market encounters appear to be 'placeless', but they are firmly nested within the Dutch cut flower network: Dutch companies run online platforms, and although physical flows are separated from trade flows, the former still frequently cross through the Netherlands.

As shown above, the changing relations within the cut flower trade following the entry of corporate retailers into the market brought about the emergence and rising importance of new market encounters: direct sales and virtual markets were established in addition to traditional auction sales. Still, the auctions have retained their important role as a sociotechnical market device. Nowadays, they assist in forging linkages between buyers and producers beyond simply the auction sales themselves, and they are a reference point for price-making processes and the valuation of flowers. Across all three market encounters, the growing power of corporate retailers can be observed. Yet, the complexity and diversity of market encounters, as well as the high importance of personal relationships, trust, and reputation within the Dutch cut flower network, challenges the notion of a monocausal relation between emerging direct sales and a buyer-driven industry. In order to assess the question of how power relations materialise in linkages between buyers and producers, an examination of the valuations of cut flowers and price-making processes is instructive.

Objectifying cut flowers: Bouquets and certifications

Materiality plays a decisive role in the process of market making. In order to be valued as a commodity, things need to be transformed from entangled beings into passive commodities with predictable qualities, they need to be 'pacified' or 'objectified' (Çalışkan, Callon 2010, 5). As I will argue in this section, in these processes of pacifying flowers an unequal distribution of knowledge and material equipment results in power asymmetries (Callon, Muniesa 2005, 1238; Çalışkan, Callon 2010, 13; Ouma 2015, 39–40). In the cut flower trade, retail chains can impose their qualifications and valuation of goods on others.

Cut flowers do not possess a value *a priori*, they need to be objectified through a process of stabilising and defining their qualities and by delimiting their quantity (Callon, Muniesa 2005, 1233). In order to be calculable, they need to be comparable and have a value for the buyer, they need to be 'singularized' (Callon, Muniesa 2005, 1233). Objectifications and singularisations are not static but constantly ongoing and highly dynamic processes. Historically, the shift of cut flowers from a highly exclusive luxury good to a year-round available, everyday gift or item for home decoration was made possible by a 'civilizing process' (Ziegler 2007, 55). This transformation included innovations in breeding, production, handling, and marketing. Today, the pacification of cut flowers can be divided into two categories: product specifications and (legal and non-legal) requirements to gain access to markets.

Product specifications

The global agro-industry has experienced a post-Fordist diversification, with more specialised and niche products (Robinson 2008, 58). In the cut flower industry, this process was driven by the market entry of retail chains. Since then, the pacifying of roses has been split into two segments with different pacifying processes.[5] Traditional florists in the specialised chain usually offer a broad range of flowers, including specialties, new and innovative varieties, and expensive high-quality flowers. In comparison, the retailers in the unspecialised market channel usually sell a narrow product range and highly standardised small to medium sized flowers. This specialisation and segmentation entailed a new valuation of flowers and resulted in changes to breeding, handling, branding, and a new delimitation of the item for sale – from single stems to bouquets.

Flower breeding is increasingly dependent on market information. Due to the high volume of flowers they sell, retail chains have a large quantity of information about consumer preferences. Hence, the knowledge about what customers want is unequally distributed and gives retail chains an advantage in terms of their relationship to producers and breeders. Although the knowledge-intensive parts of breeding are mainly based in the Netherlands, flower fashions are set elsewhere: in the corporate headquarters of retail chains, at floral designer shows, and in floral and lifestyle magazines, all shaping the producers' and customers' valuation of specific flower varieties (see Hughes 2000). Retailers play a decisive role in the selection of new flower varieties apart from agro-technical indicators like yield. The current quest in breeding (and accordingly in production techniques) for maximising the vase life of flowers is to a large extent at the request of corporate buyers (see Chapter 6). New product varieties and new market segmentation often bring about the branding of products as a common singularisation strategy. In the cut flower industry, the brand names of flower companies or the different varieties of flowers play a role during the grower-buyer exchange, as they are attached to valuation processes based on the reputation of or experience with the product quality of a particular farm or variety: 'In Holland, … people know the variety names' (IV 32, Sales Manager, Breeder). Yet, these valuations are not related to consumption patterns: 'At the retailer, they could not care less about the name' (IV 34, Managing Director, Breeder), and 'some customers do not want

---

[5] Ultimately, of course, the delimitation of these segments is generalised and not definitive. At some points, the two market segments overlap; retail chains may also sell specialised flowers, florists small flowers, and some retailers (such as those operating kiosks) work between both segments. As I will show later, growers partly target both retail outlets (see Chapter 5).

to see the name on the packaging' (IV 28, Farm Manager, Grower). Here, the far more common singularisation process relates to certifications and labels.

The most important change which the emergence of the unspecialised retail chain has brought about is the new delimitation of the items for sale, in other words a new objectification of cut flowers. In specialised retail shops, flowers are usually sold as single stems or in individualised bouquets assembled on the spot and according to customer requests. Therefore, the standard commodity in this chain is the single stem. The valuation process refers to single cut flowers that need to be both special and impeccable at the same time. In contrast, unspecialised retailers sell ready-made, mono- or mixed-colour bouquets of standardised flowers. The criteria for cut flowers to become valued and thus turned into commodities (see Ouma 2015, 31) differ substantially. Here, objectification does not concern single stems but rather bunches of flowers: flowers need to have a standardised size and a uniform quality and appearance. This trend towards mass standardisation is reinforced by the digitalisation of the auctions and the subsequent display of stock pictures of the flowers for sale. This shift in what is rendered tradeable in the cut flower industry has had serious consequences for the production (see Chapter 6) as well as for the trade and handling of flowers. Bouquets are made and valued according to the wishes of retailers: 'Some supermarkets have some pretty weird demands' (IV 82, Former Shareholder, Flower Farm). Bouquets for retailers are either assembled and packed on the farm or during the handling around the sales process. Although growers prefer to pack them on Kenyan farms due to labour costs, which are up to 75% lower compared to the Netherlands, they have to be flexible to meet the buyers' demands. The handling and packing of flowers is crucial in the process of valuing cut flowers. As previously discussed, purchases are mainly made according to a supplier's reputation. The reputation for product quality is to a large extent based on the quality of (un)packing and the presentation of flowers at the auction and during the sales process. Growers can improve their trade relations mainly by investing in handling and the unpacking of flowers (see Chapter 6).

Legal and non-legislative requirements for market access

Apart from product specifications, requirements for market access are part of turning cut flowers into tradeable commodities. Some of these requirements are set by compulsory EU legislation. Singh lists seven different legislative requirements for access to the EU market (2013, 45–9). These include phytosanitary regulations, rules on trade in endangered species, on product specifications, on secure supply chains, and on packaging material, tariffs, and the enforcement of the intellectual property rights of breeders. These regulations are an 'attempt … to harmonize the market in cut flowers' (Singh

2013, 43) – or, in other words, an attempt to standardise cut flowers. They do not attach a value to flowers in the sense of a price, but they are part of the objectification process of flowers for the EU prior to transactions. These objectifications involve a lot of bureaucracy for suppliers and traders: '[The] market will always give some restrictions. ... [I]t's really a complicated business. It is because we are dealing with diverse markets; different customers need different specifications' (IV 63, Agronomist, Supplier). Part of this work is already done in Kenya during production or transportation, for example the phytosanitary inspections carried out by the Kenya Plant Health Inspectorate Service (KEPHIS).

The most important non-legislative requirements for market access are certifications based on product standards. Standards are important sociotechnical devices within the calculation process of goods, and they can be conceived as 'socially constructed and enforced conventions' (Ouma 2010, 204). In the cut flower industry, standards play various roles at different stages in the process of qualifying flowers. For customers, b2c labels like Fairtrade or Rainforest Alliance are mainly meant as an individualisation strategy. These often deploy geographical knowledges, for example by displaying East African flower farm workers or by making supply chains transparent through a tracking system. Yet, this geographical imagery and information is often presented to consumers that are either uninterested in or uninformed about the product's background: consumer studies show that consumers hardly ever know of a flower's origins and that it does not play a major role in their purchasing decision (see FloraHolland 2015b). For retail buyers or wholesalers, certifications are less an instrument to individualise cut flowers, but more a tool of control over suppliers in the process of valuing cut flowers.

Some standards serve a similar function to legislative regulations – this especially concerns MPS (Milieu Project Sierteelt). MPS is one of the oldest certification schemes. It was initiated by the Dutch flower industry in 1993. Its aim was twofold: to develop strategies to reduce environmental impact, and to make these efforts visible in order to promote a positive image of the industry (MPS 2019). Nowadays, it is the minimum requirement for auction sales and the only label shown on the clock: 'No MPS – we're no longer friends' (IV 61, General Manager, Service Provider). Thus, MPS is important for all flower transactions. On the contrary, 'Fairtrade is only going for supermarkets at the moment. Maybe it starts also for customers on [a] small-scale, but so far, it's mainly for supermarkets' (IV 28, Farm Manager, Grower).[6] There are plenty of other b2b and b2c certificates with different priorities that

---

[6] Today, the purchase of Fairtrade labelled flowers via the auction is not even possible, since FloraHolland cannot facilitate the accounting of the Fairtrade Premium

play more or less important roles in direct sales.[7] Certifications are new socio-technical devices in the process of qualifying cut flowers that differ substantially from the traditional devices of reputation and personal contacts. They enable a qualification of commodities based on written and formal standards with formal sanctions for non-compliance. Therefore, by deploying standards, buyers – mainly corporate retail chains – found an effective way to formalise and control the valuation process of cut flowers, which was hard to access for external actors because of its informality. Today, all retail chains apply their own set of certifications. Combined with distinct national demands and product specifications, the requests for a flower's particular qualities are very specific: 'Let's say the [corporate retail chain] supermarkets, they have a 50cm [referring to the stem length] Fairtrade line, they specify that' (IV 28, Farm Manager Grower); and the requirements can be high: 'I think the quality Fairtrade wants are insane' (IV 43, Managing Director, Grower). This concerns not only the production process, but also handling, bouquet assortment, and transportation, which requires high flexibility and quality assurance in the unspecialised retail channel: '[The] way we handle general cargo is not the way we handle perishables. Perishables are supposed to be imported or air freighted under a certain room temperature, because they are perishables; that's why they are called "perishables"' (IV 62, Sales Executive, Freight Forwarder).

As shown above, the objectification of cut flowers is only partly based on its physical attributes. The valuing of cut flowers especially is related to objectification, standardisation, and singularisation processes that take place prior to or around the supplier-buyer exchange. These processes do not only refer to the physical attributes of cut flowers that are generated in its production process, but also to transport, handling, and unpacking. To a large extent, these valuations are firmly nested in the Dutch cut flower network. Nevertheless, changes in product specifications and requirements for market access have implications for Kenyan flower growers. On the one hand, farms have to follow these valuation processes and adapt to new objectifications and standardisations in order to get access to markets and products of higher value. On the other hand, the Kenyan cut flower industry was a major facilitator of these developments, for example by producing cheap mass products or by pushing their own certifications such as KFC Silver (see Chapter 5).

---

that is paid as a part of the grower-buyer transaction and is supposed to be transferred directly to the bank account of the grower's Fairtrade committee (the 'Joint Body').

[7] For a comprehensive overview of the certifications and standards used in the cut flower industry see, for example, Riisgaard 2011. The effect of standards on flower growers will be scrutinised later (see Chapter 5).

Price-setting and local knowledge

Prices are the materialisation of human and non-human actors meeting through various different forms of market encounters and their qualifications of cut flowers. They are the '[c]oncrete outcome of manifold sociotechnical relations' (Ouma 2015, 43). In order to analyse prices as a calculated, numeric outcome of economic relations, mechanisms of price-setting have to be scrutinised. The question raised here is 'who (or what) actually calculates (and how) when we say that "the market" calculates?' (Callon, Muniesa 2005, 1229). In cut flower trade, three major agencies take part in the process of price-making: buyers, traders/suppliers, and market devices that shape market encounters.

In the case of the unspecialised retail channel, the buyers' price-setting strategy is almost exclusively directed towards low prices. Consumers purchasing flowers in supermarkets mostly buy them on impulse. Moreover, ready-made bouquets are not associated with high product qualities. Therefore, '[p]rice is the only aspect that truly requires attention in order to increase satisfaction with the rose in the Netherlands, Germany and France' (FloraHolland 2015b, 9). The optimum prices for flower bouquets in these countries is estimated at well below € 10 (FloraHolland 2015b, 22–7). In order to maximise their own margins, 'buyers are trying to cut costs on all fronts' (CBI 2017b).

As a reaction to this strategy, suppliers or traders representing growers have developed complex strategies to increase their revenues. For Callon and Muniesa, the calculation of prices is always located in a continuum between qualitative judgement (ethnographic explanation) and quantitative calculation (explanation of neoclassical economics) (Callon, Muniesa 2005, 1230–2). This continuum can be observed in the sales strategies of flower traders. They have to take numerous aspects into account, such as weather conditions in Europe (the warmer it gets, the lower the prices), the quality of flowers for sale, the recent history of price developments, the purchasing strategies of competitors, and the estimated quantity of flowers offered. All this together presents a diffuse set of information upon which decisions are made over quantities, retail channels, and prices. In this process, they deploy a range of sociotechnical devices that support their qualifications, such as the reputation of their company, weather forecasts, balance sheets. Interestingly, standards and certifications are deeply involved in the objectification and standardisation of cut flowers, but they are not part of the price-setting mechanisms. For instance, Fairtrade-certified flowers used to obtain prices roughly one cent above average a few years ago, but not anymore. Buyers pay 10% of the trade price as a premium, whereas suppliers are not rewarded financially for their certifications in these transactions. Fairtrade minimum prices do not apply to the cut flower industry because of antitrust laws (IV 93, Transfair, Certifier).

In the price-making process, not only human actors but all kinds of socio-technical devices can have calculative agency. In cut flower trade, calculative devices are not only part of supplier strategies but also shape market encounters. The most important one is the flower auction. Even today, the FloraHolland auction clocks are the key reference point for the 'world price' as well as for the qualification of new varieties or suppliers. The availability of a price accessible to growers, traders, and buyers leads to a homogenisation of prices – though this effect was somewhat reduced due to the loss of peer pressure following the introduction of remote sales. The auction is run by grower cooperatives and therefore dedicated to the growers' quest for high prices (see above). Digital sales platforms brought along new forms of price-making. Here, the responsibility of bidding is shifted to the traders or suppliers as they set the fixed prices of the flowers for sale. In order to obtain high prices, traders apply complex and flexible sale strategies. One trader described his strategy as follows:

> Firstly, we use different online portals; there are a lot of different ones, but we mainly use three of them; up to 10 million of the 15 million roses we produce are sold via these portals ... The prices on these auctions are fixed by the seller, it's a bit [like] gambling. Usually, I fix the prices depending on how the varieties performed on the auction [in] the last days and how many boxes or buckets I have. So usually I add one or two cents to the auction prices as I can still sell them on the auctions [in] the next days'. (IV 84, Sales and Marketing, Flower Company)

The reason why setting prices remains 'a bit like gambling' for suppliers is related to the knowledge they can deploy in their calculations: partly it is numeric, quantitative data, but crucial parts of their qualifications depend on reputation and experience. In this regard, they make use of their knowledge from the Dutch cut flower network. Yet, corporate buyers can relate vast amounts of purchases to consumer prices and have overviews over a large variety of direct sales prices. This information is especially precious, as sales prices are the most sensitive data in the cut flower industry. FloraHolland members have access to auction prices, but no overview over direct sales prices; and other growers do not even get access to FloraHolland's database:

> Interviewer: Is it possible to get access to that [database for prices]?
>
> Respondent: No, it's not. It's only for FloraHolland and the growers, but the growers don't see all the information. ... I don't think that is possible. We don't give those prices. A lot of people think it's interesting to see direct sales, for example, of competitors, they want these prices

compared, so that's why we'll not give that out. I think it will become harder to get the prices.

Interviewer: I see, it's very sensitive.

Respondent: Yes, but you can see it on the clock (laughing).

(IV 76, Sourcing Manager, Auction Services)

Therefore, corporate buyers' databases are a powerful advantage in market encounters as described by Çalışkan and Callon: '[The] more an agency is capable of complicating its own calculation by linking it to a large number of other prices ... the higher will be that agency's capacity to determine the terms of the exchange' (2010, 19).

What are the outcomes of these price-making processes, of this 'struggle between agencies trying to impose their modes for measuring a good's value and qualities' (Çalışkan, Callon 2010, 16)? In general, cut flower prices are very volatile. Seasonal deviations are huge, with higher prices in European winter and spring and low prices in summer and autumn: at times, Kenyan growers are forced to sell their products for as low as one third of their production and freight costs in the summer (IV 84, Sales and Marketing, Flower Company). These rock-bottom prices are compensated on the flower industry's peak days: some farms generate 40% of their profit on only two days – Valentine's Day and Mother's Day (IV 42 Managing Director, Consultancy). Generally speaking, price deviations are higher at the auction than in direct sales. Here, prices are often fixed over longer periods of time, including extra payments on peak days. Also, prices of short term and single direct sales seem to be more homogeneous. Here, prices are usually fixed without lengthy discussion during a quick phone call or in a short email.

Although volatile, one general trend can be observed: the drop in cut flower prices noted elsewhere (Hale, Opondo 2005, 318; Riisgaard 2009a, 328) was confirmed by almost all interviewees, and can be seen in the development of average prices at FloraHolland (see Figure 2). These have stagnated at € 0.22 over the last ten years, equalling a decline of 9% in real prices when considering inflation rates. This development shows that corporate buyers are able to transform their knowledge into price settings in their own interest.

Conclusion: A new market order

The changing relations within the cut flower trade following the entry of corporate retailers into the market brought about the emergence and rising importance of new market encounters: direct sales and virtual markets were established in addition to traditional auction sales. These new encounters have led to a reorganisation of global linkages in the cut flower industry. Direct sales especially seem to have put forward new governance relations in the form of buyer-driven chains with corporate retailers acting as lead firms. Yet, direct sales do not causally relate to powerful buyers. And power in economic relations does not automatically derive from the size of the firms. New market orders, such as the shift in governance structures within the cut flower industry, have to be forged, constantly produced, and stabilised. The producer-buyer driven dichotomy of the GCC approach can be used to describe the outcome of shifting relations, but it does not explain the reasons for this shift or how it is realised. In the cut flower industry, direct sales are just one of many and not even the major reason for shifting power relations. Rather, corporate buyers were able to shift trade relations in their favour by influencing the objectification and standardisation of flowers to suit their own interests. Furthermore, they achieved a reduction in sales prices through the use of their knowledge in the price-making process.

New market encounters, changes in the objectification of cut flowers, and dynamic price-setting mechanisms result in a new market order for the cut flower industry. This market order introduces formality, anonymisation, and the cutting of social ties in an industry characterised by personal face-to-face contacts, reputation, and informality. Ultimately, the market entry of retail chains has not led to a simplified, buyer-driven value chain, but rather complexified market encounters, and increased their diversity in forms, volatility, and quantity.

A new market order challenges the Netherland's role as the main hub in the cut flower industry. When the market order in the cut flower industry was shifted for the first time towards production in equatorial countries, the Dutch cut flower network changed its role but still remained pivotal. Similarly, whilst undergoing fundamental changes regarding market encounters, the objectification of goods, and price-making processes, it has continued to be the central hub of the cut flower industry:

> The Dutch are in control whether we like it or not. You cannot market your flowers if you are not in the Dutch system. Yes, these are families that know everyone in the flower industry. And of course that costs us money because everybody takes his margin. I thought I could do it [marketing flowers] myself but I couldn't. (IV 22, Head of Production, Grower)

The Dutch cut flower network is the main reference point for prices, varieties, and for the forging of economic linkages. Economies of scale, especially in transport, are a main reason for this. Due to cluster effects, it is 'still cheaper to ship flowers first to the Netherlands' (IV 7, Farm Manager, Grower).

For Kenyan suppliers, this is especially important, since Jomo-Kenyatta International Airport in Nairobi, its link to international buyers, only offers a limited range of direct connections, for example to Eastern European or American destinations. When he refers to 'families' and explains that he was not able to market cut flowers himself, the Kenyan production manager indicates the important role of personal contacts and reputations in cut flower trading. The market entry of retail chains diminished the importance of these factors in valuing cut flowers and price-making. Nevertheless, they are still part of these processes and crucial in forging linkages in market encounters. Lastly, the flower grower's expression that 'of course that costs us money because everybody takes his margins' shows that Dutch flower companies are powerful in a GPN sense: their power does not relate to a position in a network, since this position has fundamentally changed several times over the last decades. Rather, these firms themselves are Actor-Networks in flux that are powerful, since they had the opportunity to create, enhance, and capture value despite changing relations (see Henderson et al. 2002, 448–9). In this effort, they were backed by the Dutch government, which supported them with policies aimed at 'increasing the efficiency of international transactions' (Levelt 2010, 90) through innovations in breeding, handling, and transporting perishables.

A supportive institutional setting and strong personal ties could lead to the conclusion that its territorial embeddedness explains the ongoing importance of the Dutch flower industry. Yet, this explanation overterritorialises relations within the cut flower industry, purifying (global) economic relations in the cut flower industry from its (local) context and turning social, political, or cultural relations into mere 'background scenery' (Jones 2008, 72). As I have shown, social contacts are not only the background for or the context to economic relations. Rather, these categories are deeply intertwined; ultimately, they cannot be separated into ontological categories. Moreover, the Dutch cut flower network does not owe its importance to its spatial location, since it is not spatially confined to Aalsmeer or the Netherlands. In contrast, the ongoing importance of the Dutch trade hub is based on its ability to spatially (in a Euclidean sense) expand, forge, and maintain these distanced linkages. The Dutch cut flower network is a place in a global sense (Massey 1991) and can be thought of as an important node created by relations in the cut flower network all over the world.

Changes in the Dutch cut flower trade network also directly relate to dynamics in the Kenyan cut flower industry, as they continue to be its most important link to European buyers. Growers are dependent on market encounters formed in and around the auctions and are increasingly involved in direct sales. In the following chapters, I will scrutinise how changes in the Dutch trade hub relate to Kenyan flower growers and especially the Lake Naivasha cut flower industry.

4

The Lake Naivasha Cut Flower Industry:
Past and Present

Over the past 40 years, Lake Naivasha has developed into the biggest cut flower producing area in Africa. Located 80km north-west of Nairobi in the Kenyan Rift Valley at 2000m above sea level, the 180km^2 freshwater lake and its surroundings are home to approximately 50 flower farms. The Lake Naivasha cut flower industry has become a major production centre, especially for European traders and buyers, and is now deeply entangled in the worldwide cut flower network. Yet, 'markets do not fall out of thin air' (Berndt, Boeckler 2009, 536), and neither do production sites within markets. Agro-industrial centres such as Lake Naivasha have a variable and contingent spatio-temporality (Coe et al. 2008, 272). Therefore, it is key to outline the historical and geographical context to current marketisation processes. In Nevins and Peluso's words:

> Our point is not only that we need to understand histories and geographies
> to show changes in commodity production but that comparisons of past
> and present commodification processes show how the very definitions
> of nature, people, and places are changing with shifting social relations
> and political-economic contexts. (Nevins, Peluso 2008, 2)

In this chapter, I will shift the focus to Lake Naivasha as a place of production for the cut flower industry by scrutinising how this area emerged as an agro-industrial cluster. In order to do so, this chapter will first outline the historical framing of Lake Naivasha as an agro-industrial centre. Subsequently it will trace the current cut flower Actor-Network.[1]

---

[1] This section focuses on the historical development and current assemblage of export-oriented agriculture around Lake Naivasha. The relation of the cut flower industry to its surrounding SES and its stakeholders will be explored in Chapter 8. As I will explain later, this delineation does not mean that the cut flower industry and the SES are part of distinct ontological categories of the economic and its (social, historical, etc.) context (see Chapter 7). These delineations are contested and part of economisation processes. Nevertheless, for the sake of clarity of argument, I will employ this distinction in this book as an epistemological categorisation.

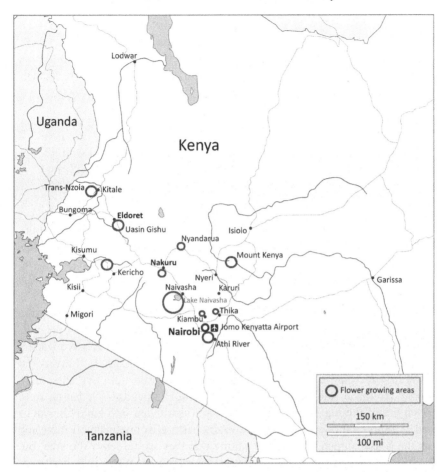

Map 1. Flower growing areas in Kenya (Cartography: Linus Zurmühlen; Source of base map: https://d-maps.com/m/africa/kenya/kenya64.gif).

Historical development: Turning Lake Naivasha into an agro-industrial centre[2]

Lake Naivasha's history is often described as a leap from a pristine natural paradise to a densely populated, urbanised agro-industrial centre. According to Mark Seal's biography on the Naivasha-based environmentalist Joan Root,

[2] This section is mainly based on archival data and interviews compiled by Gerda Kuiper. I am grateful that she shared her insights with me. Her study gives a more detailed account on the history of Lake Naivasha (see Kuiper 2019, 35–84).

Lake Naivasha was once 'a wonderland of wildlife straight out of a Walt Disney film that … is like *Doctor Doolittle* times one thousand, where 1,200 hippos swim by day and mow the grass by night amid the music of the areas' 350 species of birds'. Yet, as Seal continues, only two decades later, Lake Naivasha:

> [Had] been invaded by armies of flower growers who created some of the biggest flower farms in the world. These farms covered the lakeshore with huge plastic hothouses, inhibited the natural migration of wildlife, and attracted a desperate tide of hundreds of thousand impoverished migrant workers, resulting in slums, squalor, crime and, some insisted, ecological apocalypse. (Seal 2011, xiv)

This narrative ignores two important things. Firstly, long before floriculture emerged in the 1970s, the area was already inhabited. And secondly, it was the major transformations initiated by the inhabitants that provided the ground for the first economisation of Lake Naivasha for horticultural exports in the second half of the 20th century.

Before 1900, the area was probably closest to the picture of pristine nature with large herds of wildlife that is typically put forward by present-day conservationists. But even then, Masai pastoralists and Kikuyu traders were present. Around 1900, the arrival of the Mombasa-Uganda Railway led to the first reorganisation of the region. With the train line, British settlers arrived and made Naivasha part of their 'White Highlands'. The Masai were driven out of the region and their territory was divided into large chunks of land. A representative of a Lake Naivasha pastoralist organisation indicated that the Masai signed agreements stating that they would leave the area, but due to their illiteracy did not understand their content. When they hesitated, nevertheless, they were coerced to sign. These agreements still exist and are now contested by pastoralist community organisations, especially since the new Kenyan constitution shortened leases dating back to colonial times from 999 to 99 years (IV 52, Representative. Pastoralist Outreach Service). These estates were leased to individual European farmers who installed cattle ranches. The colonialisation of the area already created the first prerequisites for the emergence of the cut flower industry: a basic infrastructure with roads and a township (which later became Naivasha Town) was established and land ownership was coercively restructured in this period. On the one hand, the new land ownership structures created the first wage labour market in Naivasha, since Kenyans could no longer rely on their own land and were subsequently employed by the ranches. A portion of these labourers came from other parts of Kenya, representing the beginnings of the labour migration that is still today the basis of the flower farms' recruitment systems. On the other hand, after decolonisation, the large plots of land facilitated the establishment of some large-scale horticultural farms.

After Kenya's independence in 1963, only a few of the colonial settlers stayed. The rest sold their estates, partly to land-buying cooperatives and partly to wealthy foreigners attracted by the lake's scenery. The new Kenyan Ministry of Agriculture soon highlighted the horticultural potential of the area.[3] Even before flower farming took off, most of the region's produce, like pyrethrum and vegetables, was exported to Europe.[4] In the 1960s, the first cut flowers were grown in Naivasha on small-scale farms. The first large-scale growers opened up in the early 1970s. They cultivated seasonal flowers like statices and carnations. Most farms were owned by Europeans or Kenyans of European descent who had been invited or encouraged to introduce horticulture to Naivasha by the Kenyan government. Naivasha proved to be the perfect location for the production of cut flowers. Its latitude just south of the equator guarantees high insolation throughout the year which is necessary for the quick and steady growth of cut flowers; its longitude and its location 100km north-west of the Jomo Kenyatta International Airport in Nairobi give it relative proximity to European destinations for export; and its altitude of around 2,000m above sea level prevents temperatures from exceeding 30°C, which would harm the flowers. Moreover, the lake and a high groundwater level provide a steady source of fresh water, which is essential for growing cut flowers.

Although locational factors make Lake Naivasha perfect for cut flower production, and although the establishment of the industry was encouraged by the Kenyan government, the region was not automatically integrated as a 'periphery' into the 'capitalist world-economy' (Wallerstein 1974, 349). Rather, expansion phases of capitalism as described in World-System Theory (Wallerstein 1980, 129) require serious efforts by economic actors. Especially in the beginning, horticultural production for export in Naivasha was pioneering work and included a lot of trial and error. Entrepreneurs had to forge linkages to European destinations, standardise plants in accordance with local conditions of production, invent new technologies, and hire and train labourers. The story of Hans Zwager and his farm Oserian – today the biggest cut flower farm in Naivasha – is recounted by Charles Hayes and seems to be a typical report of entrepreneurship for this time (1997, 348–52): Zwager, a Dutch agro-chemical entrepreneur, bought an old colonial estate at

---

3 KNA/BV/64/50, Ministry of Agriculture, June 1970, 'Horticultural development in Kenya. Synopsis of horticulture working party draft report & recommendations for government action'.

4 AR Naivasha 1973.

the southern lake shore including a colonial palace and a ranch. He decided to 'test the market' (Hayes 1997, 248) in Europe and grow vegetables for export. When he heard about the high demand for statices in Europe, he shifted to cut flower production. After some setbacks in the beginning,

> Hans set up a new sales/distribution network in Holland and, suddenly, the estate began paying ... '[O]ur new sales organisation proved to be viable and our team soon had control on marketing and airfreight rates', says Hans Zwager. 'The problems of raising the quality of our flowers to the high standards acceptable in Europe still confronted us and, although our payroll grew larger every month, these efforts paid off. The better prices we received helped us tackle the huge debt with which we'd been saddled'. (Hayes 1997, 352)

Zwager's story shows that right from the start of horticultural production, 'investments to make markets work' (Berndt, Boeckler 2012, 205) were necessary. Making Naivasha a part of the market order of a globalised horticultural production has always involved practical, material, and ideological efforts. The historical development of Lake Naivasha as a horticultural production site reminds us that these investments also need to be examined when looking at present marketisation processes.

The Kenyan government's encouragement of horticultural production at Lake Naivasha seems to be a positive example of 'strategic coupling' – that is to say, matching the region's assets with the needs of translocal actors through an appropriate institutional framework (Coe et al. 2004). While this strategy served the purpose of strategic coupling to 'maximize the region's economic potential' (Coe et al. 2004, 472), strategic coupling also has 'dark sides' (Coe 2011, 391), since it is not concerned with non-economic development, and it 'tends toward the a-historical and a-social' (Selwyn 2016, 1772). These flaws become obvious when looking at the institutional framework for the Lake Naivasha cut flower industry after its establishment: the Kenyan state hardly interfered with exporters.[5] The industry grew rapidly and without regulation, especially in the 1980s and 1990s. In 1982, cut flowers were already being produced on 420 ha;[6] in the mid-eighties, the first farms emerged on the remote northern side of the Lake;[7] and eventually in 2002, cut flower production was officially regarded as the

---

[5]   Regulations in the Kenyan cut flower industry are examined more closely in Chapter 6.

[6]   AR Nakuru 1982.

[7]   KNA/NKU/GU/1/7/34 Minutes of the Ndabibi Sub-Locational Development Committee, 15 April 1987.

main economic activity in the Naivasha region.[8] The absence of regulation has facilitated the expansion and economic 'success' of flower farms. The adequate institutional framework for this development was the absence of public legislation – which led to low wages, precarious employment, exorbitant profits for shareholders, and environmental damage. It turns out that – at least in the case of Naivasha – the adequate strategic coupling strategy mainly served the needs of a neoliberal free trade market order. Conditions improved in the early 2000s, when most farms shifted their production from seasonal flowers to roses. Yet, this happened due to market dynamics and not because of government interventions. This shift implied a steadier production and therefore a higher demand for permanent employment and the introduction of more sophisticated production techniques, most notably the prevalence of polythene greenhouses.[9]

Diversity and similarity in the current Actor-Network

Today, the Kenyan floriculture industry consists of over 200 farms (IV 46, CEO, LNGG) located mainly in the highlands of the Rift Valley; important locations include Mount Kenya, Nakuru, and Athi River (see Map 1). The greenhouses of these farms cover a total area of over 3,500 ha (IV 63, Agronomist, Supplier). The Kenyan cut flower industry is dominated by large-scale farms that account for 97% of flower production (Bolo 2008, 37). The number of small-scale flower growers in rose production has declined constantly due to strict European import regulations and the high investments required for the steady production of high-quality flowers. Kenyan flower exports have been growing almost steadily over the past 20 years, reaching € 747 million in 2017 and accounting for over 70% of Kenya's horticultural exports (KNBS 2018) (see Figure 6).

Lake Naivasha is Kenya's central place of flower production. The basic numbers have already been outlined above: 50 to 55 farms,[10] up to 250 ha large, 40,000 employees, 2,000 ha of greenhouses, 8,000 tons of flowers per months.[11] Yet, these numbers can only give a brief overlook of the scope of the industry. They do not reveal a lot about its internal organisation, its functional division, its heterogeneity, and the actors involved. The Lake

---

[8] KNA/NKU Annual Report of the district labour officer Naivasha, 2002.

[9] The specific circumstances of rose production will be discussed later (see Chapter 6).

[10] This number fluctuates as mergers and splits of flower growing companies are common strategies.

[11] Numbers from my own data and that of the KFC, which was given to the author (unpublished).

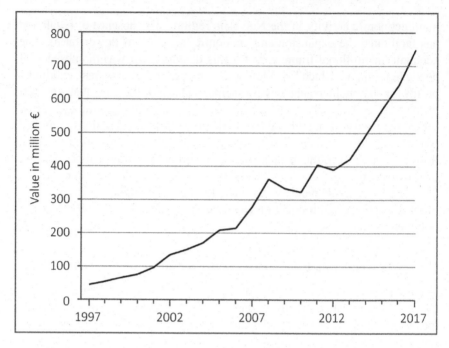

Figure 6. Kenya flower export sales, 1997–2017 (Author, KFC).

Naivasha cut flower industry cannot be reduced to a few statistics. It is a complex and diverse Actor-Network of material and social entities. Therefore, before analysing its interdependence with new marketisation processes, it is necessary to follow Latour's call (2010, 59) and describe the Lake Naivasha cut flower Actor-Network by tracing the translations of entities into it. In order to structure this account on the countless connections and complex interactions, I will trace linkages, differences, and similarities that can be divided into five analytical categories: locations, biographies, farm types, functions, and organisations.[12]

Locations

Farms at Lake Naivasha can be categorised into three groups according to their geographical location. These locations have distinct spatio-temporalities

---

[12] Actors have different roles in different categories; some categorisations overlap, others vary significantly.

(see Coe et al. 2008, 272) that also imply distinct consequences and reactions to the reorganisation of the cut flower industry. The oldest and biggest location for flower growers is South Lake. Here, the first flower farm settled in the 1970s. This farm is (at least partly and whilst under new ownership) still in business today. The farms here are connected to Naivasha Town and the highway to Nairobi by a broad tarmac road, which is partly maintained by the flower farms (see Figures 7a–c). The majority of workers either live in the settlements of Karagita, DCK[13], Kongoni, and Kwa Muhia Kamere, which immediately surround the farms, or in Naivasha Town, and with only a minority on the farms' own compounds. Most large farms with a production area of over 100 ha are situated along the South Lake road, in vicinity of the riparian land.

A few years after the first South Lake farms were established, a new flower production area emerged on the opposite site of the lake: North Lake. This part of the area is much more remote, even North Lake farm managers describe it as an 'undeveloped hinterland' (IV 4, Production Manager, Grower). This is not necessarily due to its distance from the highway and Naivasha Town, which is at most less than 20km away, but by the state of the road and transport infrastructure. The road branching off the highway was not tarmacked at all until 2016 and the first half of it has only been upgraded recently (see Figures 7a–c). This lack of infrastructure constitutes a barrier for workers as well as for flowers, and therefore 'has been a disadvantage in one way or another' (IV 72, Packhouse Manager, Grower). Regarding workers, farms here partly depend on company-owned staff buses from Naivasha Town and on on-farm housing, but they mostly recruit their employees from Kasarani, the biggest settlement in the North Lake area. Infrastructure development is partly dependent on flower farms. For instance, a newly established flower farm built the road connecting it to the lake by itself and continues to repair it once a year (IV 4, Production Manager, Grower). On the other hand, competition for resources, especially land, is much lower than at South Lake, since fewer commercial farms are located here. Land is cheaper and, even more importantly, it is available. The new farm, established in 2013, purchased 40 ha that were put up for sale by the government. Likewise, older farms here have space for expansion, a common contemporary strategy of flower growers (see Chapter 6).

Since 2001, a new form of flower farm location has been established, the Flower Business Park (FBP). An American-Israeli investor developed it after acquiring a large property 10km north-east of the lake. In time, the area was

---

[13] The name of the settlement DCK stems from the first flower company at Lake Naivasha ('Danish Chrysantemum Kulter').

Figure 7. Comparison of the road infrastructure at the three main locations of the cut flower industry around Lake Naivasha (Author).

7a. The South Lake tarmac road near Karagita.

7b. The dust and gravel road at North Lake.

7c. The paved road and gate at the Flower Business Park.

fenced off, a central infrastructure installed, and later the land was sold or leased out to farms. The investor describes his strategy as follows:

> Essentially, I put in all the infrastructure except the greenhouses. I will bring the water and everything. I will give you the cold rooms, the packhouses, the offices, the main lines, the water, the irrigation system. Everything, the reservoirs, you name it, but not related to the greenhouses. I provided it. … I also gave them local knowledge; how to hire, what to do. (IV 78, Shareholder, Flower Business Park)

The project attracted European farmers who seized the opportunity for a smooth entry into the Kenyan flower industry. Today, the flower business park hosts 210 ha of greenhouses and most farms are currently expanding their production. The park developer still provides the infrastructure (see Figure 7), including management housing. Partly as a result of the 'very selective' (IV 78, Shareholder, Flower Business Park) sample of farms approved for the project, FBP-farms try to dissociate themselves from South Lake farms with regard to infrastructure and also to reputation: '[It is] much better there [at FBP], we have our own water, are not lake-dependent, not that much gossip and bad publicity' (IV 36, General Manager, Breeder).

Biographies

The Lake Naivasha cut flower network can also be subdivided by looking at the biographies of actors working on and around farms. A look at these biographies reveals that the local flower industry is entangled in translocal networks, and therefore closely connected to other Kenyan provinces and also to the Dutch trade hub. The following categorisation is both simplistic and non-exhaustive. Yet, due to either the sheer amount or the high degree of influence of people sharing one of these backgrounds, they have to be outlined in order to explain current marketisation processes. Three types of biographies are prevalent.

Firstly, Dutch managers and shareholders have been key actors in the Lake Naivasha cut flower industry ever since its earliest days. Two kinds of biographies dominate this group: on the one hand, there are younger men educated at European universities, who proactively decided to migrate to Kenya. Their motivation is often more personal rather than based on job opportunities. This sourcing manager describes how he enjoys living in Kenya and the adventurous sides of his work: 'Life is hard for a lot of people, very hard, but it's a beautiful country. I love it, the sun is shining, and I love the sun a few hours a day. It gives you energy and the work is fantastic, I was really pioneering' (IV 76, Sourcing Manager, Auction Services). This next farm manager, in his early forties, is another typical example (IV 7, Farm Manager, Grower): before he moved to Naivasha in 2008, he was working in the car industry as an engineer. Though he 'grew up with flowers' due to the family-owned flower farm near Aalsmeer, he had no special education in horticulture. But he thinks that 'it is very similar to engineering and his education helps him a lot'. After a cross-continental journey through Africa together with his wife, they opted to live in Africa. Therefore, he quit his job, joined the family business, and took over the company's production site at Lake Naivasha. On the other hand, there are middle-aged Dutchmen with a wealth of practical experience but no university education. They were typically more or less forced to migrate to Kenya because of the downfall of cut flower production in the Netherlands. Here, the case of a fifty-year-old head of production serves as an exemplar (IV 8, Head of Production, Grower): this manager had not been professionally trained in floriculture but claimed to have 'experience in agriculture since his childhood'. Before coming to Kenya, he had worked in California where he had led two farms. Upon returning to the Netherlands in 1999, he met a flower business developer at the auction, who asked him to become his farm manager in Kenya. Ever since, he has lived in Kenya and has been employed by several farms. Unlike the younger Dutchmen, these managers strongly identify as farmers who oppose corporate structures and their administrative and financial departments: '[T]hey're just office people, they don't have a clue about roses' (IV 36, General Manager, Breeder). Both Dutch groups share hobbies, such as rally-racing, and socialise in common meeting places. The network of Dutch farm managers and stakeholders in Naivasha is an outpost of the Dutch cut flower network. Linkages forged in Aalsmeer endure in Naivasha and are the backbone of recruitment systems for farm managers, of cooperation between farms, and of connections to European buyers. Take for example the recruitment of this former head of production after he was laid off by his employer (IV 45, General Manager, Grower): when he left his previous role, he passed this news on to two of his friends among the Dutch managers at Lake Naivasha. 'The news spread like a fire', and two hours later the shareholders of another farm called him and offered him the position of general manager. This Dutch cut flower network in Kenya is actively supported by the Dutch government, represented by the Embassy of the Netherlands in Kenya in Nairobi. In accordance with a general shift in development policies, from aid to economic partnerships (Savelli et al. 2019), it sees its role as a 'broker of contacts and knowledge' with a focus on agriculture and horticulture.[14] Therefore, the embassy holds receptions for Dutch investors and high-ranking Kenyan politicians, presents itself at the IFTEX, the Nairobi flower expo, acts as a mediator, and tries to 'make trade as smooth as possible' (OB 88, Employee, Dutch Embassy).

Secondly, Indians and Kenyans of Indian descent form another group with similar structures.[15] India is one of the largest rose-growing countries: India's production areas for cut-roses total 31,000 ha (Rabobank 2016); yet, unlike Kenyan flower growers, Indian farms almost exclusively produce for domestic consumption. Therefore, knowledge transfers and capital investment into Kenya are common. Flower farm management has become a very mobile profession, so some Indian managers of Lake Naivasha farms have been headhunted from within their home country. For instance, the newly established farm at North Lake hired an Indian general manager (IV, 30, General Manager, Grower). After finishing his university education in plant science at an Indian university, this manager worked in the Indian flower industry. Although he claims to see himself as 'a grower', he gained particular experience in setting up new farms in India. Eventually, he was headhunted by a professional recruitment company, who were commissioned to find a general manager for the new farm by its Kenyan and Colombian investors. He took the offer and moved to Naivasha with his new employer promising him shares of the farm in the future.

---

[14] Brochure, 'The Embassy of the Kingdoms of the Netherlands in Kenya'.

[15] The core Actor-Networks I traced were the ones around Dutch managers or shareholders. Hence, compared to Dutch networks, Indian networks are underrepresented in the sample and, therefore, the analysis of this group is less extensive.

The third type of prevalent manager groups are black Kenyan supervisors. I explicitly refer to black Kenyans here, since the group of white Kenyans (of European descent) are actually more similar to foreign managers. They are usually trained at Kenyan universities. They are highly mobile in terms of their chosen employers and their location of employment: in order to secure higher positions within farms, they always look for 'greener pastures' (IV 57, General Manager, Grower). Therefore, these managers have experience of various different farms and environments. The following curriculum vitae of a production manager offers some insight into this type of career (IV 77, Production Manager, Grower): he holds a diploma in Farm Management from Egerton University and started his career as a greenhouse supervisor at a large farm in Naivasha. Later, a French-owned farm hired him as a senior supervisor where he worked for two years. Then his current farm employed him as a technical manager and, three years later, he was promoted to production manager. These careers differ significantly from the careers of Dutch and Indian managers described above, as Kenyans only very rarely reach the top of farm management. I encountered only two Kenyan general farm managers who both had extraordinary experience in flower farming, which in the end was what made general management achievable for them. Yet, one of these only held the position for two years, and the other is the general manager of a rather small farm with a size of 15 ha (IV 19, Former General Manager, Grower; IV 57, General Manager, Grower). On the one hand, this shows that after a period where there was a distinct 'lack of skill' (IV 68, Sales Manager, Supplier) within the available Kenyan workforce, the Kenyan educational system has been able to produce sufficient output for the cut flower industry. On the other hand, it proves that Kenyan applicants can compete for top management positions with foreigners who have privileged access to these jobs through their personal contacts. These positions are attractive to both groups: salaries are exorbitant for Kenyans and attractive for European farm managers. They range from around KES 250,000[16] per month for a senior grower, responsible for 10–20 ha, up to KES 1 million[17] per month for a general manager of a large farm (IV 68, Sales Manager, Supplier; IV 57, General Manager, Grower).

---

[16] Equivalent to € 2,272. The exchange rate between the Kenyan Shilling and the Euro fluctuates significantly. At the beginning of my fieldwork in February 2014, the exchange rate was € 1 = KES 117; in June 2019, it was € 1 = KES 113. Henceforth, I will provide conversions based on the exchange rate in July 2015, when most of the data had just been compiled: € 1 = KES 110.

[17] Equivalent to € 9,090.

The typology outlined above seems justifiable especially since segregation between these groups is common: 'There are groups I do not mingle with so much, the Indians' (IV 41, Managing Director, Grower). Although segregated along lines of race and nationality, the management network in Naivasha is quite small, especially in terms of the top management. It comprises less than 200 people, and most managers know each other: 'It's very small ... you get to know all the main suppliers and main people in the businesses. You do, ... because there are not so many people around' (IV 22, Head of Production, Grower).

The group of managers is small, then, but internally segregated. However, the socio-economic gap between these managers and the biggest group of actors within the cut flower industry, the workers employed on the farms, is even bigger. This gap is also reflected in a gendered division of labour: whereas top management is almost entirely male dominated, more than half of the field workers are female. Many of these workers also share common characteristics in terms of their personal biographies (see also Kuiper 2019, 85–126): the majority came to Naivasha as labour migrants from other parts of Kenya, particularly from the Western Province. The lack of opportunities to secure their livelihoods in these places coupled with the prospect of an industry hiring thousands of workers made Naivasha an attractive destination right across Kenya. Awareness of the active recruitment going on in Naivasha andthe opportunities the offered started to spread through personal contacts and family networks. Even after coming to Naivasha, most workers maintain tight relations with their places of origin and usually plan to return after retirement.

A closer look at the commonalities between the various biographies of actors in the Lake Naivasha cut flower network reveals that, both in management and among the general workers, mobility is a central feature. The vast majority are in one way or another migrants due to Lake Naivasha's relatively short history as a permanent settlement. As such, by looking at the biographies of the main actors of the Lake Naivasha cut flower network, it becomes clear that this network is not confined to the spatial boundaries of the region.

Farm types

Lake Naivasha flower farms can be categorised based on their size and corporate organisation. Middle-sized farms dominate in Naivasha, with only two operating on more than 200 ha. The majority of farms employ between 501 and 1000 employees, which equates to a production area of roughly 30–60 ha (see Figure 8). Thus, a vast majority of these farms would be classified as belonging to the mid-tier in European economies. A look at the prevailing forms of corporate organisation supports this categorisation. Only a few farms are part of larger corporate enterprises. These corporations operate several farms in Kenya – usually between two and five – that are controlled from a central administration, often located in Nairobi. These headquarters are responsible for sales and marketing, handling, transport, finances, and accounting for all farms in Kenya. The shareholders in these firms are international (though rarely Dutch) and often with Kenyan partners. Investments in the cut flower industry are usually geared towards long-term commitment, mainly due to fixed investments in the infrastructure of the farms. As a result, there is a relatively high level of continuity in terms of shareholders. Continuity in shareholding predominates to an even greater extent in the second type of farm organisation – owner-managed companies. Dutch shareholders especially tend to manage their farms themselves; on the one hand, due to their personal and professional backgrounds and, on the other, because they regard it as a success factor:

> The successful farms here in Kenya are those of which the owners or at least a very good manager are on top of it, because it's not something you can close on Friday afternoon and the whole will be okay, when you come back on Monday. It's a 24/7-thing – you have to be there because one mistake [and] your crop is gone or your year is gone. It's possible to make good money with it, but you have to do it right. Not everybody can do it. (IV 37, Managing Director, Breeder)

Moreover, owner-managed Dutch farms identify as family companies. In order to legitimise this claim, they often connect their Kenyan branches to the company history of the Dutch mother companies. Due to taxation, these family companies are often actually split companies that are not legally merged but owned by different members of one family (see also Chapter 3).

Breeders are an exceptional case in terms of corporate structure. They are multinational enterprises with headquarters in the Netherlands or Germany. Their small farms in Naivasha serve as facilities for testing varieties, as well as sales and marketing offices for the mother companies. Together, they form a complex corporate organisation. Genetics are owned by the mother companies and often Kenyan farms are legally independent companies that are contracted by the European parts of the corporation. Here, the conception of GPN scholars of the firm itself as 'a relational network' (Coe et al. 2008, 277), and not only as a part of a network or as a node in the chain, proves to be right. Due to the size of Lake Naivasha's cut flower industry, all of the ten major breeders and other, smaller companies operate branches around the lake who are often responsible for the activities of the companies in all of Eastern Africa. By looking at the forms of corporate organisation, it once again becomes clear that the Lake Naivasha cut flower industry is closely linked to the Dutch cut flower network; not only in terms of personal biographies, but also through internal firm networks and the construction of corporate networks.

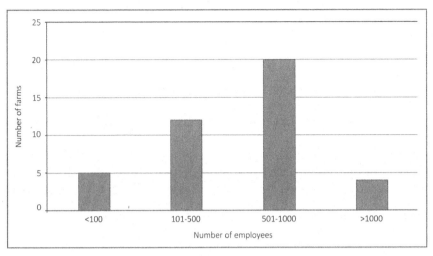

Figure 8. Size of farms by number of employees (Author, own interviews, LNGG, KFC, Happ 2016).

Functions

The Lake Naivasha cut flower network includes not only growers but the full spectrum of the industry. Although supply, transport, and other production inputs are certainly 'productive (i.e. value-added) activities leading to and supporting end use' (Sturgeon 2001, 10), and therefore have to be conceived as part of GVCs, they rarely play a role in GVC analysis. The GCC and GVC studies on the cut flower industry are good examples of this research gap (see e.g., Hale, Opondo 2005; Riisgaard 2009a). A brief look at the cost structures of flower farms makes it clear that these actors need to be considered when assessing dynamic market relations: besides labour and air freight, production supplies account for the larger part of expenses in production (see Figure 12). Supplies can be split into three groups: the 'hardware', for example crop-treatment products; greenhouses and the polythene covering them; and other supplies, such as (protective) clothing. Regarding the first two categories, two big players headquartered in Nairobi account for the largest source of demand. These Kenyan companies are not the producers of their supplies but wholesalers for the chemicals and fertilisers of 'multinational companies' (IV 63, Agronomist, Supplier), like Bayer and Syngenta. Furthermore, they offer 'after-sales services' to their customers: '[We] don't produce, we just market the products. We also do some other added values like blending fertilizer for the sake of the customers. We do the soil analysis and realise that maybe the farmer needs some specific elements. So, we blend for them' (IV 63, Agronomist, Supplier). Greenhouses usually stem from global centres of horticultural technology, such as Israel, the Netherlands, or more recently also India. Despite this duopoly, farms tend to split their orders over different suppliers to avoid exclusive dependencies. Relations between growers and suppliers are usually fixed in 'open contracts' (IV 63, Agronomist, Supplier), which determine the terms of transactions, but leave prices and amounts open. Prices are then negotiated on a weekly basis, especially for fertilisers.

Breeders play an important role in the Lake Naivasha cut flower network, although their local branches do not play a decisive role in the selection of new varieties.[18] Yet, they take part in marketisation processes by cooperating with flower farms and retailers in the process of creating new products (see Chapter 6). Some breeders also commercially propagate flowers or have a small area for growing flowers (see Table 2). Only three specialised propagators offer their services at Lake Naivasha, mainly because propagation is seen as a stand-ardised task. The main objective of propagation is to produce uniform quality; innovation and novelties are rare in this section of the flower business. As such, some of the growers run their own propagation units. Growers represent the largest share of the cut flower industry and studies and media reports often equate the Lake Naivasha cut flower industry specifically with flower growers. Growers differ substantially in size, in their internal organisation, in the production techniques they employ, in the variety of activities in which they engage, and in the retail channels they target. After being produced, flowers have to be transported to European destinations. The transport sector is subdivided and consists of Kenyan and international freight forwarders that either collect flowers from farms or receive them at their facilities close to the JKIA in Nairobi. They then book cargo space for their customers from airlines. Some of these freight forwarders specialise in perishables. Relations between farms and these forwarders are mostly long-term and fixed, although spontaneous short-term bookings also occur from time to time. Finally, a large number of service providers and consultancies assist flower farms in Kenya with forging market relations, innovating production, or cutting costs.

Organisations

Besides personal relations, biographical parallels, and corporate structures, two main industrial groups are part of the wider Lake Naivasha industry. The Kenya Flower Council (KFC)[19] brings together growers and associated businesses on a national level. Founded in 1996 and fully funded by growers, this trade association today represents 123 growers and 80 associate members

---

[18] For a detailed explanation of the process of breeding, selecting, propagating, and growing cut flowers, see Box 1 in Chapter 6.

[19] See www.kenyaflowercouncil.org.

(i.e. non-growers). These members' output amounts to over 80% of all flower production in Kenya and, therefore, the KFC is usually referred to as the legitimate representative body of the whole industry. The mission of the KFC is twofold: on the one hand, it is active in both lobbying and industry promotion, especially regarding the international flower trade. It plays an important role in shaping Kenyan legislation on the horticultural industry (see Chapter 5), works closely together with government agencies,[20] and engages in media discourses (see Chapter 7); on the other hand, the representative role of the KFC is backed by its function as a certifying body: it awards its own certifications, KFC Silver and KFC Gold. Although not very well known in Europe, KFC Silver is a rather strict standard and combines both environmental and social issues. It is seen as a baseline for quality assurance and, thus, all members have to comply with the common code of conduct. At Lake Naivasha, membership in the KFC is common, and there are only a few farmers who oppose it. Moreover, the KFC also conducts auditing and awarding for GlobalGAP, Tesco – TN10 and the new Kenyan national standard KS1758.

On a local level, the Lake Naivasha Growers Group (LNGG) is the 'twin brother' (IV 21, CEO, LNGG) of the KFC. The LNGG represents around 65% of the Lake Naivasha growers (IV 21, CEO, LNGG). Similar to the KFC, it has its own code of conduct, compliance with which is obligatory for members. Although the standard does not involve a certification or label, it is an important factor in the wider reputational systems of the farms: it became an indicator especially for retailers to see if their suppliers adhere to local legislation: '[A Retail Chain] comes to us and asks: "Are you a member of the LNGG?" – Yes, we are' (IV 22, Head of Production, Grower). The LNGG standards ban commercial activities from the riparian zone of the lake and, therefore, some (a small few) farms strongly rebel against the LNGG.[21] As one of five regional partners of the KFC, the main tasks of the LNGG are 'a bit of marketing' and mainly 'the interface between organisations, community, governments etc.' (IV 21, CEO, LNGG) at a local level. Furthermore, the LNGG represents its member farms in all initiatives around Lake Naivasha.

[20] These agencies value the KFC for its competence, as one representative told me (IV 79, Technical Officer, Government Organisation).

[21] *LNGG; Code of Practice, Objective 2*, states: 'Riparian land is defined by the land below 1906 water level (1893.3 MA5L). … The LNGG has identified the 1889 MASL contour level as the lowest level of farming around the Lake, below which no farming activities will be allowed. The 1889 contour level has been defined to limit encroachment from farming developments onto the wetlands. Riparian land therefore requires special care and LNG6 Code of Practice should be adhered to in its entirety'.

Conclusion: A different type of cluster

Since the first establishment of commercial horticulture in the 1970s, Lake Naivasha has developed into an agro-industrial cluster (see Calas 2013). In economic geography, clusters are usually defined as a 'sectoral *and* spatial concentration of firms' (Schmitz, Nadvi 1999, 1503) with an emphasis on spatial proximity and local factors. As I shall argue here, Lake Naivasha proves the case for a different understanding of clusters. The conventional cluster definition carries a strong spatial connotation in a Euclidean sense, with a bias towards spatial proximity and a binary conceptualisation of local and global linkages. Kulke's observation on the embeddedness of farms in agricultural clusters gives an example of this understanding:

> The spatial dimension shows that especially those farms are performing well which possess strong local links (in the sense of strong ties) in combination with supra-regional connections (in the sense of weak ties; Granovetter 1973). Ideally the best practice for farms is therefore to be embedded in local as well as in supra-regional networks. (Kulke 2008, 144)

This 'local fetishism' (Grabher 2006, 172) is highly problematic when analysing Lake Naivasha's cut flower industry, as it is not primarily made up by 'in-here relations' (Amin 2002, 388). As I have shown, personal biographies, corporate structures, formal organisation, and other factors prove that the network is essentially translocal and tied together by its interest in flower breeding, propagation, and growing around the lake. Thus, Lake Naivasha is a cluster, yet related to a relational (in contrast to a locational) conceptualisation of place. This conceptualisation 'shift[s] theoretical attention from the static entities that are symptoms of economic action (firms, institutions, regional clusters) to the dynamic practices and relational associations that constitute action and produce these entities' (Jones 2008, 79) and 'posits local economic activity as part of, and inseparable from, proximate and distanciated transactions, and assumes that whatever counts as the local is the product of varied spatial practices' (Amin 2002, 395).

The Lake Naivasha cut flower cluster contains a broad and heterogeneous set of actors – from growers to breeders, from small to large farms, from Kenyan to Dutch shareholders, from suppliers to freight forwarders (see Table 2). Nowadays, this cluster comprises all relevant inputs, services, and organisations, especially for flower growers. The Lake Naivasha flower network gathers twice a year – at the Naivasha Hortifair,[22] a horticultural trade fair, and the

---

[22] For a detailed description of the Lake Naivasha Hortifair and its role in the local cluster, see Calas 2013, 6–7.

Table 2. Flower farms and their specifications. Locations are not listed to maintain confidentiality, 8 at South Lake, 5 in FBP, 3 at North Lake, 1 in Nanyuki (for comparative purposes) (Author).

No.	Activities (main activity bold)			Size of Production (ha)	Employees	Average output (daily)	Origin of shareholders	Origin of top management	First year of production	Auction sales	Direct sales	Fairtrade
	Production	Propagation	Breeding									
1	X		X	12	500	40,000	Dutch	Dutch	2007	X		No
2	X	X		135	2,500	550,000	Indian	Kenyan, Dutch, British	2007	X	X	No
3	X			70	1,500	400,000	Dutch	Dutch		X	X	No
4	X			28	610	130,000	Dutch	Dutch	2001	X	X	Yes
5	X			240	4,000	1,000,000	Dutch	Dutch, British	1982	X	X	Yes
6	X			20	1,000	150,000	Kenyan, Colombian	Indian	2013		X	No
7	X			38	800	190,000	Kenyan (of Indian descent)	Indian	1985	X	X	Yes
8			X	2.5	70	*Breeder*	Dutch	Dutch	2007	*Breeder: no flower sales*		
9	X	X		9	130	20,000	Dutch	British, Dutch	2013	X	X	No
10			X	0.6	15	*Breeder*	Dutch	Dutch	2006	*Breeder: no flower sales*		
11	X		X	21	520	115,000	German	Dutch	2005	X	X	Yes
12	X			42	700	180,000	Dutch	Dutch	2002	X	X	No
13	X			80	3,000	*No data*	British	British	1982	X	X	Yes
14	X			23.5	500	90,000	Kenyan (of British descent)	Kenyan (of British descent)	2009	X	X	No
15	X			15	120	35,000	Kenyan, British	Kenyan	2014	X	X	No
16	X	X		30	700	130,000	Kenyan (of Indian descent)	Kenyan (of Indian descent)	1991		X	Yes
17	X			40	900	*No data*	Israeli-American	Indian	2001	X	X	Yes

IFTEX in Nairobi, a buyer-grower fair. These expos – as trade fairs in general – 'create temporary spaces of presentation and interaction, or temporary clusters' (Bathelt, Zakrzewski, 14) in the Kenyan cut flower industry.

Besides the KFC and LNGG, relations in the cut flower network are hardly formalised, and are rather based on kinship, personal friendships, and biographical parallels. Due to this lack of formal ties, some describe the industry as a 'family' (IV 68, Sales Manager, Supplier), while others deny the existence of a strong general network and point to its segregation:

> In Holland traditionally we have this open culture between farms, and you can be competitor, but you still work together on production issues or common issues. But in Kenya you don't see it a lot. And maybe the Dutch among themselves, they are more willing to learn from each other. But maybe the Indian owned farms have also their own networks or the Kenyan owned farms. It is not so much in the culture of here that you work closely on common issues. [It's only] if you know them personal. Within the Dutch farms it is easy to communicate. (IV 28, Farm Manager, Grower)

Segregated networks based on personal relations are the basis for cooperation, such as in the inter-farm trade of flowers (see Chapter 6). This is even true for relationships to government bodies; one flower farm director described his cooperation with Kenyan officials as follows:

> This is based on the relationship you have and the reputation you have. As I said, we have been in Kenya for quite some time and we have some good connections with some institutes, government bodies and whatever. Also the people we employed. Some of them have been in industries for twenty years. They know quite some people when it comes down to exports, agencies etc. So, as long as the relation is there, it's enabling. If not, if you would be a new entrant here you struggle. (IV 34, Managing Director, Breeder)

As we will see later, these forms of cooperation play an important role in reactions and responses to new market orders, as they partly strengthen the resilience of farms by offering them additional flexibility (see Chapter 6).

5

Linking to Buyers: The Making of the Global Cut Flower Market at Lake Naivasha

'As long as people love, get married or die, we will sell roses'.[1]

The translocal cluster of the Lake Naivasha cut flower industry is deeply entangled in the reorganisation of cut flower production, trade, and retail, and therefore also in the emergence of a new market order. As I have shown in the previous chapters, the market entry of corporate retailers brought along with it the emergence and rising importance of new market encounters. Corporate buyers were able to shift trade relations in their favour by influencing the objectification and standardisation of flowers in their interest. Moreover, they achieved a reduction in sales prices through the use of their knowledge in price-making processes. Ultimately, the market entry of retail chains has not led to a simplified, buyer-driven value chain, but has rather complexified market encounters and increased their diversity in forms, volatility, and quantity. Considering this complex network of trade relations, the process of connecting Lake Naivasha to global markets, that is 'the on-going, and relatively autonomous, material and ideological processes of linking different social and structural elements' (Bair, Werner 2011, 992), requires further attention. This sort of analysis has been largely neglected by GCC scholars (Bair, Werner 2011). Yet, a detailed account of the forging of linkages is necessary to explain how new power relations unfolded, why standards became an important market device in the cut flower industry, and why production has been reorganised. In this chapter, I will examine how dynamics in cut flower production relate to developments in the Dutch trade hub and the emergence of a new market order. I will first analyse how flower growers in Naivasha are linked to (European) buyers and how new relations between farms in Naivasha and buyers and consumers in Europe influence the local cut flower industry. A detailed examination of these relations is necessary in order to understand to what extent the reorganisation of the cut flower industry has contributed to the rising importance of corporate retailers and, vice versa, how

---

[1]   IV 4, Production Manager, Grower.

retail chains are driving dynamics in the Lake Naivasha cut flower industry. These questions will be addressed in Chapter 7.

Forging linkages between growers and buyers

The trade statistics for 2017 show that the Netherlands is by far the most important export destination for Kenyan cut flowers with a market share of 52% (see Figure 9). Other European countries like the UK (15.7%), Russia (3.8%), Norway (3.7%), and Germany (3.7%) are far behind. These numbers reveal that the Dutch flower trade hub is Lake Naivasha's main link to international flower vendors. Therefore, the new market order in the Dutch trade hub is key to Kenyan producers. As shown in Chapter 4, this market order implies more complex market relations. Sales and marketing services and departments have gained importance in order to create profitable connections within this complex configuration. These departments are either closely tied to growers or are contracted as sales and marketing partners.

This complex configuration requires scrutinising the multitude and coming-into-being of producer-buyer relations. Most GVC and GCC studies refrain from this challenge and are dedicated to the analysis of a single dominant chain. In investigations on the Kenyan cut flower industry, this has primarily been the direct sales link to British supermarkets (see e.g., Hale, Opondo 2005). Yet, considering the heterogeneousness of market encounters and the way these imply different objectifications of cut flowers and distinct price-making mechanisms, the focus on single chains is simplifying and too narrow. Rather, I want to follow Bair and Werner's call 'for a deeper engagement with the processes that engender the forging and breaking of links between circuits of commodity production, people, and places' (Bair, Werner 2011, 992).

As the national trade statistics indicate (see Figure 9), the perspective of Lake Naivasha growers is that the EU is the only import region that is able to sustain the flower industry all year-round (IV 21, CEO, LNGG). Only a few newer farms target what they call 'untouched markets' (IV 30, General Manager, Grower), for example Japan, Australia, and the Arabian Peninsula. Kenya's exports are limited by JKIA's direct flight connections; cargo flights to destinations outside Central Europe are especially rare. Therefore, a large portion of all flowers, even those going to these 'untouched markets', pass through the Netherlands. For this reason, most growers also refrain from transatlantic trade, although they see the USA as an interesting export destination.

In order to connect their products to these export countries, Kenyan flower growers make use of all existing market encounters (see Table 2). Auction sales still play an important role, not only at the Dutch trade hub but also in the sales strategy of many flower farms. Some farmers even fully commit

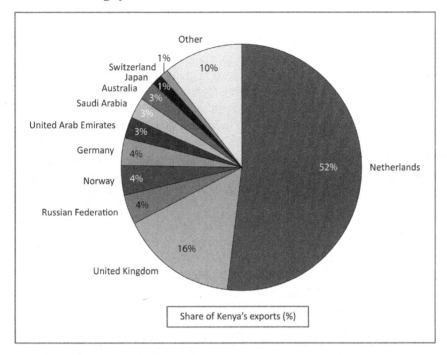

Figure 9. Export destinations of Kenyan cut flowers, 2017 (Author, ITC).

to this market encounter and sell all of their produce in this way. There are several reasons for the ongoing success of auction sales among Kenyan growers. FloraHolland's 'all-or-nothing' policy towards its members deters farms from resigning. Even farms focused on direct sales are dependent on the auction's agency as a 'vitrine' (see Chapter 3), especially when testing or advertising new products:

> When you have new varieties, you have to put them on the auction. Because of the price pressure ... and the incredible increase in cost, here in Kenya people are not looking much into new varieties; there are only a few people who can afford it ... For them, the auction is the easiest, you prepare, you send, and you're priced, there is quality inspection and it is easy going. (IV 76, Sourcing Manager, Auction Services)

Furthermore, FloraHolland provides a fast and secure accounting and payment system for its growers, which is crucial as most bills are paid by cash flow and not via credit (see Figure 12). In addition, though critical of the extreme volatility of prices at the auctions, many growers still want to benefit from profits on the cut flower vending peak days (mainly Valentine's and Mother's Day), when prices can increase tenfold and profits are much higher than compared to direct sales. Lastly, the auction involves different objectifications of cut flowers than direct sales, valuing high quality, big head size, and small niche products. Yet, the auction did not sustain its role as a major market encounter automatically. Rather, the linking of actors via this sociotechnical device is based on 'maintenance work' (Çalışkan, Callon 2010, 20). This task is performed by actors around the auction and FloraHolland itself. They offer a variety of services linked to auction sales, such as unpacking or quality controls, and have a 'sourcing office' (IV 76, Sourcing Manager, Auction Services) in Nairobi.

In the last few years, direct sales have gained an importance similar to that of the auction trade for Kenyan growers. Direct sales provide several advantages for growers. First of all, the transaction costs are lower, since auction fees and intermediaries can be avoided. Based on annual agreements – though usually not in the form of written and formal contracts – prices are less volatile and more predictable for growers, and the demand for flowers is fairly stable and calculable. Here is a manager of a large grower explaining a recent deal: 'Well, it is easier for us as well. I don't have to worry about bringing my crops in fresh for Christmas or for Valentine's, I can put out the same quantity, minimum amount, money on the table and cash flow' (IV 45, General Manager, Grower). Due to their size, some large farms are dependent on direct sales, since it is only they that guarantee the necessary demand for a high output: '[B]ecause of the nature of the company, which is huge and has millions of stems, we have to sell to the huge supermarkets' (IV 22, Head of Production, Grower).

The diversity and complexity of distribution channels and market configurations produced by the reorganisation of the Dutch trade hub is reflected in the strategies of the growers at Lake Naivasha. Over the past twenty years, flower growers have learned to flexibly navigate between auction sales and direct sales, florists and retailers, importers and sales agents. Contrary to Hale and Opondo's observation that farms targeting direct sales 'tend to rely on it almost entirely' (2005, 306), the interviewed farms covered the full spectrum, from those with 100% auction sales to those with 50% auction sales, from those with 50% direct sales to those with 100% direct sales (see Table 2). Furthermore, apart from these two main channels, farms create new market encounters themselves, for instance by supplying to other growers that need to meet the demands of retailers. In some cases, this flexibility is strategic, but often farms have no other choice – due either to the particular varieties they grow or their failed attempts to sell all flowers via one sales channel.

The analysis of market channels shows that a focus on order and simplicity, as is put forward in many chain studies, is inadequate. This focus views flower farms as a passive starting point for two distinct value chains upon which control is exerted. Yet, they are rather 'in the middle of a network' (Hughes 2000, 180). By acknowledging the complexity and 'disorder' of these networks, it can be analysed how 'they dismantle current structures or practices, disrupt the existing order, displace standing relationships and destroy the status quo' (Marshall, Goodman 2013, 288).

New buyers – New power relations?

The nature of linkages between Lake Naivasha's flower growers and European buyers confirms the findings on market encounters in the Dutch cut flower trade hub (see Chapter 3): connections are ephemeral as they are rarely based on contracts and farms operate flexibly between different retail channels and market encounters. They actively try to strengthen their position by investing in sales and marketing services. The multi-stranded network of trade relations also challenges the common view on power relations within global agro-industries. These represent global agro-industries as tightly controlled by corporate retailers once they cut off intermediaries and establish direct connections (see e.g., Lawrence, Burch 2007; Aufhauser, Reiner 2010). However, a look at the Dutch trade hub has already revealed that corporate retailers mainly exert power by influencing the objectification of goods and by deploying their knowledge on prices (see Chapter 3). Therefore, an investigation of how power asymmetries are created, how they unfold, and how they materialise in market STAs is necessary, instead of just describing the industry as 'buyer-driven' in an expressive, yet generalising way. As Berndt and Boeckler have noted (2010, 564), supply chain capitalism brings along diversity in market relations and with it indirect and flexible governance models. This flexibility and the multitude of power relations is hidden in everyday processes of inclusion and exclusion (Goger 2013). So, what do everyday interactions between growers and buyers in the cut flower industry actually look like?

First of all, it has to be noted that direct contact between growers and buyers takes place only infrequently. Corporate retailers usually approach growers via wholesalers, trade agents, or their sales and marketing departments (and vice versa). Market encounters mainly take place either in the Netherlands or at flower expos like the IFTEX, with a few exceptional farm visits by retailers either around these expos or in preparation for regular transactions. Written contracts between growers and buyers are rare in the cut flower industry. Therefore, direct and formal control is also not a major issue. In these rather exceptional cases, retail chains contract large farms for regular supply and usually fix the volumes and prices of flowers for a year. For the few farms participating in these transactions, the financial security they provide is favourable, whereas the fixed amounts put them under pressure to meet production targets: 'I really have to make more production otherwise we lose orders' (IV 45, General Manager, Grower). This pressure – also implied by informal agreements – is one of the few forms of governance in the classical sense of the GVC framework that prevails in the cut flower industry. Here, governance refers to the coordination of transactions; the cut flower industry with strong lead firms would be assumed to have captive relations. Yet, these hierarchical relations hardly surface within transactions except in the fixation of production volumes. Rather, the unequal distribution of power materialises in the normalisation of practices around these transactions (Ponte, Gibbon 2005). Corporate retailers closely examine larger farms with whom they intend to engage for a longer period – not for their ability to produce quality flowers or to pack bouquets ready for sale, but for their practices and reputation regarding social and environmental issues. For instance, this manager describes how a corporate retailer inspected their farms as a prerequisite for direct sales:

They have been here, all around the farm. … They were coming here with their white coats on and clipboards. … And you have to show the environmental guy [that] we have done this, we have done that. … On the social and environmental side, which has become almost overriding, we had a meeting with a gentleman from [a corporate retailer]. They want our flowers and we want [to do business with] them, but there is a quid pro quo; the social environmental has to be build up from scratch, our buildings, making sure our housing is organised, and making sure we are doing something for the community – this is almost a requirement now – which is good, it's only that it will cost money. And for this particular company: we are going anywhere until we make profits. … For instance, they require us to have a demonstrable ongoing project which is socially related. (IV 22, Head of Production, Grower)

These checks are part of the retailers' strategies to realign given practices in their interest, namely the demand for and trend towards traceability. Nowadays, supermarkets want to sell growers 'as their own farm' (IV 61, General Manager, Service Provider). In order to do so, they have to take control of compliance with a public discourse of socially and environmentally sustainable flower production.

The analysis of power relations between buyers and growers shows that buyer-driven structures or captive governance relations are not as obvious and common as often stated (see e.g., Hale, Opondo 2005). Rather, power in the cut flower industry, whether legislative or 'industrial' (Bair, Palpacuer 2015), is 'diffused in a Foucauldian (capillary-like) sense whereby it is always present in all social interactions' (Dicken et al. 2001, 93). In order to fully understand these relations, it has to be analysed 'how control over market access and control over production processes relate to each other' (Harvey 2007, 53). Regarding Lake Naivasha's connections to global flower buyers, this mainly concerns the regulation (or, more precisely, the restriction) of market access.

A neoliberal model case?
Regulations in the Kenyan cut flower industry

'Supplying the European market is not for everyone'.[2]

Restriction on market access is the main regulatory tool in the cut flower industry. In this section, I will address the questions of why regulation of cut flower production is almost exclusively related to producer-buyer linkages, what role public legislation plays (if at all), and how these observations fit into the post-political condition of neoliberal capitalism.

Before examining industrial governance and the interplay of growers and standards, I will first have a look at the regulatory gap within public legislation that private standards filled. The non-interference of the Kenyan state with flower farming has been a mainstay of the industry since its beginnings in the 1970s. Of course, labour, environmental, and phytosanitary legislation exists; yet it is either too general and not adapted to floriculture, or simply not as effective as private standards. A good example is the regional legislative framework for water abstraction and sanitation. It is very sophisticated but less efficacious than industry standards. Kenyan policies directed towards the flower industry have been mostly supportive and 'enabling' (Neilson 2014, 57), and not regulatory. As a major foreign currency earner, the industry is part of economic policy strategies, such as the Economic Recovery Strategy, the Strategy for Revitalisation of Agriculture, Kenya Vision 2030, and the National Horticultural Policy (Rikken 2012). Therefore, while farm managers complain about the incapacity and corruption of the Kenyan government, taxation is one of the few issues directly affecting their businesses. Farmers criticise the multitude and complexity of Kenyan taxes and its high financial burden. Rikken has described this taxation system as 'uncoordinated, duplicated and inconsistent' (2012, 35). As a result, farms have to put a lot of administrative effort into taxation and levies. On the other hand, it opens up space for favourable terms. Reports on tax evasion in the cut flower industry are rife (see e.g., Redfern 2011, Mayoyo 2014) and tax avoidance strategies are deeply entrenched in the corporate structures and sales strategies of flower growers.

---

2   CBI 2017d.

Some scholars evaluate this institutional framework for the cut flower industry because of the lack of interference as a positive:

> An enabling policy environment. Both government support and lack of interference have been important factors in the industry's phenomenal growth. A fairly strong intellectual property protection regime, the availability of skilled manpower, functional quality-control and regulatory policies, and other government incentives have fostered the industry's rapid growth rate. The government's limited involvement in production and its hands-off approach to business operations have created space for strong private sector participation. (Bolo 2008, 47–8)

This evaluation follows the neoliberal dogma of free entrepreneurship, self-regulation, and of public legislation focusing on private property rights, free trade, and free markets (Harvey 2005). The position is backed by the KFC, which considers self-regulation as a 'main principle' (IV 20, CEO, KFC) and strongly lobbies for governmental support and against regulation. For instance, on its homepage, the KFC sees one of the reasons for the industry's success in '[a]ctive government support mainly by facilitating trade through the provision of incentives in the form of nil or reduced duties and other taxes on imported inputs crucial to the sector' (KFC 2019). The strategy of the Kenyan state and of its proponents, such as the KFC, promotes the narrative of 'making value chains work for development' (Taglioni, Winkler 2016). In this strategy proposed by the World Bank, institutional frameworks have been reduced to business enabling environments, facilitating the market access of private actors.

Therefore, regulations restricting market access are powerful control instruments. Part of these also fall under public legislation, namely EU-regulations over market access (see Chapter 3). In order to ensure market access for Kenyan companies, the KEPHIS[3] cooperates and carries out randomised phytosanitary checks of flowers at the airport. Yet, even these checks show that private regulation of market access is far stricter and more effective in the cut flower industry: first, the rules that KEPHIS seeks to enforce are less strict than, for example, MPS standards; KEPHIS mostly checks for invested and damaged crops, while MPS tries to control the underlying usage of chemicals and fertilisers (IV 63, Agronomist, Supplier). And secondly, controls are not very strict, or as one sourcing manager puts it, 'KEPHIS is a joke' (IV 76, Sourcing Manager, Auction Services).

---

[3]   The Kenya Plant Health Inspectorate Service is a government agency in charge of ensuring the quality of agricultural inputs and produce.

Like in almost any other agro-industry, codes of conduct are 'mushrooming' (Barrientos et al. 2003, 1511) in floriculture as well. Within the GVC governance framework, certification schemes and associated standards are theorised based on its role to reduce complexity in transactions between producers, retailers, and customers. Standards are seen as a set of formal institutions 'that transmit information to customers and end-users about a product's technical specifications, its compliance with health and safety criteria, or the processes by which it has been produced and sourced' (Nadvi 2008, 325). Yet, there is more to standards than just transmitting information to buyers about production conditions. Standards have already been identified as an important market device for the pacifying of cut flowers in the analysis of market encounters at the Dutch trade hub (see Chapter 3). They enable a qualification of commodities based on written and formal rules with formal sanctions for non-compliance. Therefore, standards provide an efficient tool for external actors like corporate retailers to formalise and to control the valuation process of cut flowers. This understanding links to a conceptualisation of standards in convention theory. Here, they are conceived of as a form of quality convention, that is 'a set of shared values and ... legitimized procedures' (Ponte, Gibbon 2005, 22) on which the qualifications of the products are based. By influencing these conventions, powerful agencies such as lead firms are able to impose their qualifications of goods on others and govern 'through the market' (Ouma 2010, 203). Therefore, an analysis of certification schemes must not only consider what information they are meant to transport, especially since these are often based on vague notions, such as sustainability (Kuiper, Gemählich 2017) or a problematic understanding of development (Moberg, Lyon 2010, 13). Rather, Barrientos et al. (2003, 1517) remind us to always question which agents are responsible for introducing codes of conducts and why they might do so.

In the cut flower industry, certifications began to emerge in the 1990s. Today, the Flower Sustainability Initiative Basket of Standards lists 28 of them, only including certification systems benchmarked against GlobalGAP (FSI 2015). This is surprising, since consumers show little interest in this information or the stories that roses carry (see Chapter 3). The multitude and diversity of b2b as well as b2c standards renders the interpretation of them as a tool to reduce complexity in transactions disputable. Farms comply with multiple certifications in order to get access to different retail channels that require distinct standards or even combinations of them, depending on the country and buyer. Some of these are broadly spread such as MPS, KFC Silver, and GlobalGap, while others are niche certifications only required for single buyers. Once farms comply with the basic standards, getting additional certificates is mainly an administrative effort that does not necessitate any profound changes in production or environmental behaviour. Therefore, farms tend to have as many certificates as possible to be eligible as suppliers to retail chains and to increase their flexibility in sales channels.

I want to use the example of Fairtrade to further elaborate on the interface between farms, standards, and market access. Fairtrade provides an interesting case study because it has quickly gained in prominence within the flower industry in recent years. The first Fairtrade-certified flower farm in Naivasha received its label in 2003. Only 12 years later, 15 farms (around one-third of the farms in Naivasha) were certified. Moreover, this b2c certification is prominent in consumer markets: in 2017, 835 million Fairtrade flowers were sold, and 51% of these were grown in Kenya (TransFair 2017). Fairtrade is an atypical certification: unlike other schemes, it did not originate from the flower industry itself but stems from a broader political movement. The original aim of the movement was to profoundly transform international trade and to decrease inequalities in trade relations, or in the words of a representative of Fairtrade: 'Fairtrade is the only certification scheme that aims to change an existing market' (Group Discussion 93, TransFair). Fairtrade is best known for its effort to improve small-scale producers' access to global markets. In more recent years, it started including products produced by hired labour, such as flowers, and entered into mainstream value chains (Smith, Barrientos 2005).

As with the vast majority of other certification schemes, Fairtrade awards its certificate for complying with a product-based standard. Additionally, Fairtrade includes a 'premium' as a unique feature. Fairtrade buyers pay a premium of 10% of the commercial price, which is meant to be invested in 'socio-economic and environmental projects' for the workers (Fairtrade Africa 2019). This fund is managed by a Fairtrade Premium Committee, containing elected workers and advisors from the management (Fairtrade International 2014, 9). Apart from this premium, Fairtrade's requirements are similar to those of other standards. Most farms participating in certification schemes like Fairtrade are best practice farms (see Hale, Opondo 2005, 309), for whom the effort to comply with Fairtrade's standards is low: 'So if you are KFC-certified, you find that to become Fairtrade-certified is somehow easy because most of their standards go hand in hand with Fairtrade' (IV 15, Fairtrade Manager, Grower). Although compliance with Fairtrade standards is no obstacle for most farms, the application and compliance procedures require administrative effort and costs, as one production manager described it: 'It gives you a lot of headaches. It's a lot of work, it's not that you say, ok, we are Fairtrade ... no, it's a lot of work to continue with Fairtrade and do it in a proper and right way' (IV 12, Head of Production, Grower). The observation that compliance is a more bureaucratic and financial rather than structural process (see Raynolds 2012) is mirrored in the Fairtrade application process of a recently Fairtrade-certified farm (OB 10, Fairtrade Manager, Grower; IV 15, Fairtrade Manager, Grower):

it cost around KES 500,000[4] to acquire the certification. These costs were mainly connected with the audit and in setting up the administrative structures, whereas changes in the production process were negligible. After the first, intensive four-day audit by FLO-CERT (Fairtrade's audit and certification body), the audit team suggested improvements and requested ideas and plans from the farm on how they might achieve these improvements:

> [T]hey send to you a mail: "..., now you have to give us what you're suggesting to improve. What are your plans to improve on this?" So to suggest which measures you are going to take as a farm to work on the issues. So once you suggest, they also confirm what you've suggested. If they're not satisfied, they send it back and say: "we're not satisfied with this. Can you give us another suggestion?" So we have to give them a new suggestion on this. So if they don't accept they keep on coming back to us and telling us: "we're still not satisfied", and then we have to work on it again. So you have to give a solution that according to what they feel is good. (IV 15, Fairtrade Manager, Grower)

On the one hand, this back and forth of suggestions and plans shows that compliance with standards is a 'messy and contested process' (Ouma 2010, 205). On the other hand, the process is based on plans and formalities, not on structural changes. This is also reflected in the way proof is given. 'Evidence' is uploaded instead of being gathered as part of an audit of implemented measures:

> Now we are in the final stage: there are some issues that were picked that we need to rectify. So we are now giving evidence that we've rectified them. So maybe there have been some procedures that we never followed very well, so we need to rectify. Then we upload the evidence to FLO-CERT. ... They have the system that we communicate to them. We have the E-SAT system they opened, so when they want the evidence, we just upload, browse, and we send it to them. (IV 15, Fairtrade Manager, Grower)

As this application process reveals, standards are sociotechnical devices in marketisation, not only in the sense that they enable the qualifying and standardisation of flowers. They are also the result of bureaucratic and technical articulations, they are 'material and discursive assemblages that intervene in the *construction* of markets' (Muniesa et al. 2007, 2, my own emphasis).

The impact of a Fairtrade certification on farms is in some ways contradictory. To a limited extent, it improves working conditions and the environmental impact of flower growers (see Happ 2016). Still, as Raynolds noted,

---

4   Equivalent to € 4,545.

'conventional quality and efficiency norms guide production practices on certified farms' (2012, 515–16). A Fairtrade Manager confirmed this: '[It's] just the same flowers. We are just going to grow them the way we always grew' (IV 15, Fairtrade Manager, Grower). On this point, the premium distinguishes Fairtrade from other certification schemes. Dolan (2007), who carried out fieldwork in Naivasha ten years ago, analysed the premium as a 'governing' tool. She concluded that workers were mystified about Fairtrade and perceived it as another form of charity from 'the white man' (Dolan 2007, 253). A decade later, employees were aware that under Fairtrade a part of the profit is set aside for them. Workers from non-certified farms also knew about Fairtrade and expressed the hope that their farms would become certified because they hoped to profit from the premiums. In the meantime, the premiums play an important role in providing social infrastructure on and around Fairtrade farms (see Chapter 7). Yet, the premium also generates criticism by farm managers who strongly refuse its monetary dimension:

> Fairtrade is … crap. Great wonderful ideas. All the certifications started to have wonderful ideas, but the moment you start dealing with money, [that's] what Fairtrade is about with all the extras for the supermarkets. Then you have to come back [to them]; some project to help your employees and whatever. But the problem is money. Money? No, no, no. Money in Africa is going to get to the wrong place and the wrong hands. (IV 22, Head of Production, Grower)

Although the allocation of Fairtrade premiums on farms is partly dependent on the management's consent, it is the only point where Fairtrade really undermines existing power relations – by assigning money for social and environmental projects to labourers and improving their position against capital.

On the other side, certifications like Fairtrade put farms under financial pressure. Producers have to carry the full financial burden of certification schemes. In Fairtrade, fees vary after the initial audits. Depending on the size of the farm, growers have to pay between € 2,000 and € 3,000 per year (IV 75, Flower Product Manager, Fairtrade Africa). At first sight, these costs seem to be moderate. Yet, farms pay for several certificates and face a financially precarious situation anyway. Moreover, trade prices for Fairtrade flowers are no higher than for conventional ones (see Chapter 3). And lastly, as an 'extra', the Fairtrade organisation offers promotion services to certified farms. Yet, these efforts seem to have limited effects, since according to Fairtrade's own data Kenyan farms in 2015 only sell an average of 23% of their flowers under Fairtrade terms (IV Flower Product Manager, Fairtrade Africa), although all are produced under the same conditions.

Regarding power relations in the cut flower market, the shift to certifications and especially to Fairtrade has led to a 'depoliticisation' as defined by Swyngedouw (2014).[5] Certifications do not 'fundamentally question the existing state of the neo-liberal political economic configuration' (Swyngedouw 2014, 123). Instead, they have become a substantial part of this configuration as they are part of the cut flowers' objectifications by buyers. Moreover, Fairtrade offers technical solutions, such as the premium, which fit into the existing globalised capitalist system with its market-based, monetary solutions. Thus, certifications obscure the workings of the market instead of questioning them (see Luetchford 2011). This acceptance of the status quo is not the only depoliticising effect of the introduction of certifications in the cut-flower industry. It is also a good example of what Swyngedouw describes as 'the post-democratic inclusion of different opinions ... in stakeholder arrangements of impotent participation and "good" governance' (Swyngedouw 2014, 123). There is a gap between those who are capable of translating the vague notion of 'sustainability' or 'fairness' into concrete measures and those who are responsible for the implementation of these measures. The interpretation of sustainability is mainly left to the creators of the standards of the certification system – mostly actors from the industry or activists. It is therefore not part of a public and democratic legislative process, a situation exacerbated by the Kenyan state having interfered very little in the cut-flower industry. But while industry actors and activists set the definition of sustainability, responsibility for the implementation of a 'sustainable production' is mainly put on the shoulders of consumers and workers. The choice to promote sustainable production is left to consumers, who can select sustainable – that is, certified – products. On the production side, it is the workers who are (mainly implicitly) made responsible for changes in the production process (see Chapter 6). Regarding laws and state regulations, the effects of the rising importance of certifications are twofold and contradictory: on the one hand, many certifications require compliance with national and regional regulations; therefore, they strengthen the enforcement of the existing institutional framework. On the other hand, farms primarily comply with industry-based, voluntary, non-state regulations. In the case of tea plantations in Darjeeling (Besky 2008), farm managers even used the existence of certifications to argue in favour of the abolishment of more stringent national legislation. Industry-based regulations do not have the democratic, public nature of state legislations. Recently, forms of 'hybrid governance' (Bair 2017) have emerged in the cut flower industry. Together with the Kenyan government, the KFC has developed a legislative minimum

---

[5] For a more detailed discussion of this argument, see Kuiper, Gemählich 2017.

standard for export flowers, the KS1758. Thus, legislative and industrial forms of governance have become entangled.[6]

Conclusion: Governance by regulating market access

Certification schemes are an influential device in reshaping grower-buyer relations in the cut flower industry. Even standards aimed at changing existing power relations, such as Fairtrade, fail to do so and in the end even serve to reinforce them. This is mainly because they are geared towards production and not towards the trade of cut flowers (see Hughes 2001, 392). Yet, power inequalities do not only exist on farms in relations between labourers and managers, but also in trade relations between producers and corporate buyers. By making various standards a prerequisite for market access, retailers have deployed them as a tool to enforce their power. In conclusion, it can be noted that the cut flower industry is predominantly buyer-driven. Yet, modes of governance and the exertion of power do not conform to the direct control measures of GVCs and GCCs. As Ponte and Gibbon have noted before:

> It has shown that the historical trend from hierarchical to tendentially looser forms of co-ordination between lead firms (or 'buyers') and their immediate suppliers, and the related movement towards a 'network world', do not necessarily mean that global value chains are becoming less 'driven' than in the past, but that they are driven in different ways. In many cases, ... this results in relatively loose forms of co-ordination but high levels of drivenness (or, theoretically, vice versa). (Ponte, Gibbon 2005, 21–2)

In the cut flower industry, these loose forms of coordination mainly concern the regulation of market access and the objectifications of cut flowers through standards. Here, corporate buyers are able to capitalise on their knowledge about consumer markets and their buying power. As I will show in the next chapter, these loose forms of coordination are also visible in the production of cut flowers.

---

[6]   The KS1758 also shows the limitations of public legislation: government actors are responsible for audits without having the capacity to fulfil this task. Therefore, KFC members, who are benchmarked against the new standard, are the only farms officially complying with the new standard. As a consequence, membership has risen by 25% in the first year after implementation (IV 92, CEO, KFC).

6

Growing Roses: Reorganising Flower Production at Lake Naivasha

'A farm is not a machine, there are always challenges'.[1]

Dynamics in the cut flower industry are not only based on the external relations of the flower farms, but also related to internal modes of organising cut flower breeding, production, and trade. In economic geography, firms have often been conceived of as single nodes or boxes with little attention paid to internal dynamics (Coe et al. 2008, 277). Although constituting a single legally defined entity, farms are not internally homogeneous actors. External relations and dynamics may have heterogeneous and arbitrary implications for distinct parts of companies, as they may for instance change the capital-labour relations within farms (Selwyn 2013, 78). Therefore, firms should rather be conceived of as 'relational network[s]' (Coe et al. 2008, 277). Looking behind the fences of the flower farms at Lake Naivasha and scrutinising their internal mechanisms is key when trying to understand the interdependencies between market dynamics and flower growing. In order to understand the dynamics of reorganisation in terms of cut flower production, a short look at how farms are assembled materially and socially is first necessary.

The greenhouse is the most essential part of any flower farm (see Figure 10). It also tends to be front and centre in any visual representation of the farm, such as on bouquet sleeves or in Fairtrade brochures. Yet, in order to grow and pack cut flowers, further technical facilities are necessary: water pumps, waste water cleaning, irrigation and fertigation systems, spray rooms for chemicals, workshops for maintenance, vehicles for transport, etc. After production, flowers are brought to the packhouse, where they are graded, bunched, and then cool stored. Administrative and social buildings also complement these structures on the farms: offices, sometimes housing for managers and/or labourers, a canteen, toilets, etc. On most farms production is organised based on a top-down hierarchy (see Figure 11). Even farms striving for flat hierarchies follow the overall structure of a general manager overseeing

[1] IV 61, General Manager, Service Provider.

Figure 10. Workers harvesting in a greenhouse (Author).

production, packhouse or post-harvest, and HR-management. Below this level, these sections are subdivided and headed by supervisors or – depending on the farm size – another management level. At the bottom of the hierarchy, general workers make up the vast majority of employees. Most of them work in the greenhouses, maintaining and harvesting flowers. Others spray flowers, pack or transport them, or are responsible for security.

In this chapter, I will show that the reorganisation of flower growing at Lake Naivasha has a two-sided relationship to the cut flower industry's new market order. On the one hand, it implies a financial precariousness for growers, high pressure on the labour force, and a tight management of flower growing to mitigate low prices. This includes strategies such as high flexibility, expansion, and constant innovation. On the other hand, the new market order is dependent on the flower growers' ability to innovate handling and production, to produce more flowers of uniform quality for low prices, and to constantly create and grow new products. Marketisation is a process that is never complete and full of friction. Therefore, this chapter will give examples of crises in the reorganisation of flower growing at Lake Naivasha before concluding with more general remarks on the fragility and stability of the new market order.

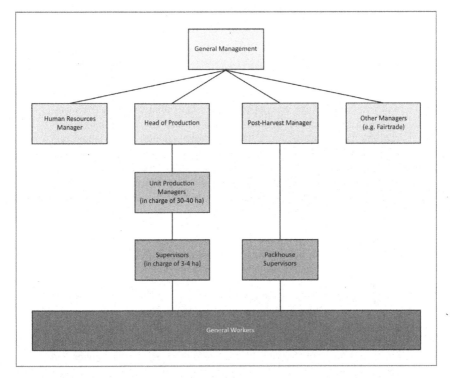

Figure 11. Farm hierarchy depending on the size of the farm. Smaller farms, for instance, have no unit production managers (sometimes also called 'senior supervisors') (Author).

Financial precariousness

'Farmers have a lot of assets, a little in the pocket and nothing in the bank'.[2]

Increasing financial precariousness is probably the most significant change the new market order has brought with it for flower farms. This development has two sides: it is a direct consequence of the market entry of corporate retailers and the shift to bulk production; yet, in turn, this marketisation process is largely based on lower prices and also higher costs for flower growers.

In the early years of the Kenyan flower industry, profit margins were enormous (up to 50%). This flower farmer remembers the gold rush era of the industry:

[2]   IV 68, Sales Manager, Supplier.

Box 1: Making Flowers

New varieties of flowers are created through lengthy and elaborate processes of breeding. Breeders manually cross varieties, plant the seeds, and search for suitable plants by trial and error. This usually entails at least three rounds of planting, testing for indicators like productivity, disease resilience, colour, size, thorns, etc., and subsequent selection. This way, breeders come up with around one new variety per 100,000 seedlings from the first round. Growers then purchase royalties for varieties from breeders. Before the crops can be planted, they need to be propagated, that is to say they are reproduced. The propagation of roses entails grafting, which describes the process of merging the parent plant of a rose variety with a durable rootstock. Propagation is necessary in order to plant new varieties but also to constantly replace plants destroyed by diseases or other external factors. Today, farms plant between 60,000 and 70,000 plants per hectare. These last for around five years; sometimes for up to ten years depending on maintenance and the demand for new varieties and investments. Lake Naivasha farms mainly grow intermediate roses, that is single stem roses with a size of 40 to 60 centimetres. Other common rose categories are the larger hybrid tea, the smaller sweethearts, and spray roses with multiple blooms per stem. The overwhelming majority of roses are grown in greenhouses covered with polythene that has to be renewed regularly. Open air plantations expose roses to weather extremes and reduce the controllability of the growing process. In greenhouses, cut flowers are either grown on treated soil or on hydroponics, a mineral nutrient solution, for example one composed of coco peat. Flowers are irrigated by drop irrigation which enables fertigation, that is the dissolution of fertilizer in irrigation water which is then sprayed with chemicals to protect against diseases. They require daily maintenance, for instance labourers need to pluck surplus buds, weed around the plants, and bend flowers to make them grow straight. Production can be timed by cutting back stems based upon a projected growth time before harvest. Depending on the variety, the density of plants, and production management, the yield is between 100 to 300 stems per m^2 and year. Roses take on average between eight to thirteen weeks until they are ready for harvest. Greenhouse roses are harvested every morning, depending on the desired cut stage of the flowers which is mainly determined by the opening of the bud. After harvest they are graded, that is sorted by size, and sometimes bunched, which is bouquets being put together and wrapped in plastic foil. Finally, they are cooled to slow down the deterioration process and shipped in cold transport.

Twenty-five years ago, when I started this company, the margins were enormous; you could not fail to make flower farms work. But over the years, the market has changed unbelievably. You used to be able to send almost anything in a box, people would pay huge margins. I was able to send one box to a client in Paris years ago with three different varieties. It was great – people paid for it and it was a lot of fun. But then people realised there is good money in it and farms started to expand everywhere, and the usual standards set in just like in any other business and the prices came down. (IV 22, Head of Production, Grower)

As he indicates, these times are now long gone. Over the past years, costs for labour, transport, and production supplies have tripled, whereas trade prices have stagnated or even fallen. To understand this development and its implications for growers, a look at the cost structure of flower farming proves instructive (see Figure 12).

First of all, it must be noted that flower farming implies a high amount of 'spatially fixed' capital (Harvey 2001). Production and technical infrastructure are expensive to purchase and set up; hence, capital costs are high especially in the first five years after opening or expanding a farm. Building a greenhouse (30% of the total amount), preparing the soil, installing drip irrigation (15%), building supplementary buildings (15%), and purchasing royalties for flower

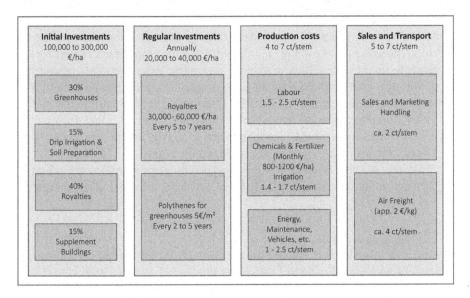

Figure 12. Investments and running costs of flower farms, 2015 (ct = Eurocents) (Author).

varieties (30–40%) add up to between € 100,000 and € 300,000 per hectare. The running costs of flower farms are predominantly determined by labour and the supply of chemicals and fertilisers. The Collective Bargaining Agreement (CBA) of 2014 sets a basic wage for newly hired workers of KES 5,401 gross[3] (Anker, Anker 2014), yet salaries vary greatly depending on the employer and the workers' experience. Generally speaking, labour costs, including welfare, add up to € 0.015 to € 0.025 per stem.[4] Depending on the credit period and if a farm recycles its waste waters, the costs for chemicals and fertilizer are between € 800 and € 1,200 per month and hectare. Together with irrigation costs – mainly for maintaining the technical infrastructure and not for water abstraction fees – production costs excluding labour total € 0.014 to € 0.017 per stem.

In addition to these daily expenses, running a flower farm requires regular investments. Greenhouses are covered with polythene that has to be replaced every two to five years, costing about € 5 per m². Approximately every five years, royalties are renewed or new varieties are planted. Breeders charge between € 30,000 and € 60,000 per ha for new varieties. Farms have faced a sharp increase in these costs over the past ten years. Total production costs rose by over 50%, with a rise in labour costs of over 100%. Hence, cutting expenditure became more important. Growing flowers for European customers in Kenya also creates significant costs outside of the producing farm. Air freight is now the single highest outlay. Prices have risen steeply over the past 15 years and vary between US $ 2 and US $ 2.10 per kg. Combined with costs for transport to and from the airport and freight handling, transport costs sum up to about € 0.04 per stem, thereby exceeding the total production costs. Moreover, the new market order with complex market encounters forces farms to invest in handling, marketing, and sales; these costs are comparable to that of a farm's whole Kenyan labour force. The activities relating to this second block of expenses are flexible, often outsourced or carried out by the farms' mother companies in the Netherlands (see Chapters 3 and 4), whereas the costs directly related to production are perceived as the core business of flower farming and, therefore, are managed on farm.

Despite the high costs for transport and handling, growing flowers in Kenya is 'much more competitive' (IV 7, Farm Manager, Grower) when compared

---

[3] Equivalent to € 49.

[4] The following cost structure has been assembled from various interviews with farm managers and an annual financial statement from a flower farm. For reasons of anonymity in relation to this very sensitive data, the name of the latter is not disclosed nor is the number of the interview given in order to prevent the drawing of any conclusions on the identity of that specific firm.

to the Netherlands. The main reason for this is the lower production costs. Maintaining and harvesting roses is largely manual work and not automatable, therefore the amount of labour required has remained relatively stable at around eight to ten workers per hectare. Even after switching to Eastern European migrant labourers, Dutch flower farms face labour costs more than 30 times higher than in Kenya (IV 84, Sales and Marketing, Flower Company). Moreover, climatic conditions increase production costs for Dutch growers: the growing periods are longer and greenhouses need to be heated year-round.

Therefore, Kenyan farms enjoy the benefit of more appropriate conditions in comparison to Dutch growers when it comes to dealing with stagnating revenues and low trade prices. The average price on FloraHolland auctions remained relatively stable at € 0.20–0.22 between 2008 and 2018 (see Chapter 3). Yet, these prices contain higher valued varieties compared to the intermediate roses that are the main crop in Naivasha. As such, the Lake Naivasha growers who were interviewed for this book often obtained only € 0.08 in off-season, are 'happy' (OB 73, Packhouse Manager, Grower) with € 0.18, and average between € 0.10 and € 0.15 over the year. Depending on crop productivity (between 100 and 300 stems/m^2), annual yields amount to a maximum of € 30 per m^2. The capability of Lake Naivasha flower farms to sustain profitable or at least non-deficient production, when facing these low trade prices and revenues, is one of the main pillars of the new cut flower market order. In European supermarkets, consumer prices of € 3–5 for bouquets of 9 to 14 roses are common, equalling € 0.20–0.50 per stem. Considering corporate retailers' margins of over 30%,[5] dumping prices for producers is inevitable. Low consumer prices are essential for the unspecialised or 'abundant' (Ziegler 2007) retail chains. The vast majority of flowers in supermarkets are purchased on impulse, based on prices below € 5 for a bouquet of uniform quality flowers (see Chapter 3). Supermarkets do not offer the floral services of specialised florist retailers and focus their business model on economies of scale in contrast to high-value products. Therefore, their valuation of cut flowers depends on their availability in high amounts and uniform quality, and their low prices. According to marketisation scholars, 'fixing a price is always the outcome of a struggle between agencies trying to impose their modes for measuring a good's value and qualities' (Çalışkan, Callon 2010, 16). Due to the powerful impact of retail chains on price-setting mechanisms (see Chapter 3), this mode of valuation has become dominant over the last few years. This sales strategy combines high volumes with low prices and would not have been possible with the Dutch flower growing industry, as

---

[5] In 2016, the gross margin in German retail was at 32.7% (Statistisches Bundesamt).

van Liemt had already noted in 1999: 'Many growers do not make a profit; a significant number are expected to cease production in the not-too-distant future' (1999, 22). In contrast, Kenyan growers who grow the adequate product (intermediate roses) are able to produce for low prices and to expand their production to increase volumes.

At the same time, the new market order terminated the 'gold rush era' of the Kenyan cut flower industry. Rising costs and stagnating or sinking prices eventually resulted in low profit margins. Nowadays, most Kenyan farms only make profit between December and April. Annual profit margins are usually well below 10%, and farms with production costs just above average or yields just below average struggle hard to operate profitably at all. In order to make a self-sustaining minimum profit in absolute terms, the majority of farms chose to expand their greenhouses in the last decade (see below). One farm manager describes the new market order as follows:

> So it has to come from the hectarage now. But the profit per hectare has gone done drastically. But that is competition, that's the free market. On the other hand, I think this is the way how you can grow roses the cheapest. ... I don't see it go back to areas where you have to put artificial light and nobody wants to work on it. (IV 37, Managing Director, Breeder)

Apart from production and transportation costs, Kenyan flower farms are dependent on two financial factors in their growing of 'bulk' flowers. Firstly, currency fluctuations either threaten or favour Kenyan growers. Production costs are paid in Kenyan Shillings, transport costs are charged in US-Dollars, whereas revenues are mostly in Euros. Hence, a devaluation of the Euro against the US-Dollar increases air freight costs; a devaluation of the Shilling against the Euro increases production costs. Secondly, flower growers rely on constant cash flow. They are mid-tier family businesses and external equity invest-ments are rare. Therefore, farmers tend to 'reinvest every financial gain they make' (IV 68, Sales Manager, Supplier) or loan money to expand or reinvest in their farm infrastructure. This is also the main reason why FloraHolland's instant and guaranteed payment system is still a strong argument for growers to sell via its auctions.

The necessity of instant cash flow and the perils of financial precariousness came to the fore on one of the largest farms at South Lake in 2013 and 2014. The farm was taken over by a corporate investor from India in 2007. From 2010, the new shareholders stopped investing in the farm and diverted parts of the cash flow for unclear reasons. The lack of investments soon resulted in a deterioration of production infrastructure. Broken polythene was not replaced and bills for chemical and fertilizer supply were not paid (IV 29,

Sales Manager, Supplier). In 2013, the farm lost its MPS certification due to multiple cases of infested produce (IV 9, Former HR-Manager, Grower). The lack of certifications broke the farm's linkages to most buyers. Cash flows dried up and workers were not paid for several months. After they went on strike, production came to a halt in 2013. Finally, two banks that were the farm's biggest creditors appointed receivers as the new farm management. These banks had to invest over € 4 million in the first two years of receivership to get the farm back to full production (IV 87, Sales Manager, Import/ Export). Although an exceptional case, this particular example shows how much farms rely on constant cash flows from sales in order to reinvest in essential production facilities.

The new market order with low prices and high amounts of uniform products is largely based on the ability of Lake Naivasha growers to satisfy this demand. Yet, the ongoing increase in costs and the stagnation of prices puts pressure on many flower farms that have already reached the limits of profitable production. As such, financial precariousness is common among flower farmers especially considering unmanageable external factors like currency fluctuations. Farms have to work as efficiently as possible and cut their expenses. Farms with higher costs are under constant risk of insolvency:

> Let's look at the reality; this is not an easy business now. And I would not give this company in Kenya [his employer] more than a fifty-fifty chance of being in business this time next year. ... I would never describe it as a collapse – but it's definitely a downswing at the moment or a levelling out. (IV 22, Head of Production, Grower)

Strategies for coping with low prices: Expansion and flexibility

Farms deploy different strategies to cope with low prices and to operate profitably despite low margins. Some of them seem close to what the GVC framework describes as upgrading, that is to say they improve the link of the farms to the GVC in order to gain access to more profitable positions (Gereffi et al. 2001, 2–5). The making of new products and innovations in production and handling will be discussed later (see below). But first, I want to draw attention to two processes that are a necessity for farms in order to maintain and stabilise the new market order: expansion and flexibility.

Firstly, many small- and middle-sized farms at Lake Naivasha have expanded their production. In this regard, the spatial expansion of market orders scrutinised by geographies of marketisation (Berndt, Boeckler 2012, 204) can be taken literally. Since growers started producing for supermarkets, many of them have built new greenhouses. This step became necessary to counterbalance the loss of profit due to the drop of margins and to meet retail chains' requests for higher amounts of supply: '[This] type of clientele, you have to supply them as much as possible' (IV 41, Managing Director, Grower). Greenhouses were enlarged massively especially in the late 2000s and early 2010s. Technically, building new greenhouses is quick and simple: one farm set up five new hectares of greenhouses within two months, which included the planning phase. During its construction, a newly established company constructed one greenhouse on three hectares every 15 days. Yet, growth rates have decreased, particularly because land and other resources have become scarce and expensive (see Chapter 7):

> I think expansion has come to a limit not financially but environmentally, [in terms of] resources, water, labour, and all these things. Management is important because people have started to reach the boundaries of the current system and I think, in Kenya, there will be not much expansion, if any. (IV 40, Managing Director, Breeder)

This scarcity of resources especially affects farms at South Lake. On the contrary, the FBP has withheld land for expansion. Moreover, there are operational reasons for the slowdown of expansion. Middle-sized farms with production areas between 30 and 70 ha are able to maintain flexibility in their production.

This leads to the second fundamental approach of flower farms to cope with low prices: flexible production strategies. These have been common in the cut flower industry for a long time (Barrientos et al. 2003, 1514). Initially, they were mostly related to the seasonality of consumer demand in Europe. The traditional seasons for cut flowers in Europe prove how much the new market order is based on equatorial production: peak season lasts from December to May, in other words European winter, and low season refers to European summer. For Kenyan growers, this seasonality offers the advantage that the low season is adjusted to coincide with Kenya's coldest months, with lower insolation equalling lower production (see also Riisgaard 2009a, 329). The new market order implies two distinct processes regarding the seasonality and flexibility of production: the flexibility of daily production has increased, whereas the market entry of retail chains has mitigated the seasonal volatility of demand, at least in regard to quantities (see Riisgaard, Gibbon 2014).

Figure 13 shows the seasonality of flower exports between 1995 and 2009, the time period when corporate retailers pushed into flower purchases. The diminishing variance of export quantities implies a fairly stable amount of production over the course of a year. In contrast, revenues continue to be volatile. This volatility causes financial precariousness with profitable operations only between December and May. Yet, it does not imply a significant reduction of output on most farms. The perennial crop prevents this:

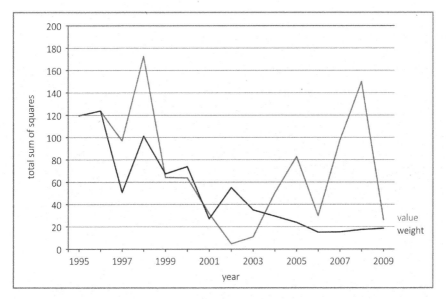

Figure 13. Seasonality of Kenyan flower exports, 1995–2009. As an indicator of the monthly variance of exports, the total sum of squares equals the annual sum of the squared differences of the monthly export means and actual exports. Thus, lower sums equal lower variance and hence lower seasonality, and vice versa (Author, KFC).

at equatorial locations, roses grow and need maintenance year-round. Direct sales and long-term agreements with buyers can help farms mitigate price volatilities. In these agreements, peak prices are lower, yet minimum prices are higher: '[If] you go to June, July, August prices go very low. That means, we are making more money than bringing it to the auction because of the contract' (IV 45, General Manager, Grower). These contracts or agreements usually only fix the average or total amount of supply for a time span between three months and a year. The actual weekly supply is then agreed upon a few weeks or days before harvest.

Farms at Lake Naivasha deploy several strategies to increase their flexibility in production. The most common one is closely related to the seasonality of demand and the contractually fixed amount of supply: the timing of production. The flower harvest can be timed by cutting sprouts of roses. For this purpose, the growth period between the cut and the planned date of harvest, for instance the delivery day of an order or a 'peak day', such as Valentine's Day, has to be projected. This way, farms manage to produce a maximum daily output three times as high as their mean production. This strategy involves high opportunity costs for growers as they deliberately destroy partly grown roses. Moreover, it is risky, as the time span for harvest is small: peak days require supply for a specific single day. Although much effort has been put into prolonging the vase life of roses, cut flowers perish at the latest 14 days after and thus cannot be stored. One Lake Naivasha farm has a cold store where they keep roses until the 'market is ready' (OB 14, Farm Coordinator, Grower), which is to say when the price is acceptable. Yet, storing flowers is only possible for up to two days; hence, the scope of this technique is very limited. As such, precise projections and timing are key. Yet, as Callon (1998a) reminds us, the pacifying of things, their transformation into controllable goods, is never complete and overflows, in other words unforeseen outcomes, are common. These overflows mostly relate to unexpected weather events during the growth period.

Yet overflows also occur through small delays in handling and transport, as caused by the ban of night flights at Jomo Kenyatta International Airport in Nairobi between 2015 and 2018. This production manager describes the process of timing production output and how they try to contain overflows on his farm:

> What we do, we have a production forecast on every variety. … One thing that guides us is the breeders' recommendation, but we are going higher than the breeders' recommendation. We also have the variety character-istics; so you know for this variety even if you target 300 stems/m², you can't get, you'll just get 200. … Also, we have the market requirements. Like now the market is really bad. So, we have to be very low in the targets. So, those are the things that guide us; the market's requirements, breeders' recommendations. Also, sometimes like [in] April, May, and June, [it's] very cold and wet; so weather guides us. … We have … the daily weather readings. For the weather forecast, you go to the internet. … This is today; you can read it, radiation, temperatures, wind. … In the years I have been in practice, I have known the varieties so well; I can tell you each variety and, in this greenhouse, I can go below or above five per cent. (IV 77, Production Manager, Grower)

As a result, farm managers try to minimise their risk by applying socio-technical devices, such as weather forecasts or computerised fertigation, and their experience in farming. Failing targets involves high follow-up costs: for instance, booked air freight has to be rearranged or cancelled. Furthermore, a failure of supply is one of the few situations in which buyers exert direct pressure on farms: 'If you miss a target and you have not communicated, you are in for it! [he laughs]' (IV 72, Packhouse Manager, Grower). As a reaction to high opportunity costs and risks of overflows, some farms deploy a weakened technique of timing:

> We do it a bit, that we cut a bit back. All the rejectable stems we cut out and some extra blind shoots, we cut out [so] that we have more for

those [peak] days. But we don't do it to the extreme. You can even cut flat your whole production, but we don't sacrifice current production, current good production, for those days. We don't do it, but other people do that. (IV 28, Farm Manager, Grower)

However, it is not only through the timing of production that farms can increase their flexibility. They also make use of various market encounters to profit from higher prices or mitigate lower prices in both direct and auction sales (see Chapter 5). Furthermore, growers broaden the scope of their possible buyers by supplying to other farms. Through inter-farm trade, smaller producers in particular get access to buyers demanding quantities far too large for their own production. This way, the receiving larger farms can flexibly respond to production shortages or broaden their portfolio of varieties for bouquets. This manager of a medium-sized farm describes his cooperation with a large grower:

We sometimes sell to [a large grower]. … They sell a lot of flowers to [a German retail chain]. … They were looking for extra and then they came to us. And then [the sourcing company of the German retail chain] found our farm very good to work with. So it is a partnership with them, so we do a little bit together. And they are more specified in that range of products. That is 35cm length and [the large grower] has much more of those flowers, and we are smaller in that range. We are a bit more in intermediate. For them it is really the mainstream and for us [it] is more of the by-products. (IV 28, Farm Manager, Grower)

These cooperations are based on direct and personal contact, often between managers who have close ties. They show that marketisation is often ambivalent and contradictory (Muniesa et al. 2007, 3). Usually current marketisation processes result in the cutting of social ties (Berndt, Boeckler 2012, 199), but in this case it even encourages cooperation. Lastly, a few farms try to diversify their activities. One farm started growing tomato seeds for European seed companies, a field where they can make use of the knowledge they have gained through the growing of cut flowers. Yet, diversification only plays a minor role, since flower farms and especially managers strongly associate their profession and activity with the main product, cut flowers.

Maintaining and stabilising the new market order in the cut flower industry requires flower growers to be both flexible and also to expand production. Overflows, such as the failure of production timing, indicate that these efforts are always partial and imperfect (Callon 1998a, 252). The need for flexible producers also shows that a market order based on corporate retailers as main buyers does not necessarily lead to an advantage for large-scale producers. In the last few years, the most profitable enterprises have been middle-sized farms. These are able to adapt flexible strategies quicker, as their administrative and operational structures are more agile. In contrast, the production costs of large farms are fixed for a certain time. The largest farms in Naivasha underwent several phases of expansion and downsizing in the last few years as a reaction to varying market orders. These phases of contraction and expansion are extremely costly due to the capital-intense infrastructure of flower farming.

The making of (new) commodities

The production of non-traditional export products in the Global South often entails the introduction of new plant varieties that suit the demands of buyers and consumers in the Global North (Robinson 2008, 59). Accordingly, the marketisation process in the cut flower industry after the entry of corporate retailers includes new objectifications of cut flowers at the main trading place in the Netherlands (see Chapter 3). Apart from the traditional valuations based on reputation, personal contacts, and the physical display of flowers at the auctions, certifications became more important. Moreover, cut flowers are now standardised as a mass product of uniform quality sold in bouquets rather than as individual stems. This new market order seems to bring with it upgrading possibilities for flower farms. Product upgrading could be possible through a move to more profitable products (Humphrey, Schmitz 2000, 12), since the required varieties – intermediate roses – suit Lake Naivasha's conditions. Secondly, a portion of of the bouquets is packed on the farms themselves in line with the buyers' demands – opening the opportunity for functional upgrading, that is to say the introduction of new, more complex functions, such as processing (Gibbon 2001, 63). In the following sections, I will scrutinise how the new objectifications of flowers are asserted on farms; if they cause dynamics that qualify as upgrading and if the concept of upgrading, as defined by GVC scholars (see e.g., Gereffi 1999; Barrientos et al. 2011), is at all helpful to describe these dynamics. In this regard, it has already been noted that the objectification of flowers during market encounters is increasingly dependent on market information. This information is unequally distributed and gives retail chains an advantage in their relationships with producers and breeders (see Chapter 3). Yet, the pacifying of cut flowers does not only take place during market encounters (see Çalışkan, Callon 2010, 5–8), but also reaches back to the breeding, planting, and packing of flowers.

Breeding

The breeding of roses is a cumbersome and tedious process based in large parts on trial and error. Global rose breeding is dominated by less than ten breeders, headquartered in the Netherlands, Germany, and France. These are multinational companies with farms all around the world, including Naivasha. For most of them, Kenyan farms in general and Naivasha growers specifically are the largest customers: 'The main market for us as breeders is Kenya' (IV 37, Managing Director, Breeder). The ten largest breeders sell royalties on average for around 50 ha of flower production in Kenya, in total 500 ha. This total number results from a renewal of 10–20% of the 2,800 ha in total production and an additional expansion of production of 150–200 ha per year in Kenya. Breeders' farms are small and usually consist of greenhouses for trials and a 'showroom' where various varieties for sale are presented in full flush to potential customers. Since the use of GMO is forbidden by MPS, breeding relies on the crossbreeding of varieties. This is done by manually pollinating the roses and then subsequently seeding them. Crossing and selecting the first round of seeds that go for trials is not a very laborious process, yet it is a delicate moment. As such, these tasks are performed by top-level employees in (or near) the European headquarters: 'It is not complicated. It's only that it is quite knowledge-intensive. Especially the first selection, there is a lot of experience involved in that. We have one … main breeder. He is based in Holland but he travels all over the world. So … he is doing the first selection' (IV 34, Managing Director, Breeder). What follows is a laborious process of three rounds of planting seedlings followed by selection, each round scaling up the number of plants per variety, and in total amounting to millions of plants over the course of several years:

> [W]e do over 100,000 pollinations per year. These 100,000 varieties usually give us about 1,000,000 seeds and each seed is individual. About half of those million seeds germinate, the other half is not viable. Of these half million seedlings within a year, they bring the selection down to 12,000 to 13,000 individuals. What we get here [in Naivasha] is about 2,500 individuals and we have another small site in Karen, Nairobi which receives … five plants per variety. In Karen, they select 150 and in a good year we get six or seven varieties. It is not a very efficient business; we go down from half a million seedlings to ten varieties globally in a span of seven years. (IV 40, Managing Director, Breeder)

Crossbreeding creates new varieties at random. Afterwards, these lively beings have to be turned into commodities, they have to be 'civilised' (Ziegler 2007, 55). The actual pacifying of roses is done during the selection of varieties passing on to the next round of testing. Flowers become commodities 'because they are valued according to specific criteria' (Ouma 2015, 31). There are two groups of criteria in this selection process: first, a set of over 20 indicators examines the physical attributes of the plant, such as scent, disease resistance, productivity, vase life. This compilation of indicators shows that valuations of cut flowers is already occurring in the breeding process. These indicators are 'neither intrinsic nor extrinsic' (Callon, Muniesa 2005, 1234), they are based on the physicality of the roses, yet geared towards the expectations of agencies on its material qualities (Çalışkan, Callon 2010, 5). Traditionally, the actors expressing their expectations about the quality of cut flowers were growers who mainly opted for productivity and disease resistance (see below). Nowadays, buyers have become powerful agencies in this process and have shifted the sets of indicators to better serve their own interest. These concentrate on vase life or clear and extraordinary colours (e.g., orange). Retail chains are even more influential in the second criteria for selecting varieties: market feedback. Due to their high turnover, retail chains – apart from FloraHolland – possess the most information on consumer preferences and prices. Breeders, on the other hand, fully rely on secondary data about how their (future) varieties (will) 'perform' and hence cooperate with buyers:

> We don't do specific market research, we don't go out and converse with people, but we do a lot of different things. We send batches to packers and now with the direct markets, not so much with the supermarkets themselves, but the guys who are selling to the supermarkets. But then they say 'Yes, we like it' and maybe our grower can plant it. (IV 32, Sales Manager, Breeder)

Some breeders specialise in varieties for the unspecialised retail chain. For them, it is important to get their varieties 'approved' by retail chains:

> For example, it [the target market] can be the retail [chains]. If it's that and it gets approved by [a German supermarket], it can be a big variety. Because those guys are slow in their selection. So once that it gets approved they get stuck in to it and there will be millions and millions of stems. So I need to sell a lot of hectares for that. (IV 34, Managing Director, Breeder)

Thus, retail chains shape the new market order in their interest by making use of their knowledge in price-making mechanisms and in the objectifications of cut flowers during market encounters (see Chapter 3), as well as in the process of selecting new varieties (see also Hughes 2000, 180). Breeders are dependent on feedback from buyers, since 'they can have the technically perfect flower, but it needs to be sellable' (OB 38, Managing Director, Breeder). Due to the long process of testing and selection, breeders plan several years ahead. Therefore, they are bound to their specialisation on a certain market segment:

> [In] 2003, 2004 more and more breeders started moving, we have to select and breed specifically for this upcoming market because otherwise

we end up nowhere. It takes time before you change your thinking that your main product in five or ten years will not be on the market anymore. And the breeding will always ... think ahead, because when we start crossbreeding now [in 2014], we crossbreed for 2018 to 2020. And what will the market need? First the market of our clients [the growers], but also the client itself ... But you will grow for this market. What the buyers need and want is quite difficult. (IV 37, Managing Director, Breeder)

In order to be more flexible, breeders scaled up crossingbreeding to create more possible varieties. Due to the elaborate trials, this implies large investments in testing facilities. For instance, breeding requires around 70 employees per hectare, compared to between eight and 11 for growing. Ultimately, three to five new varieties per year are a satisfying result for breeding companies; hence, success rates are low and risks are high: 'Every year we try to come up with five new varieties, we try to get them to market. Sometimes it is zero and other times it is eight, nine, but the success rate is 0.00001 per cent' (IV 34, Managing Director, Breeder). Over the years, the large breeders have built up portfolios of 50 to 80 of those 'successful' varieties. Breeders call varieties successful once they have sold 'anything' of it, 'half a hectare or whatever' (IV 32, Sales Manager, Breeder).

Yet, their catalogues also contain varieties that are planted on 100 ha or more. Through these outstanding varieties, breeders are able to take part in shaping market relations. Although they are dependent on knowledge from buyers and are not selling products to retail or consumers themselves, breeders can intervene in market relations by creating exclusivity or a supply shortage through the limitation of their royalties. This way, breeders may shape marketisation processes in their favour and extend demand for their varieties. One breeder describes this strategy:

If we said we got this new massive nice one, it looks spectacular. And we can say: you can plant one hectare. And two months later: let's sell another ten hectares to all these other farms. Actually, there was a guy, he was surprised to see his prices were going from hero to zero. Because he just flooded the market. So, the idea being, that if you limit it then this is how to establish the variety in the market. I mean you should always sell longer instead. So we have one that is called *Yellow Submarine*. It's very popular. It is a yellow. And we just limit it. And so we got nonstop request at all the shows. *Yellow Submarine, Yellow Submarine, Yellow Submarine*, that's all they wanted. And because we limited it that's lasting until now. (IV 32, Sales Manager, Breeder)

Exclusive varieties generate higher turnovers for breeders as prices for producers are higher.

In their market encounters, breeders and growers usually exchange only 'a piece of paper' (IV 34, Managing Director, Breeder), entailing a patent, and instructions for planting and maintaining the crop. Three to four plants are enough for propagation, which is left to the growers' responsibility. This implies new pricing systems: mostly, they are now based on production area and turnover, whereas in the past they referred to the actual number of plants sold. Royalties entail expiry dates, the maximum area for production, and the number of plants. Before these contracts come into being, growers have to decide on which variety to plant.

Planting

Lake Naivasha flower growers possess a diverse portfolio of rose varieties on their farms. A range of around ten varieties per 30 ha increases their flexibility in market encounters. Moreover, the seasonality of the cut flower market is also reflected in the greenhouses of flower farms. Growers need different varieties in order to meet seasonal demands, as these are linked to distinct colours: red for Valentine's Day, yellow for Easter, white and pink for Mother's Day, etc.

The selection of which varieties are planted is one of the most sensitive moments in the production of cut flowers. It implies high investments for royalties (€ 35,000–60,000 per ha) and ties producers to the variety for five to seven years – unless they uproot it earlier, which costs even more because of expenses for propagation and the interim loss of production during the initial phase of planting. The fixity of investments is especially problematic for flower growers facing the volatility of the new market order, which requires flexible producers (see above). The financial precariousness challenging many farms further complicates investments. On the other hand, the new market order forces producers to regularly invest in new varieties. Varieties have an 'economic life' (IV 28, Farm Manager, Grower) or a 'lifecycle' (IV 76, Sourcing Manager, Auction Services); new and especially exclusive varieties generate higher revenues. Therefore, growers need to constantly renew their portfolio:

> Normally the newer ones are better on the market. In other farms, they have planted nowadays some older varieties again, because they thought: maybe in the past they were still productive and still there is demand. But we have never done it. We have never planted a variety again. Okay, we have planted varieties in Kenya that we had tried in the Netherlands. But not replaced with the same variety. (IV 28, Farm Manager, Grower)

Hence, farms cannot escape the necessity of investing in new varieties. The important question is: how do they decide on which variety to plant? In her study on Dutch gerbera growers, Ziegler noticed that 'flower farmers seldom (perhaps never) have the perfect information they need for a "rational" decision, or anything approaching it' and that the choice is therefore often depicted as a 'gamble' (2007, 105). Among Lake Naivasha growers, similar reasoning prevails. The choice is based on 'pure experience' (IV 8, Head of Production, Grower), and in Kenya it is often also perceived as a 'gamble' (IV 45, General Manager, Grower). Although being some distance away from making rational choices based on infinite information (as presented in the *homo oeconomicus* -model), farm managers try to minimise the uncertainty of the valuations of new varieties. Production performance indicators are important factors in this process. They are transmitted by breeders and their validity is then often tested in trials. This farm manager describes the indicators of growers' valuations of a rose variety:

> It should be productive, that is one of the first things to get. It should grow nicely, so you should look how it grows. Then transport is also very important. You can have a perfect flower here on the farm, but if it is not working in transport, if it gets damages, then it is useless. Then it should be tolerant for diseases. (IV 28, Farm Manager, Grower)

Moreover, it is also the case for growers that valuations of varieties by external market agencies play a decisive role. Projections about the market performance of varieties depend on knowledge about consumer and buyer preferences. For growers, this information is either accessible through the auction, or through large corporate buyers. This opens the door for retail chains to influence the selection of the varieties planted. They exert control either through specific requests for certain types of flowers, personal contacts during farm visits and at flower expos, or cooperation with breeders and growers. This farm manager describes how feedback from buyers affects his choice and is weighed against production performance indicators:

> You listen to the market very much. Some people from the supermarkets sometimes are coming to the farm. For example, for our latest orange, somebody from [a British supermarket], he saw it here in the green house. He said: 'Oh, that colour is the best'. And then of course you take it in your consideration. We have planted it now and everybody is still saying: 'Oh, the colour is so good'. So you have to listen to the market. But also [the farm's sales manager] in the Netherlands, what he feels. The response of the market. We trial varieties on … this exhibition that is now going on in the Netherlands. This trade fair. … We ask potential customers what they think about it. And then if they say that this variety is the best in the Netherlands, he doesn't look at production. He only receives the flower and says: 'Ah, this is beautiful and the market likes

it'. So me here on [the] farm and also [a shareholder], we should still feel that and if you look at the growth: does it give the numbers? And we are finally the people to decide it. Because if you only listen to the market you end up with poorly producing varieties. (IV 28, Farm Manager, Grower)

This strategy proves that, similar to selection processes during breeding, in their choice of varieties, farm managers' valuations entail quantifications (productivity, vase life, etc.) and qualifications (customer feedback, experience) alike (see Berndt, Boeckler 2012, 208). Their qualifications in particular expose growers' selection processes, and as a result the objectification of cut flowers, to other agencies. Flower farms themselves can influence these qualifications by choosing their possible buyers, whom they then contact for feedback. For instance, some farms explicitly try to avoid supermarkets and therefore do not involve them in their choice of varieties. Yet, as planting a variety can impede or enable market relations, most farms include retail chains in their selection process. As a consequence, Lake Naivasha growers increasingly choose varieties suitable for a specific segment of the unspecialised retail chain: the upper supermarket segment, which requires intermediate roses with medium head size, reasonable quality, and long vase life; in contrast to the lower supermarket/discounter segment which requires the smaller super sweetheart roses with maximum productivity at minimum prices. This segment seems to be the most promising market channel for the majority of farms, as its product suits the climatic conditions at Lake Naivasha very well and prices are moderate in comparison to the discounter segment.

Packing

Besides breeding and planting, new objectifications of cut flowers also take place during their packing. In market encounters, mono- and mixed-coloured bouquets are now established as a new item for exchange besides single stems (see Chapter 3). First of all, this implies changes in production: synchronised maturity and uniform looks, quality, and size are fundamental for bouquets. Yet, the main change these new products entail concerns the packing of flowers. These are now not only prepared for transport, but a portion of them at least are ready-packed for retail. The preparing of bouquets ready for sale requires sophisticated harvest and post-harvest activities. After cutting, flowers are 'graded', which includes sorting for length, removing excessive foliage and bad flowers, and finally composing bouquets of flowers of a similar quality and at the same cut stage. As such, for immaculate bouquets of uniform flowers, the timing of production and harvest is fundamental. This task is even more intricate for mix-colour bouquets, since they require diverse varieties with distinct growth periods and cut stages. Furthermore, packing bouquets entails risks for growers as bouquets are only accepted by buyers if all components meet their requirements.

The objectification of cut flowers as bouquets by corporate retailers occurs not only in actual market encounters, but reaches back to production and handling. In direct sales, packing is often done according to the customers' specifications. Farms store packing material by customers, assort bouquets according to their specifications, and wrap it in plastic sleeves with the supermarket branding: 'They bunch the flowers up depending on the customers. ... There are ones who need 18, there are ones who need 20. We go by customer specification' (OB 26, Packhouse Manager, Grower). To fulfil these specifications, some farms also cooperate with one another to be able to supply a broader range of bouquets (see above). Due to the more elaborate grading process compared to single stems for auction supply, processing flowers for bouquets requires more work, especially during peak days. One manager said, for instance, that his farm of 40 ha employs 200 workers for grading and increases the workforce to 350 in preparation for Valentine's Day (OB 81, Financial Director, Grower). Hence, labour costs are higher for packing bouquets, especially when considering that farms need to adjust and invest in their handling facilities, and that wages for packhouse workers, including bonuses, are higher than for 'general' workers (see also Gibbon, Riisgaard 2014, 115–18).

The introduction of new, highly productive varieties and the processing of cut flowers seem to provide possibilities for flower farmers to upgrade. Yet, whilst at the same time being inevitable for growers, the planting of new varieties turns out to be a risky investment. Preparing bouquets opens new market channels, but it is both laborious and expensive. Moreover, these efforts are not rewarded financially: flower prices have dropped mainly because of these bouquets of new varieties, which are sold in European supermarkets and produced with higher expenditure for the growers (see Chapter 3). Hence, the classic approach of GVCs to upgrading, as the improvement of an economic actor's link to a GVC in order to gain access to more profitable positions (see e.g., Gereffi 1999), does not get to grips with these dynamics. Ponte and Ewert (2009, 1637) define upgrading more broadly as 'reaching a better deal'. Their observations about the South African wine industry (Ponte, Ewert 2009) show some parallels to Lake Naivasha's cut flower growers: the improvement of product quality, production management, and processing were accompanied by an increasing demand for bulk wines, by higher risks, and by limited rewards for producers. They conclude that in terms of reaching a better deal, for firms (or more generally speaking for developing countries) the best option may even be 'downgrading' (Ponte, Ewert 2009, 1648). The cut flower case shows that unprofitable upgrading or downgrading sometimes does not even represent a better deal, but is rather the only option for producers. This relates to Havice and Campling's reinterpretation of upgrading by linking it to the articulation debate (Havice, Campling 2013). They criticise the inclusionary bias of mainstream upgrading definitions and note that upgrading should be used to reflect upon the uneven geographies of capitalist development more generally. As shown above, the 'non-linear dynamics of upgrading' (Havice, Campling 2013, 2611) prevail in the cut flower industry. New varieties and the preparing of bouquets have come at great costs for producers, and have produced moments of upgrading and downgrading, as well as of the marginalisation and the exclusion of producers not able to invest in new varieties and flower processing.

Ultimately, the making of new commodities did not benefit most producers (and breeders), but opened the door for influence and control to be exerted by corporate retailers. In this way, retail chains are able to use their market knowledge to affect the objectifications of cut flowers in their favour within market encounters, during breeding, and in the planting and packing of cut flowers.

Making farms profitable: Innovations in production and handling

'To compete in this market channel and segment, low production costs, a professional organisation and excellent planning are extremely important'.[6]

As I have shown, the making of new commodities has not led to a more profitable situation for Lake Naivasha growers. Financial precariousness, obligatory flexibility in production and market relations, production standards, and certifications have all put pressure on farms. This leads to questions of how farms cope with such an unfavourable market order and how some of them have even managed to operate profitably? Here, three factors are decisive: minimising production costs, raising productivity, and increasing the quality of produce in order to obtain higher prices.

Farms try to achieve a minimisation of production costs and a rise in productivity mainly through technological advancement in their production. Regarding means of production, cut flowers are a typical non-traditional agricultural export product. These require sophisticated industrial inputs, technology, and technical knowledge, all imported from abroad (Selwyn 2016, 1776). Bearing in mind that markets are sociotechnical agencements composed

---

6   CBI 2017a.

of heterogeneous elements, these means of production are not situated outside the market. They are not simply tools, resources, or capital invested *into* the market, but actors *within* the market (see Çalışkan, Callon 2010, 3; Müller 2015, 77). Marketisation entails assembling these heterogeneous elements 'that may be human and non-human, organic and inorganic, technical and natural' (Anderson, McFarlane 2011, 124). Thus, reassembling markets can imply a more prominent role of distinct actors. In the new cut flower market order, this is concerned with production technologies. As shown in Table 3, farms try to minimise costs for inputs such as fertiliser, chemicals, and water, increase the controllability over production, or raise the crop productivity by investing in a wide range of technologies. As the 'civilizing' process of cut flowers through breeding is never complete (Ziegler 2007, 100), these tools are used to tame overflows, that is the remaining unintended processes during cut flower growing, such as plant diseases. Some of these technologies are widely applied, for instance lightweight greenhouses and fertigation; some are currently spreading, such as hydroponics. Meanwhile, only two of the most advanced farms employ crop heating. Most of these technologies come at high cost and require significant investments that are hard to realise for most farms. Yet, in the long term they pay off. For instance, a combination of fertigation and hydroponics enables the recycling of waste water. The water and the dissolved nutrients may be reused. An agronomist I interviewed (IV 63, Supplier) and the 'Green Farming Demonstration Project' (Ketter et al. 2015a; Ketter et al. 2015b) promise up to 65% less water use, 30% savings on fertilisers, and over 20% more production through the application of fertigation techniques.

The increasing prevalence of production technology has also changed managers' attitudes towards flower growing. Many managers still strongly identify as farmers and stress the agricultural aspects of flower growing instead of the industrial ones. Yet, innovations in production such as complex fertigation mainly require technological knowledge. The mechanisation of production and the introduction of new technologies often involves tinkering. Investments into innovations have to be calculated and their benefits modelled. One farm manager noted that growing flowers resembles his previous job in the car industry and described it as 'very similar to engineering' (IV 7, Farm Manager, Grower). Engineering is an appropriate term, as it describes a deeply sociotechnical process – technology needs to be allocated, tested, installed, applied, and maintained. Ultimately, increasing productivity and reducing costs with production technology is based on assessments of risk, investment, and the benefits of technology. This farm manager describes how he tries to balance costs, product quality, and productivity:

We have quite high-producing varieties and I think we know how to grow quite well. And the climate in Naivasha is very good. And then we are [also] fairly good in giving the plants a proper amount of water. ... Even in our Dutch farm we were always high producing. So it is also *how* we are growing. But you should also understand, ... most of the times if you have high production the average price of the flowers is also lower. So it's not automatically that you can say [that] a farm with 250 [stems per m² productivity] and another one is 150 so the one with 250 has double turnover, no. A rose plant can produce a number of kilogrammes of biological material. ... so maybe ... the sales price of a stem times the productivity is maybe on a high producing farm sometimes similar to a low producing farm. But, of course, you try to optimise it. If you have higher production and good turnover, you try to have both values on a higher level of course. Then you have more turnovers for your farm. (IV 28, Farm Manager, Grower)

It is not only the use of technology that has to be managed in production, but work flows also have to be organised. Proper crop maintenance is the second decisive means for lowering costs and increasing productivity. This task is carried out manually and consists of spraying, weeding, removing excess foliage, and pruning 'non-productive stems' (OB 26, Assistant Production Manager, Grower). Since only the productive parts of the plants remain, the use of fertilisers can be minimised. Furthermore, crop maintenance is necessary to prevent diseases and hence increase productivity. As these tasks are solely performed by general workers, farm managers try to uphold the quality of crop maintenance mostly through strict hierarchies and tight control over labourers. Yet, as Selwyn observed in the case of fruit production: 'Improving fruit quality means training workers to avoid waste and inefficiency, and to perform new tasks that contribute to the production of higher quality and priced fruit' (Selwyn 2016, 1780). The same applies to the cut flower industry. Crop maintenance is a delicate task, and although most general workers are not formally educated, training on the job and experience increases the accurateness of labourers.[7] Therefore, it is important for farms to keep their workforce stable.

A third strategy to make farms profitable, besides reducing costs and raising productivity, is to obtain higher revenues. In order to increase the prices of their produce, farms mainly have to intervene in handling and transport. The valuation of cut flowers in market encounters at the Dutch trade hub is related to the suppliers' reputation, which is to a large part based not on production processes but on the quality of (un)packing and the presentation of flowers at

---

[7]   Kuiper writes in great detail about hierarchical management systems and the skills needed for crop maintenance and harvest (Kuiper 2019, 131–52).

Table 3. Innovations and technology in production (Author).

Technology	Targets	How does it work?	
Higher Crop Density	Increased yield	Planting more plants per m² than average; selecting highly productive varieties	
Greenhouses and Polythene	Increased controllability of production	Replacing old (wooden) greenhouses with light steel ones; new polythene protects against condensation and enables the regulation of ultraviolet and infrared light and has a higher durability; more expensive	
Hydroponics	Increased controllability of production Recycling and saving of fertilisers and water Increased crop productivity	Replacing soil with artificial soil or soilless hydroculture, e.g. coco peat; enables the control of run-off, involves higher costs (2-3%)	
Crop Heating	Increased crop productivity	Running heated water through pipes close to the crops during low temperatures, especially in the morning to extend growth period; water is heated by solar panels or geothermal energy	
Computerised Fertigation	Increased controllability of production Recycling and saving of fertilisers and water	Combination of irrigation and fertiliser in a (pulse) drip irrigation system controlled by software; pulse drip irrigation waters for a few seconds with high pressure and then pauses; increases plant intake of nutrients and water	
Biological Pest Control & Integrated Pest Management (IPM)	Saving of spray chemicals Longer access times to greenhouses for crop maintenance	Using live organisms, predators and antagonists to control pests such as mites and plant diseases	

the auction and during the sales process (see Chapter 3). Decisive indicators for the presentation of flowers are a neat appearance of bouquets and the freshness of the products. Farms can take several measures at different points along the way, from greenhouses to buyers, to ensure a high quality. It begins with the harvest, where cut stages have to be timed well. Here again, the skills of general workers are essential: 'It's all about the cut stage ... Make sure that the leaves are clean; that's all. You have to get to the greenhouse and you tell the people who cut, this is the cut size today! And you monitor it. ... You make sure that your teams are up to date' (IV 76, Sourcing Manager, Auction Services). The same applies to the packhouse work where the bouquets are assembled. In an effort to raise the quality and rapidity of packing, specialised packhouse team work has spread amongst farms since the early 2000s (Gibbon, Riisgaard 2014, 113). Regarding transport, minimising quality loss is the main target. This is achieved by preventing physical damage to the flowers, by the constant cooling of flowers, and by reducing the time between harvest and delivery to the buyer. Innovative farms already start with these measures on the way from the greenhouse to the packhouse, by installing railway systems to accelerate on-farm transport. After grading, flowers need to be cooled to slow down their decay. Here, farms can invest in new technologies, such as vacuum cooling, to increase the preservability of their crop. Eventually, at the airport, freight forwarders take over responsibility for the cold chain. Quality in transport is mainly measured by the ability to keep breaks in the cold chain as short as possible, for example by having cold stores close to the runway or using specialised cargo flights. After the flight to Europe, farms can still increase the quality of their flowers by investing in unpacking labour and technology. Although investments into post-harvest processes raise flower values, many farms prefer to invest in production technology, which they perceive as their core profession. Sales and management departments, often outsiders to the production process, prefer the former:

> My thing is post-harvest. If you have ten heads and two are bad, get it back, it's very simple, until you get it right! I see farms with the same varieties, the same altitude, it's five cent difference. Now, if you have 20 hectares and you have a production of 150 stems [per m^2], that's 30 million [total stems per year] and 5 cents between. That's a lot of money! It's incredible that they don't care, ... that flowers are in the sun for four hours. (IV 76, Sourcing Manager, Auction Services)

More and more, the new market order turned the task of running a profitable Lake Naivasha flower farm into a question of innovative production technology, cost-efficient production, and rapid and smooth handling. These measures enable farms to decrease their production costs, raise productivity, and increase the value of their produce. Large farms usually have more capital for investments into these technologies. Nevertheless, in the last years, some middle-sized farms have led the way in innovating flower growing. On these farms, the management is closely involved in the production process and willing to try out and invest in new technology:

> There are people who want to make money and there are people who enjoy the process like [a flower grower] ... He doesn't care about money, he cares about the product. ... He wants to grow at his best. There [are] a lot who do it for the money, which is okay, but he wants to do it good. He thinks about things and he dares to invest. He invests in a Dutch organisation who comes there for the fumigation, for chemicals, because he says he doesn't have all that knowledge. He spends a hundred thousand Euros or something every year to do soil samples, machines. ... He thinks about things; he knows what exactly is in the water. He goes further and further and further. Most people don't do that. (IV 76, Sourcing Manager, Auction Services)

This example shows that the innovation of production is based on capital, production management, and technology. It also proves that marketisation and the reorganisation of the cut flower industry is a profoundly sociotechnical process, assembling heterogeneous human and non-human actors (Çalışkan, Callon 2010, 8–13). Close assemblages of capital, production management, and technology help farms in innovation processes. Access to capital as well as knowledge about production technologies simplifies testing or investing in them for production management. These close assemblages occur mostly on middle-sized farms: within these, the shareholders and the management have tight relationships or are even identical. The general management of these farms is usually involved in production or at least knowledgeable about it. Meanwhile, large farms are usually run by business managers or by farmers too busy with accounting to take care of the production themselves. Combined with their higher flexibility compared to the large farms (see above), innovations in production and handling have turned middle-sized farms into the most profitable enterprises of the last few years.

Labour management

In the preceding sections, I have scrutinised how the current marketisation has reassembled and reorganised actors in the cut flower industry. So far, the analysis has mainly focused on farms from a manager perspective and their relation to other actors. In this section, I want to draw attention to how the new market order links to capital-labour relations in the cut flower industry.[8] The employees at Lake Naivasha, as of today approximately 40,000 with the vast majority of them being categorised as 'general workers', played an important part in the Kenyan cut flower industry right from its start in the 1970s. To a large extent, cut flower production (and handling) both is and will in the foreseeable future continue to be manual work. The number of employees per hectare has changed only a little over the past decades and lies between 8.5 (IV 45, General Manager, Grower) and 12 (Gibbon, Riisgaard 2014, 112). As such, the availability of cheap labour has been a locational factor for many enterprises when first looking to establish their farms. The availability of labour in Naivasha is mostly based on migrants from other Kenyan regions; most notably from the Western and Nyanza provinces, as a survey by Kuiper has shown (2017, 110). Obviously, workers are essential to flower production as the maintenance of the crop and the harvest rely on constant effort. Lastly, much of the attention from the media and NGOs has been focussed on working conditions. Apart from the issue of environmental damage, the topics most targeted by various campaigns have been health risks, low wages, and sexual harassment (see e.g., Food & Water Watch 2008).

These factors show that labour plays a crucial role in both historical and current marketisation processes within the cut flower industry. GCC and GVC studies have mostly conceived of workers as passive objects who are at the mercy of external market forces and powerful lead firms (Selwyn 2013, 77). A marketisation perspective enables us to turn this story around and perceive of labour as a form of agency constitutive of global economic connections (Riisgaard 2009a, 326; Selwyn 2013, 77). Selwyn offers such an approach when he argues for a bottom-up conceptualisation of upgrading (2013). According to him, 'action by labour may co-determine processes of local development' (Selwyn 2012, 217). Thinking of labour as agency within global markets is not intended to obscure poor labour conditions or exploitative relationships. Rather, it shifts attention to 'how value is produced not only through firm–firm or firm–state relations, but also through the labor process' (Goger 2013, 2633). This value creation through the labour process may be (and often is) rooted in poor working conditions, starvation wages, or health risks.

In the Lake Naivasha cut flower industry, however, value creation is more and more based on a stable, experienced, and trained workforce, which

---

8   This section focuses on the relation between labour and current marketisation processes. As such, workers' realities and their everyday struggles cannot be acknowledged to a satisfying degree here. My colleague Gerda Kuiper has contributed much more on this particular issue and writes extensively about the lives of labourers in Naivasha (Kuiper 2019).

has potentially positive effects on labour conditions. Labour efficiency and accuracy is decisive in the process of reducing costs, raising productivity, and increasing product quality (see above). Here, the cut flower industry has characteristics that are similar to grape production in Brazil. A study by Selwyn on the industry (2016, 1780) showed that producers aiming at product and process upgrading are dependent on trained and efficiently performing workers. In the Kenyan cut flower industry, general workers are often regarded as 'unskilled labour'. Yet, investments in training on the farm and experience in executing various tasks[9] make long-time employment attractive for farm managers. All farm managers I spoke to about labour turnover expressed their pride about the low rates on their farms. Even the manager of a crisis-ridden farm claimed a very low turnover: '[It's] actually nothing; it is below two per cent' (IV 45, General Manager, Grower). In their sample of Kenyan flower farms, Gibbon and Riisgaard (2014, 109) detected an average length of employment of 5.8 years.

.Hence, in contrast to many other industries in the Global South, the cut flower industry values stability in its work force:[10] 'People who are experienced ... will work hard and will feel that they know it. So, if you have a million stems or 600,000 stems, they will still do it within the same hours. So, at the end it is cheaper' (IV 45, General Manager, Grower).

There are two sides to this aspired stability of workforce: the management strategies to achieve it and the workers' agency in terms of employment conditions. Regarding management strategies, it first has to be noted that pater-nalistic attitudes towards employees are still rife among (foreign) managers. 'Happy' is probably the most common description used by managers when discussing their labour force. Although they acknowledge the toils of farm work, they perceive it as fair employment. One general manager of a large farm describes his opinion on working conditions and his relationship to workers as follows:

> I think 95% of the workers here just want to work as long as they get their salaries ... They don't complain. They don't complain. They work really hard. ... I am not a saint. I always tell them: 'Don't need to work hard for me as long as you come on time for your job and you leave when it is time'. And when they need overtime, we request, we put it

[9] Kuiper writes about how difficult the ostensibly simple tasks of weeding, harvesting, and grading actually are (Kuiper 2019, 149).

[10] In her study on the Sri Lankan apparel industry, Goger (2013) depicts it as another exception. In a similar manner to the cut flower industry, she traces this back to a process of upgrading *through* labour that is necessary for the apparel industry to survive within volatile market relations.

as announcement two days ahead. So, everybody is happy; bonuses are paid, name it, they are quite happy. (IV 45, General Manager, Grower)

What I find especially notable here is that when asked about salaries, farm managers could not recite them (in contrast to the overall labour costs), but insisted they were above average, or at least more than the minimum wage set by the Collective Bargaining Agreement (CBA). In general, low wage levels are often legitimised by paternalistic reasoning. For instance, a Dutch manager is 'proud to give them food' and thinks it is 'the most honest way to give the people a good living' (IV 1, Farm Manager, Breeder). Yet, at the same time, higher wages are seen as a 'real danger' (IV 43, Managing Director, Grower). And not only because of the producers' financially precarious situation, but because managers assume employees are satisfied with their wages or that it is better to create employment opportunities for masses than to pay fewer employees well:

> I think, let's create in a country, where 40% isn't employed, as many simple jobs as possible. But on the other hand, we need to find the money somewhere. ... Where do they find it? It's very simple to double the salaries. You think that it's good for the country? I don't think so. So, of course, when you are used to have a salary level like in Europe and you compare it with this, you will be shocked. But come here and find out to understand how it is working and what is good for the country. (IV 37, Managing Director, Breeder)

For farm managers, wage levels are a tool for stabilising their workforce. The remuneration system in most farms is geared towards this goal with yearly increments of payments. Although the attitudes of farm managers persist, paternalistic modes are no longer prevalent in the everyday practices of labour management on farms. Paternalistic forms of labour management resemble familial relations. The farm is conceived as a private space and the farm manager as the final authority within this space (Gibbon, Riisgaard 2014, 96). In the cut flower industry, labour management is now rather oriented towards lean modes (Goger 2013, 2637) based on the following principles: small teams performing multiple operations, the training of workers in multiple skills, self-management of teams, and an orientation towards performance measurement and problem solving. In cut flower production, this includes the 'responsibilisation' (Riisgaard, Gibbon 2014, 268) of workers: teams in greenhouses are overseen by one or two supervisors and responsible for all the tasks for a section of the greenhouse, from weeding to harvest, including the quality of the end product. In packhouses, workers are paid bonuses if they grade more stems than the required daily minimum. Responsibilisation gives workers more variety and more freedom in the organisation of their work, but it also includes strict control on the output. Hence, levels of (self-)discipline continue to be high. Building on convention theory, Gibbon and Riisgaard (2014) depict these management systems as a compromise of 'industrial' and 'civic' (in contrast to traditional, 'domestic', or market-oriented approaches). Flower farms significantly differ regarding their modes of labour management, and some of them still have traditional management systems with strict top-down hierarchies and workers performing a single task day in and day out. Gibbon and Riisgaard (2014) called this domestic labour management. Yet, the general trend at Lake Naivasha farms is a shift towards civic and industrial forms. In accordance with these categories, labour management in the cut flower industry is characterised by a stabilisation of workforce, a formalisation and legalisation of employment, and responsibilisation (see Riisgaard, Gibbon 2014).

The managers' aspirations of a stable workforce not only impact on modes of labour management, but also on the workers' agency. Selwyn (2012) argues that the ability to disrupt capital accumulation due to the role of the workers in the production process provides them with structural power. Flower farms are dependent on the reliability and performance quality of their workforce. As shown, these factors directly relate to production costs, productivity, and product quality. Following Barrientos et al. (2011), this means that the attempts at economic upgrading by the farms lead to an improvement of employment conditions, or social upgrading. They argue: '[I]f economic upgrading requires high and consistent quality standards that are best provided by a stable, skilled and formalized labour force, then economic and social upgrading may be positively correlated, especially when they increase worker productivity' (Barrientos et al. 2011, 332). Yet, as Selwyn (2013) shows in the case of Brazilian grape production, working conditions only improve if the workforce is able to transform this structural power into associational power. Associational power refers to the organisation of labour, such as in unions. In the Kenyan cut flower industry, associational power is most notably achieved through the Kenya Plantation and Agricultural Workers' Union (KPAWU), which represents employees in collective bargaining.

These structures eventually lead us to question whether the increased structural power of the workers is translated into a change in capital-labour relations and an improvement of working conditions. Although violations of labour rights persist on some farms, labour conditions have certainly improved in the last few years. Flower farm workers were indeed able to transform their structural power into associational power. The degree of unionisation is high: according to the KPAWU, around 70% of Lake Naivasha farms were unionised (Kuiper 2019, 158), and 59 farms signed the CBA of 2011–13. Thus, the number of workers working under the CBA is relatively high. The growing importance of the CBA also has an effect on standards: whereas Kenya legislation does not require unionisation, Fairtrade and the KFC do. Here, the cut flower industry differs from other agricultural sectors, such as the tea sector in India, where, according to Besky (2008), Fairtrade certification undermined existing union power. The CBA, among others, limits working hours to 46 hours per week, regulates overtime pay, rest days, and annual leave, and specifies the minimum requirements for work safety and medical assistance.[11]

Contrary to many other industries where a lean mode of production resulted in a casualisation of labour,[12] the share of casual and seasonal labour diminished drastically on flower farms. This is an effect of a less volatile demand and the aspirations of a stable workforce (see above), but also of restrictions on seasonal labour in the CBA. Thus, most workers confide in stable employment relations. Farm managers try to compensate variances in demand by a flexible workforce able to perform various tasks and by scheduling annual leave predominantly off-season, as this farm manager describes:

> Actually on weekly basis … they work for 46 hours. They can work one day longer when you give them time-off at another day. We try to compensate with those hours. And you can for short period neglect some other activities. If you harvest more, then you do a bit less weeding or you compensate a bit with how you do the sprays in the afternoon. If it is sprayed anyway, you can send the people home. In our farm we don't hire more people. We still try to do with the same. But, therefore, it is not very ideal to have big fluctuations. We always try to have small fluctuation, because then we can handle the labour. (IV 28, Farm Manager, Grower)

During the main season, overtime is frequent. It is paid (1.5 times higher than regular work) and announced beforehand, but workers are expected to consent. The manager's statement also reflects the focus of an industrial-civic labour management on discipline, the fulfilment of tasks, and a rhythm of work determined by management and supervisors (see also Kuiper 2019, 131–47). These principles show that the workers' agency is limited to basic conditions of employment, but it very rarely extends to the organisation of production and labour within farms, which adhere to the buyers' objectification of flowers and management's realisation of these objectifications.

Current marketisation processes also limit workers' agency on capital-labour relations in one decisive dimension: salaries. Absolute wage levels increased in the last years but are still far from what a report commissioned by Fairtrade defines as a living wage: the CBA sets the wage for newly

---

[11] Collective Bargaining Agreement between Agricultural Employers' Association and Kenya Plantation and Agricultural Workers' Union, 2011–12.

[12] See, for instance, the study of Barrientos and Kritzinger (2004) for the case of the South African fruit industry.

recruited labourers at KES 5,401,[13] whereas a worker with over 15 years' experience earns KES 10,252[14] (Anker, Anker 2014, 40). Anker and Anker (2014, 47), however, calculated a living wage of KES 18,542[15] for Naivasha. The CBA awards different allowances to workers, for instance for transport, housing, and 'safari', but still these do not compensate for the remarkable gap. Furthermore, Riisgaard and Gibbon (2014, 281) show that the real value of basic wages as determined in the CBA, fell between 2002 and 2011. These low wage levels are an essential part of the new market order, as it is based on low consumer prices and hence on financially precarious producers who cannot afford significantly higher labour expenses. Therefore, managers do not regard Kenya as a low wage country anymore (IV 43, Managing Director, Grower), although real wages are declining. This is supported by paternalistic arguments against higher wages (see above). Certification schemes, aimed at improving working conditions, have only a little effect on wages in the cut flower industry, as they do not focus on monetary but 'social' wages, including welfare packages (Riisgaard, Gibbon 2014, 277). These findings correspond with a meta study on standards that shows that certification has no positive effect on wage levels (Oya et al. 2017).

Reorganisation in crisis: The EU-East African Community Economic Partnership Agreement and disordering the cut flower trade

The new cut flower market order is characterised by the dominance of large corporate buyers and producers who have found a way to operate their farms profitably (albeit on a low level) by making their production and market linkages more flexible, by cutting costs, by increasing productivity and product quality, and by keeping a stable workforce under tight control. Low consumer prices in Europe are not possible without the ability of equatorial producers to cope with financial precariousness. Yet, there are limits to these orderings of the cut flower market. Marketisation is never complete; it is a process full of ruptures, contradictions, controversies, and it includes processes of inclusion as well as exclusion (Callon 1998a, 252; Bair et al. 2013, 2545; Ouma 2015, 10). Hence, crises are not the exception, but the rule during the emergence of new market orders: '[B]reakdown and failure ... [are] as much constitutive of performances as construction and stabilisation' (Boeckler, Berndt 2013, 425). Crises can have multiple causes. They can refer to the general crisis tendency of capitalism due to overaccumulation (Harvey 2001), but also to

---

[13] Equivalent to € 49.
[14] Equivalent to € 93.
[15] Equivalent to € 169.

the failure of the framing of goods, or of the economisation of 'nature' as resources (Ouma 2015, 176).

In this section, I want to shift the focus away from ordering processes and draw attention to disorder in the cut flower market agencement. Accounts of crises are rife in the cut flower industry. Some of them seem to fit into the assumption of network theory that networks are 'supposedly resilient and handle crises' (Marshall, Goodman 2013, 283). A story often told by flower farm managers is how stable the industry remained and how it kept on producing and delivering flowers during the post-election violence in Kenya in 2008. Although Lake Naivasha was one of the hotspots of turmoil (Lang, Sakdapolrak 2015, 2014), many farms claim they 'didn't stop producing flowers for one day' (OB 81, Financial Director, Grower) and export figures saw an all-time peak. Yet, other crises reveal the disorder inherent to networks, which can be caused by either change or stability: 'Every change is potentially unbalancing; every stability is also potentially unbalancing when other connected processes change' (Marshall, Goodman 2013, 283). In the following pages, I will scrutinise a significant moment of crisis in the cut flower market STA: the imposition of import levies after a delay in the negotiations for the EU-EAC (East African Community) Economic Partnership Agreement (EPA) shows how financially fragile the new market order is.

Tariff- and quota-free import into the EU has been a facilitator of the Kenyan cut flower industry since its first days (Hughes 2000, 181). Free market access has been an 'ostensibly solid point' (Ouma 2015, 176) taken for granted in market relations between equatorial flower growers and European buyers. Until 2000, these regulations were assured by the Lomé Convention, giving the African, Caribbean, and Pacific Group of States preferential access to European markets for most agricultural and mineral exports (Hurt 2003). In 2000, the World Trade Organisation declared the Convention as being against its rules, since it is not based on reciprocal terms. Thus, the Coutounou-Agreement between the EU and the African, Caribbean, and Pacific Group of States followed in 2000. In the agreement, the expiry date for non-reciprocal preferential access to the EU-market was set to end in 2007.[16] Its regulations were supposed to be replaced by EPAs, which the EU intended to reach with blocs of states. For Kenya, the correspondent bloc is the EAC, which further

---

[16] *Official Journal of the European Communities, 15.12.200, L 317/3, 'The Cotonou Agreement', Article 37, Procedures, 1* states: 'Economic partnership agreements shall be negotiated during the preparatory period which shall end by 31 December 2007 at the latest. Formal negotiations of the new trading arrangements shall start in September 2002 and the new trading arrangements shall enter into force by 1 January 2008, unless earlier dates are agreed between the Parties'.

includes Burundi, Rwanda, Tanzania, and Uganda. Yet, the first five years of negotiations from 2002 to 2007 only resulted in an interim EPA between the EU and the EAC, which was in force until October 2014.

When this deadline came closer without a final agreement in sight, the quota- and tariff-free market access taken for granted proved to be a 'crucial source ... of relationally disruptive and even destructive dynamics' (Ouma 2015, 176). In 2013, the cut flower industry in particular became nervous and pleaded with the EAC via the *Daily Nation*: 'Sign the trade deal with EU' (Xinhua 2013). So, why had the EAC not signed the deal earlier? Kenya is the only EAC member not included in the United Nation's list of Least Developed Countries (LDC). LDCs are granted preferential access to all markets under the 'Everything but Arms' treatment, independent of specific trade agreements. Kenya as a lower-middle income country, however, falls under the Generalised Scheme of Preferences (GSP),[17] which includes tariffs on cut flowers in its Standard GSP category.[18] Therefore, interests among the five EAC members differed significantly (Kwa et al. 2014, 39–40). The proposed agreement would have lifted all tariffs and quotas for EAC exports, but simultaneously removed restrictions for EU exports to EAC countries.

Eventually, the Kenyan government was in favour of reaching a deal with the EU, although sceptical about the effects on smallholders and on the manufacturing industry, and especially about the Most Favoured Nation clause[19] (Kwa et al. 2014, 40). The four EAC-LDCs opposed it, since they were not offered additional access but risked losing tariff revenues of US $ 161.5 million per year (Kwa et al. 2014, 42). The EU was not willing to renegotiate terms[20] and insisted on a deal with the EAC bloc instead of the individual countries.[21] As the EAC could not agree on a common position either, the

[17] See *Regulation (EU) No 978/2012 of the European Parliament and of the Council of 25 October 2012 applying a scheme of generalised tariff preferences and repealing Council Regulation (EC) No 732/2008.*

[18] In contrast, GSP+ does not include tariffs for cut flowers. Yet, Kenya has not ratified an ILO- and a Genocide Convention, which are two of the 27 conventions required to qualify for GSP+ (Kwa et al. 2014, 42).

[19] 'The Most Favoured Nation clause seeks to guarantee quota free access to the EAC for European exports, where the EAC member states enter into preferential pacts with other blocs' (Sambu 2014).

[20] Lodewijk Briet, head of the EU-delegation, told the *Sunday Nation*: 'The EU Parliament insists on respect for Human rights and the Most Favoured Nation clause, giving us a symmetrical access in time and in scope for EU's 28 member states' (Sambu 2014).

[21] Christophe De Vroey, the head of communication at the EU delegation in Kenya: 'EU is negotiating on behalf of its 28-members and, therefore, we expect the EAC to do the same on behalf of its five members' (Gibendi 2014).

deadline was missed and, starting on 1 October 2014, an import levy of 8.5% was applied to Kenyan cut flowers exported to the EU.

This tariff severely disrupted the current marketisation process; it revealed its frictions, its precariousness, and how a seemingly ordered market STA can become disordered. It imposed two burdens on flower growers: obviously, it created expenses. Some producers were able to split costs with buyers, but most were forced to pay themselves: 'So far the buyers are now not willing to pay anything. We are just stupid producers and they dictate the market' (IV 28, Farm Manager, Grower). Furthermore, the export of cut flowers was complicated by the extensive bureaucratic processes the tariffs involved. A manager explained to me in October 2014 that 'currently we are shipping through our lawyer's office' (IV 25, Head of Production, Grower). This created additional costs. These two burdens put the relation of Lake Naivasha growers to the current cut flower market under pressure. Major principles that underpinned these relations, which have been discussed in previous sections, were thrown into jeopardy: the delay in transport through customs controls impacted on the product quality, which relies on the rapidity and smoothness of transport. Furthermore, it decreased the producers' flexibility. The rising expenses caused by tariffs and higher transaction costs seriously threatened the financial model of the farms. These expenses 'eat the whole profit' (IV 36, General Manager, Breeder), or even exceed it: 'I can imagine for some farms it is really unbearable, for other farms they say a lot of our margin has gone to that EPA' (IV 28, Farm Manager, Grower). Reduced revenues and the insecurity caused by the negotiations impeded necessary investments into an expansion of greenhouses, new varieties, or production technology. Many farms simply went into 'survival mode' (IV 25, Head of Production, Grower).

Ultimately, this rather small change in market access regulation would have over time resulted in the expulsion of the majority of growers from the cut flower market. Hence, the Kenyan flower industry put serious effort into lobbying for an agreement. The KFC especially engaged in rearticulating the market STA, by investing 'material and ideological work to link up relations of production and complexly structured social formations' (Bair, Werner 2011, 992). Although the KFC was not part of Kenya's delegation (IV 20, CEO, KFC), its voice became the most prominent in the debates about the EPA. The cut flower industry in general, and the KFC in particular, featured in every newspaper article of the Nations Media Group on the topic. It also found its way into studies by the EU (Kwa et al. 2014). These reports highlight the importance of the flower industry for the Kenyan economy and how the delay on the agreement puts it under serious threat. In this way, the cut flower industry managed to push aside arguments from other industries and groups, such as small-scale farmers or the manufacturing industry, that were sceptical of the agreement (Kwa et al. 2014). Consequently, the Kenyan government urged for the signing of the EPA. On 17 October 2014, just two weeks after the tariffs were imposed, Tanzania, the main opposer of the contract, relented (see Mutambo 2014).[22] After a rapid ratification by the EU – stimulated by a personal intervention by Kenya's president, Kenyatta (Otieno 2014) – Kenyan exporters regained free market access at the end of December 2014.

This short disruption of the market order reveals that 'provisional outsides' (Bair et al. 2013, 2544), such as the temporary imposition of tariffs, are a constitutive part of marketisation. It also shows that disorder in markets can lead to the creation of a new order (Marshall, Goodman 2013): the disorder caused by the imposition of tariffs eventually resulted in an extension of the free trade paradigm allowing a quota- and tariff-free import of EU-goods into the EAC in the long run.

Conclusion: The stability and fragility of the cut flower market order

It has now become clear that the ongoing marketisation of cut flower production at Lake Naivasha is characterised by a growing influence of corporate retailers. On the other hand, the reorganisation of cut flower production is the foundation of the role of corporate retailers in the global cut flower market. (Kenyan) Growers are an important factor in the making of markets. The following statement of a long-term industry insider regarding new possibilities in the US illustrates the growers' role in market-making:

> I am quite sure that when Obama visits Kenya next month, direct flights to the US will be introduced. ... Still, buying flowers in the US is different than in Europe, where you buy them with your groceries. But the market had to be made first in Europe as well and we will probably do the same in the US. (IV 68, Sales Manager, Supplier)

The new market order is based on low consumer prices and requires producers who are able to operate under these precarious circumstances, especially considering the rising costs of flower production. Expansion and flexibility became necessary strategies for producers in order to maintain and stabilise this new market order. Moreover, in order to obtain stable prices, growers need to invest regularly into new varieties. Yet, the making of new commodities does not ultimately benefit most producers (and breeders), but rather opens the door for greater influence and control from corporate retailers. In this new market order, running a profitable Lake Naivasha flower farm requires

---

[22] It has not become clear on what terms Tanzania made its decision.

innovative production technology, cost-efficient production, and rapid and smooth handling. These measures enable farms to decrease their production costs, raise productivity, and increase the value of their produce. Apart from technology, producers' strategies entail a stable and experienced labour force. In this regard, the cut flower industry is a remarkable case where a new market order based on corporate retail chains led to a stabilisation of employment and improved working conditions. Yet, in terms of wage levels, this effect is limited, as low real wages are an essential part of the new market order. The imposition of import levies after a delay in the negotiations for the EU-EAC EPA revealed how small changes in the market STA can result in existential crises. This leads to the more general question of how stable or fragile is the market STA at Lake Naivasha?

From a regional development perspective, Lake Naivasha is firmly linked to the new market order and its potential is strategically coupled to the needs of the flower GPN. 'Regional assets' (Coe et al. 2004, 472), such as a large and cheap labour force, climatic conditions, and a strong network of breeders, suppliers, and growers, seem to fit the 'rapidly changing strategic needs of global production networks' (Coe et al. 2004, 471). Furthermore, growers actively seek to create, enhance, and capture value[23] by adopting innovative and flexible production strategies. Thus, the strategic coupling between Lake Naivasha's regional potential and the needs of the global cut flower market seem to 'maximize the region's economic potential' (Coe et al. 2004, 474). Yet, the growers' financial precariousness and low wage levels show that the value that can be created and retained within the new cut flower market is limited, and it thus also reveals the limits of strategic coupling. The role of Lake Naivasha's cut flower industry in the cut flower market is based on financial fragility.

At the same time, the farms are spatially fixed to Lake Naivasha because of their financial precariousness. The farms have invested heavily in their production infrastructure. Greenhouses, packhouses, and irrigation systems are immovable assets often worth several million Euros. Since most shareholders are part of the European mid-tier rather than agricultural investors, and high surpluses are rare, a lack of capital prevents them from simply moving their production facilities. Hence, the Lake Naivasha cut flower industry is a good example of how 'the inscription of social relations in matter lends them a degree of fixity' (Müller 2015, 77).

Therefore, the attitude of the Lake Naivasha cut flower industry towards the rising competition from Ethiopia is not surprising. Governmental support, low taxation, and even lower wage levels in Ethiopia are often used as leverage

---

[23] Here, value refers to economic rent.

in public debates about regulation in Kenya.[24] On the other hand, industry actors stress the locational advantages of Kenya in interviews. These are not only seen in environmental factors (which are similar to Ethiopia anyway), but mainly in the regional industry's maturity:

> The production of flowers in Ethiopia is not similar to Kenya; Kenya is much more advanced, because the industry is much older, and the staff is experienced. You find workers who have worked in the farms for 10 to 15 years. These are qualified workers. In Ethiopia, they have not got to that level. (IV 75, Flower Product Manager, Certifier)

In conclusion, though financially fragile, the industry shows locational stability. It is not only dependent on global market relations, but is at the same time firmly entangled in Lake Naivasha's social-ecological system, which therefore requires further attention.

---

[24] See, for instance, *Kenya Today*, 25–31 October 2010, 'Ethiopia Woos Kenya's Leading Flower Farmers'.

7

The Cut Flower Industry in the Social-Ecological System of Lake Naivasha: Setting the Scene for a New Market Order

'Naivasha is the most dynamic system I ever came across around the world'.[1]

Since the early 2000s, concerns have increased that global cut flower production might cause a collapse of the local SES around Lake Naivasha. Media reports began to appear with alarming headlines, such as '*The tragedy that is Lake Naivasha*' (Hunter 2009) and '*Lake Naivasha is dying*' (Riungi 2009). NGO reports critical of labour conditions (see e.g., Kenya Human Rights Commission 2012) and scientific works on the ecology of the lake (see e.g., Harper et al. 2011) reinforced this image of Lake Naivasha's endangered state. Often, apocalyptical scenarios are linked to the cut flower industry, which, for this purpose, is portrayed as a profoundly unsustainable business, both socially and economically.

So far, this book has discussed Lake Naivasha mainly as a hub for the production of cut flowers and focused on the internal dynamics in the industry. Here, I conceived of Lake Naivasha as a translocal agro-industrial cluster, referring to a relational instead of a locational understanding of place (see Chapter 4). Yet, as the quoted apocalyptical scenarios show, the framing of the cut flower market, creating an inside and an outside of it (see Callon 1998a), also refers to Lake Naivasha's SES. In the process of marketisation, boundaries are established between what is included in market relations, what counts as economic and what does not. Thus, the framing of markets 'constitutes powerful mechanisms of exclusion, for to frame means to select, to sever links' (Callon 2007a, 140). These processes of inclusion and exclusion specifically relate to agencies usually termed as 'non-economic' actors (see e.g., Coe et al. 2008, 280), for instance stakeholder groups or environmental objects.

As such, this chapter will answer questions on what agencies the new market order creates and, more generally, how the Lake Naivasha SES system

---

[1] David Harper (OB 39, Stakeholder Conference).

relates to the new cut flower market order following the entry and growing dominance of European retail chains in cut flower sales. In order to do so, I will scrutinise the role of the cut flower industry in place-making processes at Lake Naivasha. Afterwards, the interdependence between the new cut flower market order and the SES is analysed on three different levels: firstly, the relationship between marketisation and nature will be outlined; secondly, the economisation of social welfare will be discussed; and, lastly, I will take a closer look at the struggles for control over the discourses surrounding the Lake Naivasha cut flower industry.

Place-making: Lake Naivasha and the cut flower industry

'Naivasha belongs to nobody'.[2]

After some time in the field, my colleague and I were invited to represent our research project at a stakeholders' conference in November 2014. The conference was organised by Imarisha Naivasha, a government-initiated organisation for stakeholder coordination at Lake Naivasha. When we entered the venue, a luxury tourist and conference resort right on the shores of the lake, I only had a very rough idea about how to include the social-ecological system of Lake Naivasha in my study. So far, my research had been focused on the local cut flower industry. Thus, I had approached the area mainly as a production site, as a 'node' (Hopkins, Wallerstein 1986, 160) or a 'box' (Gereffi et al. 1994, 2) in the commodity or value chain, as a location that offers preferable conditions for growing cut flowers. What followed during a full nine-to-five day of presentations, discussions, and networking turned my perspective upside down. The 130 participants hardly perceived Lake Naivasha as one of the major global production sites of the cut flower industry. Instead, they talked about it as a precious yet fairly stable environment, mainly defined by ecological criteria. Also, the boundaries of 'Lake Naivasha' were blurred that day. While the floriculture industry and, for example, the LNGG delineate Lake Naivasha broadly as the water body itself and the surrounding few kilometres of land, the stakeholders thought of it much more as an ecological system that is defined by hydrological relations, wildlife habitats, or vegetation zones. Terms like 'catchment area' and especially 'Lake Naivasha basin' were ubiquitous in the 24 stakeholder presentations.

This day puzzled me in several respects. How do these perceptions of Lake Naivasha that go way beyond a mere 'institutional setting' (Dannenberg,

---

[2] IV 80, Deputy County Commissioner, Naivasha.

Revilla Diez 2016, 169) relate to the cut flower industry? Why were apocalyptical scenarios, as put forward in both the relevant literature and the media, absent from the stakeholders' considerations? And it also triggered a very basic yet central question: what is actually being referred to when people talk about 'Lake Naivasha'?

In GCC, GVC, and GPN literature, places of production are mainly looked at regarding their input into economic processes. Social, ecological, and political dynamics are regarded as context into which economic activities are embedded. These conceptualisations separate and prioritise the economic from all other processes – they 'purify' (Latour 2002) it. Yet, as the stakeholder conference revealed, these prioritisations are not only questionable from a conceptual perspective, but are also inappropriate descriptions of Lake Naivasha's role in the cut flower industry.

Ecological and hydrological approaches

So, how do stakeholders conceive of Lake Naivasha? The way they demarcate the scope of their activities and the region in general can give some insights. As mentioned above, many stakeholders are concerned with Lake Naivasha's ecology. Therefore, the most common demarcations are based on an understanding of Lake Naivasha as an ecosystem or as a hydrological system. These approaches are rooted in diverse scientific studies from natural and environmental sciences. Analyses of Lake Naivasha's hydrology, its catchment area, its inflow and discharge are rife and have a long-standing tradition (among many others, see Lowery, Mendes 1977; Ase 1987; Verschuren et al. 2000; Becht, Harper 2002; Everard, Harper 2002; Everard et al. 2002; Otiang'a-Owiti, Oswe 2010; Awange et al. 2013). Many stakeholder groups refer to these conceptualisations, some with a strong and close attachment to academia, some with loose interpretations. The governmental organisation for water regulation, the Water Resource Management Authority (WRMA), provides a good case. As the name implies, the Lake Naivasha Catchment Area Protection Order of 2011 limits its authority to Lake Naivasha's catchment area. The catchment area or 'Lake Naivasha Basin' cuts across political boundaries of districts, divisions, and locations, as it is defined purely by hydrological means. The basin is defined by a map that is rooted in the research of a Dutch WRMA intern with close relations to the research institutions that have contributed to the studies above (Jong 2011). A WRMA officer describes the demarcation of the area as follows:

> Our mandate is the rivers that drain into the Lake. That means it is their source to the end which is the Lake. Mostly, the biggest catchment for the Lake Naivasha basin is River Gilgil, Malala, and Karate. So, anything that

is within their catchment, say the small streams flowing into the bigger stream, is all that we cover in the Lake Naivasha Basin. It's not a big research, because when you use the satellite photos, the DEMs, Digital Elevation Models, they can clearly show you the rivers that flow into Lake Naivasha, Elementaita, and Nakuru. Basically, if you download a satellite image and come up with maps showing which rivers flow into which basin. [The Dutch intern] came up with a schematic drawing of how the rivers flow into the Lake. So, we have that schematic drawing and we also have the DEMs which we can view using ArcGIS, QGIS, and other software analysis programs. ... The schematic drawing; we came up with the first abstraction survey that was done in 2010. With the schematic drawing, they came up with a very easy way of identifying all the rivers that flow into the lake. The guy ... from Netherlands came up with a very simple map showing how each and every main water system is connected to the Lake; how a small stream flows into the other. (IV 64, Officer, WRMA)

This demarcation shows how ecological reasoning prevails in the definition of what Lake Naivasha is. This reasoning is even prioritised over administrative boundaries in the allocation of governmental authority, sometimes causing confusion over responsibilities, as a WWF officer explains:

Now, Lake Naivasha is in the county of Nakuru, but the source of water, the surface water of Lake Naivasha, comes from the county of Nyandarua. So, if Nyandarua decides to do some things, it will affect Nakuru and if Nakuru and Nyandarua are not talking to each other, ... those are the kinds of things, those are the complexities. (IV 49, Project Coordinator, WWF)

Yet, not only parastatal or large and internationally funded organisations refer to these conceptions of Lake Naivasha. Small stakeholder groups who work on social or educational topics also put these forward, albeit less explicitly shaped by scientific methodologies. The 'unique' (IV 27, Director, WRMA) ecological setting 'of global significance' (IV, CEO, Imarisha) predominates stakeholders' visions and work in Naivasha. The 'global significance' of the local ecosystem was institutionalised in 1995, when the region was declared a Ramsar wetland, that is to say that UNESCO officially recognised it as a 'wetland of international importance' (UNESCO 2/2/1971). The efforts of many stakeholder groups also focus on conserving this picture of the area, for example by participating in ecosystem monitoring or environmental education. Bird counting is especially popular among small community groups.

What I found striking about this regionalisation of Lake Naivasha[3] is its unidimensional focus on a locally confined ecological or, even more specifically, hydrological system. It leaves aside social, economic, and all global or external dynamics. Therefore, at first sight the cut flower industry plays only a minor role. All these factors are mainly seen as an external driver of change of the 'natural' system.

A global sense of Lake Naivasha

Ecological conceptions prevailing among stakeholders contrast with an approach towards Lake Naivasha as a box in the cut flower value chain, as derived from the GCC and GVC framework. Yet, it is evident that the cut flower industry is a major driver of the Lake Naivasha SES and there are various relations between the industry and ecological systems: the industry is by far the biggest employer in the region with its 40,000 workers; it is the major income generator, the biggest water abstractor, and its 2,000 ha of greenhouses cover large parts of the immediate surroundings of the lake. So how can we make sense of these contrasting conceptions of one and the same place?

A global sense of place as proposed by Massey (1991) and Amin (2002) can help overcome the dichotomic understanding of ecology and economy and of the local and the global. Lake Naivasha can then be thought of as a node in a relational network. As a place, it is only produced by linkages and networks. These linkages are not constrained to the economic or ecological sphere, but they are social, political, cultural, and ecological. In order to reconstruct this place, one has to trace the myriad linkages and networks between all kinds of actors. Actor-Networks constitute their own, distinct spatialities and define scales and also places by themselves (Murdoch 1998, 361; Law, Mol 2001; Bosco 2008). As had emerged during the stakeholders' conference, the Lake Naivasha Actor-Network apparently confines itself to local and ecological relations. The role of the cut flower industry in the SES is deemphasised; it is, of course, often seen as an important stakeholder, but as one among many. Even industry representatives themselves play along by referring to Lake Naivasha as a 'natural environment' (IV 41, Managing Director, Grower). Only a closer look at the stakeholders' work and at their perceptions of Lake Naivasha reveals that the cut flower industry is a focal point within the Actor-Network.

---

[3] Since I focus my analysis on stakeholder groups, these observations mirror dominant discourses in the public debate about Naivasha, but underrate other interpretations of Lake Naivasha, such as a source of food and income for fishery (see Dittmann 2018). These interpretations are less connected to scientific observations.

All stakeholders I interviewed have direct relations to the cut flower industry in one way or another. Some of them are coercive, for instance the membership of many flower farms as plot owners within Lake Naivasha's riparian zone in the Lake Naivasha Riparian Association (LNRA), an organisation 'adjudicating on land ownership and ... taking care of environmental issues' (IV 56, Monitoring Officer, Environmental NGO) in the riparian zone. Moreover, due to their role as commercial water abstractors, flower farms are automatically part of the Lake Naivasha Water Resource Users Association (LaNaWRUA), an organisation for stakeholder representation and inclusion in water resource management. In these organisations, flower farms are highly respected and active members (see below). Yet, other stakeholder groups also have a pragmatic and cooperative attitude towards flower farms. This is especially surprising for environmental organisations, as international organisations paint a very negative picture of the industry (see e.g., Food & Water Watch 2008). In contrast, on a local level, flower farms are seen as a major facilitator for sustainable development. A project manager of an international development organisation describes the cooperation with flower farms: 'In fact, we wanted to bring these flower farms on board. We want them to chip in their local private contributions' (IV 50, Project Manager, Development Agency).

The cut flower industry maintains different forms of relations to other stakeholders. Firstly, they support community and environmental organisations in small informal ways. Environmental groups are offered access to farms or small boats for ecosystem monitoring; community organisations use the farms' premises for educational purposes; or flower farms provide food or other material for community events. Secondly, the cut flower industry is the biggest donor in the region. This concerns all kinds of projects, singular or long term, small amounts or millions of Euros, environmental or social. By looking at the sources of these funds, it also becomes clear that a locally confined approach towards Naivasha is inadequate. Big sums in particular do not stem from local farms, but directly from European retail chains. Some stakeholders take advantage of the attention Lake Naivasha and its flower industry have gained in Europe (see below). They reach out to supermarkets to support their interest, as this chairman of several stakeholder groups describes:

> There are two key things that drive people to join some of these organizations ... One is interest, which comes very fast. The second thing is the influence; I have an interest, how can I influence decisions made? Somebody in the UK – let's say [a British supermarket] – somebody in Germany – let's say [a German supermarket] – has an interest, because he is buying flowers. ... So, everybody is looking at how to use that interest to join some of these organizations, so as to influence issues

that might affect them or work for their interest. So, I will not even say it is passion, no; it is the issue of interest and influence. (IV 52, Representative, Pastoralist Outreach Service)

European retail chains also co-finance projects by development agencies that entail obligatory shares of private self-financing (IV 55, Project Coordinator, Development Agency; IV 49, Project Coordinator, Environmental NGO). Linkages of non-industry actors with buyers from Europe contradict an understanding of the flower industry as a box embedded in the local context as put forward by the GCC, GVC, and GPN frameworks (see above). They reveal that – as suggested by a flat ontology – agencies exist across pre-defined scales, defying any 'transcendent predetermination – whether the local-to-global continuum in vertical thought or the origin-to-edge imaginary in horizontal thought' (Marston et al. 2005, 422). If places and scales only exist in linkages of actors, the question is: how are these linkages forged?

Some of the relations – especially in cases of informal cooperation, where organisations contact flower farms – are based on personal networks, for instance through befriended flower farm managers or workers. But, mostly, the entanglement of the cut flower industry in Lake Naivasha's Actor-Network is based on the work of a few central actors. Two types of actors can be distinguished: firstly, organisations play an important role. The regional and national lobby groups of the industry, the LNGG and the KFC, are especially active in linking the flower industry with other actors. In many stakeholder groups, the industry is represented by these organisations. Moreover, the groups also often initiate new projects themselves, for instance the Water Allocation Plan, an institutional framework to limit water abstraction. Even the plan itself acknowledges this initiative: 'The process of developing the Water Allocation Plan was started in 2005 by the Lake Naivasha Growers Group (LNGG) who engaged consultants and participated in the development of the initial WAP which was submitted to WRMA in 2007' (Water Allocation Plan Naivasha Basin 2010). And secondly, a few individuals heavily engage in the linking of actors, both within and outside the flower industry. Among these are researchers, conservationists, and farm managers, but all of them have various roles in the Actor-Network. The most striking case is that of the Managing Director of a large flower farm, who is simultaneously the president of the KFC, LNGG's and Imarisha's chairman, and the President of Union Fleurs, the international association of flower growers. His name popped up in almost all interviews with stakeholders when they were asked how they got in contact with the flower industry. Here are three examples:

It was a collaboration, so from the flower the industry. We have [the Managing Director], he has the key participation; then it was [the] WWF, through our previous conversation manager; and our country director. (IV 49, Project Coordinator, Environmental NGO)

[The Managing Director] met one of the programme coordinators in Kenya over a cup of tea, just as we are seated ... There was this discussion even before I came to Naivasha: 'We have this money for private sector, we have this programme that acquires money from the private sector. Then Imarisha has this money; then we can come in and have this partnership'. From there, they exchange contacts and the partnership was formalised. (IV 50, Project Manager, Development Agency)

Some of the flower farms are included in the ... projects ... but these are small amounts, a couple of thousand Euros or something, and that is it. So, no link actually; directly only with a person [the Managing Director]. You have heard of him of course because he is involved. We got into this project through him. (IV 55, Project Coordinator, Development Agency)

The analysis of the making of Lake Naivasha as a global place reveals the deep entanglement of the cut flower industry within the local Actor-Network and the multitude of relations across pre-defined scales. Lake Naivasha became a place of global interest, due to its status as a Ramsar site, but also due to the linkages of its many actors to external actors. The cut flower industry facilitated the process of 'globalising' Lake Naivasha's Actor-Network. Today, Lake Naivasha is a hotspot for stakeholder groups who utilise the financial and organisational structures that the cut flower industry to a large extent helped create. Therefore, marketisation not only concerns the internal reorganisation of the cut flower industry, but also dynamics in non-economic relations.

Intensified marketisation, stakeholder competition, and natural resources

If marketisation processes in the cut flower industry also concern dynamics in non-economic relations, the question is: how do these processes relate to Naivasha's ecology and society? The scope of this question exceeds the inclusion of the environment or nature in GVC or GPN literature. This simply conceives of the environment as a supplier of inputs and outputs and 'fails to connect the processes of production, distribution and consumption to the natural environment in which they are fundamentally grounded' (Coe et al. 2008, 278). This shortfall can be overcome by focusing on the economisation of nature or parts of it. An economisation perspective analyses in which way and what parts of nature at Lake Naivasha are rendered as economic and how these processes are, or are not, regulated (see Çalışkan, Callon 2010). The cut flower industry is not the only actor taking part in the economisation of nature at Lake Naivasha. Due to its history, a lot of different interests meet in the region. The dynamic development of land use in this area, as well as the local setting with a fresh water source and unique flora and fauna, created a complex network of numerous stakeholders (see Chapter 4). These include diverse groups with distinct backgrounds and interests, who utilise part of its nature as resources in order to generate income. For instance, fishermen rely on the water body of the lake and a sustainable fish stock; Maasai pastoralists need regular access to the lake to water their livestock; and hotels are built on scenic plots in the riparian land and valorise wildlife as a tourist attraction.

Current marketisation processes in the cut flower industry relate to the economisation of nature through the cut flower industry, and have ultimately resulted in an intensified competition over resources with these other stakeholders. Regarding these processes, three dimensions of marketisation are decisive: expansion, the technical innovation of flower production, and the regulation of cut flower production through industry-based standards. In the following pages, I want to concentrate on land and water as the most contested resources. A closer look reveals the interdependencies between these marketisation dynamics and the economisation of nature.

An increased economisation of land is the most obvious result of the expansion of flower farms that the new market order brings about (see Chapter 6). Ever since colonial times, land has been a source of conflict around Lake Naivasha due to contested land titles, coerced leases, and a fuzzy delineation of the riparian zone because of fluctuating lake levels (Lang, Sakdapolrak 2014, 189; IV 56, Monitoring Officer, Environmental NGO). Flower farms have taken a major role in these disputes for several reasons. Their greenhouses simply cover huge areas, and the owners deny access to their properties, too. All farms are fenced off and guarded by security. Land close to the lake shore in particular has become scarce over the last decades. Hotels have mushroomed along South Lake Road, environmentalists have established conservancies, and the creation of Hell's Gate National Park just south of the Lake restricted a huge area from being put to other use. Supplying huge amounts of flowers to retail chains encouraged many farms to expand their greenhouses in order to generate minimum profits, which resulted in an intensification of competition. Availability of affordable land has become an issue for flower farms especially at South Lake, whereas for other stakeholders accessibility of the riparian land is the bigger problem. Since many farms are located close to the lake, they block access to the water for other stakeholders. This particularly concerns pastoralists, as confirmed by a pastoralist community leader who describes the relationship to flower farms as follows: 'I would say it hasn't been positive, because the pastoralists think the flower farms are denying them the rights to graze in the riparian, because of the fences and the closed corridors. So, basically their relationship hasn't been quite good' (IV 52, Representative, Pastoralist Outreach Service). As hinted at in the quote, the riparian zone is the nucleus of the competition over land. Legislation is strict about its use: 'Cultivation is illegal, building permanent structures is illegal, logging is illegal. Also, under the Fisheries Act, poaching is illegal, under the Wildlife Act, poaching is illegal' (IV 56, Monitoring Officer, Environmental NGO). Nevertheless, competition is fierce regarding the use of this zone: pastoralists demand access to the lake via public corridors, 14 of which have been defined (IV 52, Representative, Pastoralist Outreach Service). The Kenya Wildlife Service demands free access to the lake via corridors for the wildlife which congregates on the riparian land. On the other hand, it is pleased by the protective effect of fences around the riparian zone (IV 60, Senior Warden, Conservancy State Corporation). The expansion of flower farms intensifies this competition. For some farms at South Lake, the riparian zone is the only option for expansion; therefore, two of them grow roses in it. Moreover, public corridors were blocked as either a consequence of expansion or of the desire to evict pastoralists from the immediate surroundings of the farms (IV 71, Executive Director, Policy NGO). These conflicts, which carry consequences for the new market order, are to a certain extent mitigated by adherence to private standards, another pillar of the new market order. The code of conduct by the LNGG prohibits cultivation in the riparian zone. Moreover, the increased public attention through media and NGO reports, as a consequence of direct sales, empowered pastoralists. Therefore, conflict resolving strategies by flower farms are spreading, as this pastoralist representative explains: '[S]ome of these issues have been fading away, because you find some flower farms agreeing with a group of pastoralists to graze in their farms. Some have been allowing them to use their roads to access the lake; some have been giving water to their livestock' (IV 52, Representative, Pastoralist Outreach Service).

Water is another contested resource at Lake Naivasha which the cut flower industry relies upon. Roses produced at Lake Naivasha have a water footprint of seven to 13 litres per stem (Mekonnen et al. 2012). Considering the millions of stems harvested daily around the lake, the flower industry is the single biggest abstractor of fresh water in the area. Similar to the economisation of land, different marketisation processes produce distinct and partly converse outcomes in the abstraction of water. For instance, the expansion of production increased water abstraction. Yet, this was partly mitigated by technical innovations in production, such as drip irrigation and hydroculture, another pillar of the new market order (see Chapter 6). The interplay of marketisation and economisation of resources is most visible in the institutions regulating water abstraction and discharge. State regulation of water usage is based on the Kenya Water Act of 2002, introducing water permits and block rate water pricing (Kuhn et al. 2016, 377). Within these regulations, the regional WRMA office is the key authority. Its tasks include the issuing and control of permits, the ensuring of proper water allocation, quantity and quality, and the collection of fees (IV 27, Director, WRMA; IV 64, Officer, WRMA). Following a GVC and GPN approach, these regulations constitute the institutional framework into which cut flower production is embedded: they 'shape the environment for the embedded companies and are key determinants for economic success' (Dannenberg, Revilla Diez 2016, 170). There are two flaws in this approach: it neglects questions of implementation and efficacy, and it represents institutions as static and independent of global economic linkages. In the cut flower industry, water is not only a vital resource of the global market, but its regulation has also become entangled in the new market order.

In order to understand the relation between institutions and marketisation, it first has to be noted that the implementation of the existing framework lacks efficacy. The reasons for this are primarily the WRMA's deficiency of accurate data on water availability and abstraction has resulted in their loss of authority (Verstoep 2015). These problems are well-known among stakeholders at Lake Naivasha:

> [I]f it is a flower farm or another industry or whatever; there is need for proper water allocation and regulation. If WRMA would function correctly, then there would not be any issue because it is clear and they follow up correctly on how much water we have and who is taking water out according to a legal permit. (IV 55, Project Coordinator; Development Agency)

Hence, it is rather simple to evade restrictions and fines. For instance, data from a WRMA abstraction survey indicates that water users avoid the restriction of water allocation in case of shortages. The restrictions refer to the permit issued to water abstractors. In the case of low lake levels, abstractors are only allowed to use part of the amount allocated by the permit. Yet, flower farms simply hold permits exceeding their average amount of required water. More than one third of water users abstract less than their permit allows them; the actual abstraction at Lake Naivasha is 44% lower than the authorised abstraction. This is also a consequence of the low financial impact of costs for permits, abstractions, and fines (see Kuhn et al. 2016). The fee for commercial irrigation water is KES 0.75[4] per cubic metre and typically accounts for less than 0.1% of the production costs of a flower farm.

---

4   Equivalent to € 0.007.

Besides regulating water abstraction and management, the Kenya Water Act of 2002 also created a new organisation for conflict resolution and service provision – the Water Resource Users Associations (WRUAs). The WRUAs have a double role in the institutional framework. On the one hand, they are responsible for ensuring compliance with the rules set by WRMA; on the other hand, they are a platform for stakeholder participation. In the Lake Naivasha basin, the LaNaWRUA is responsible for large parts of the flower farms. It has taken a pioneering role in merging stakeholder participation and rule enforcement. Since the internal organisation of the association was not clarified, the WRUA itself came up with an approach that is based on representatives from stakeholder groups, as the chairman of LaNaWRUA describes:

> Actually, we are the pioneers; we are the guys who were constructed first by WRMA ... So, ... we thought of how to move this forward. So, we came up with the idea of categories; pastoralists, individual people with private shareholders, flower farms, and large-scale farmers, we have tour operators that are the hotels, and we have ... the water companies. ... We categorised ourselves in those groups and invited each category to a wider meeting. There were some trainings on the roles of LaNaWRUA, benefits to members, and all that. After everybody knew all that, we asked each category to go back to their people and tell [them] what they heard and, after 30 days, they brought along two representatives who sit on the LaNaWRUA committee. (IV 52, Chairman, LaNaWRUA)

Interestingly, the WRUA is not only enforcing regulation, but also lobbying in the interest of its members:

> The main interest is that we are able to influence some of the issues affecting us as an association. We are able to lobby some decisions on how we want things done here as an association. We are able to advocate when it comes to issues of what the law is saying. We advocate and force WRMA to enforce on issues of the rules of water resources. (IV 52, Chairman, LaNaWRUA)

This model favours the flower industry, since – compared to other stakeholders – it is well networked and regionally and nationally organised into stakeholder groups. Hence, the cut flower industry takes a very active role within the WRUA and when it comes to matters of individual engagement: at the time of my fieldwork, both the vice-chairman and the treasurer were flower farm managers. The WRUA opened the door for the cut flower industry to join in with the process of shaping institutions instead of just adhering to them. Nowadays, this influence even exceeds the borders of the Lake Naivasha basin: with the introduction of a system of payments for ecosystem services, semi-private forms of environmental regulation have been expanded to the highlands surrounding the basin (Rouillé et al. 2015).

This impression is backed by another process. Scholars as well as policy makers and development agencies have identified the lacking efficacy of the governmental institutional framework as a major problem (see e.g., Verstoep 2015; IV 71, Executive Officer, Policy NGO). Hence, projects to strengthen the sustainability of water usage are rife. These usually involve stakeholders or are based partially on private funding, again opening the door for collaborations with the cut flower industry. The example of the Water Allocation Plan (WAP) underlines this point. The WAP limits water abstraction for different user groups depending on the availability of water, which is measured according to the lake level. This plan itself states that:

> [The] process of developing the Water Allocation Plan was started in 2005 by the Lake Naivasha Growers Group (LNGG) who engaged consultants and participated in the development of the initial WAP which was submitted to WRMA in 2007. This draft has been exposed to stake-holders and revised to form the current version.[5]

The WAP mirrors the cut flower industry's interests in several ways. Flower growers are dependent on a steady availability of water, ideally of high quality to reduce costs for water treatment. Due to fluctuating lake levels in the last years, farms had to invest in their water abstraction systems, many of them drilled boreholes to diversify their supply. Hence, they endorse an integrated approach to which all stakeholders are committed, and which secures the availability of irrigation water. Furthermore, the flower industry is supportive of measures enhancing the image of a sustainable environment at Lake Naivasha (see below). The WAP is explicitly justified, among other things, by this argument:

> Without any limits in place, allocation of the resource will continue to increase in response to the increasing demand. This may result in any of the following consequences:
>
> ... Bad publicity for the horticultural and floricultural export industry which may be seen to be over exploiting the water resources to the detriment of other water users; Loss of export markets (for agricultural products) and tourism potential due to the bad publicity associated with economic activities around the lake.[6]

---

5   WAP Naivasha Basin 2010.
6   WAP Naivasha Basin 2010.

Large WAP billboards, displaying water levels and the current abstraction status, next to the entrance gates of the flower farms publicly demonstrate their adherence to this regulation. Taking influence in these institutions also simplifies market access for growers, since certifications schemes regulating access to European markets demand compliance with regional legislation regarding the use of resources. Not surprisingly, the WAP aims to 'make compliance to WAP conditional to market access' and 'establish compliance to WAP as a criteria for certification'.[7]

The institutional framework for water abstraction including the co-development of institutions such as WAP links to the new market order in several ways. The increased public attention for the Lake Naivasha cut flower industry due to direct sales urges farms to engage in projects propagating a sustainable image of the industry and its surroundings. The capital-intensive, technically advanced production technology gives the industry an edge compared to other stakeholders such as smallholders or horticultural farms. As a consequence, the cut flower industry often appears to be the most compliant stakeholder group at Lake Naivasha, as for instance the LaNaWRUA chairman confirms:

> They are guys who are very cooperative and I really enjoy working with them because ... they are very compliant. No issues in their operational areas, no issues with abstraction and pollution. Actually, they are my study case; for any errant abstractor, I try to encourage them to go and see what these guys are doing. So, for me, they are benchmarks since they are really cooperative and make my work easier. (IV 52, Chairman, LaNaWRUA)

The examples of land and water have shown that the economisation of nature and its regulation do not lie outside global economic relations. Resources are not only static inputs for production, and institutions regulating them are not only a frame firms are embedded into. Rather, the transformation of nature into resources as well as the regulatory institutions are dynamic and interdependent with current marketisation processes. The new market order did not lead to a unidirectional, singular impact on Lake Naivasha's nature, but has produced distinct and partially converse outcomes: resource use especially regarding land has intensified due to the expansion of production areas. At the same time, technological innovations in production resulted in a higher efficiency of water use. Moreover, increased publicity and the heightened interest of external actors has led to the development of new, elaborate institutions regulating

---

[7]   WAP Naivasha Basin 2010.

resource use. Yet, these institutions simultaneously enabled the cut flower industry to exert influence on regulations to the benefit of their interest.

The economisation of social welfare

It has already become clear that Lake Naivasha, as a global place, is primarily created through the cross-scalar relations in which the cut flower industry is deeply entangled. Hence, the flower industry is a constitutive part not only of Lake Naivasha's ecology, but also of its society. The expansion of floriculture increased the demand for labour in the area and was thus one of the main factors for the massive increase in population. Since the establishment of the first flower farms in 1969 up until 2009, the number of residents increased from 50,787 to 376,243 (KNBS 1969, 2010). It has to be noted that the boundaries of the administrative unit 'Naivasha' have changed during that period. Yet, population density increased even more sharply, from 16.7 people per km^2 in 1969 to 124 people per km^2 in 2009 (KNBS 1969, 2010). Not only did the cut flower industry shape Lake Naivasha's society indirectly, but it is also intertwined with its social networks. It also impacts heavily on social dynamics outside actual labour relations, by providing basic medical, educational, and transport infrastructure – partly on the premises of the farms, partly in the public sphere. This stakeholder summarises the importance of flower farms for the development of Lake Naivasha's society: 'There would be no Naivasha without the flower industry; even the town, may be some cows would be grazing around here' (IV 50, Project Manager, Development Agency). In this section, I will address the question of how marketisation relates to the role of the cut flower industry in Lake Naivasha's society by focusing on corporate social welfare projects as a form of private governance. These projects are often discussed under the term Corporate Social Responsibility (CSR) (see Bair, Palpacuer 2015). The arguments about why firms engage in activities outside of their core economic activities can be subsumed under two categories (Bair, Palpacuer 2015, S6): from an internalist or instrumental perspective, CSR projects are a strategy to enhance the performance of a firm. In contrast, an external or environmental view argues that CSR is a reaction to external pressures, for instance by the media or NGOs.

Investments by flower farms into social infrastructure build on a long-standing tradition at Lake Naivasha. Before the first flower farms emerged, most ranch labourers relied on the social infrastructure, such as housing or medical services, provided by their employers. The local government, however, was not prepared to have these facilities available for the large number of labourers migrating to Naivasha during the expansion of the flower industry. Thus, unplanned settlements have developed all around the lake close to the flower farms.[8] These settlements lacked (and to some extent still lack) basic infrastructure, such as sewage systems, water supply, schools, and hospitals. In the early days of the flower industry in particular outbreaks of diseases like typhoid were common.[9] As formulated in instrumental perspectives on CSR (Bair, Palpacuer 2015, S6), flower farms were forced to take action in order to secure the livelihoods and hence the stability of their workforce. Two strategies arose: a few of the largest flower farms created their own facilities on their compounds. These included housing for workers, hospitals, and schools. Other farms were not able or willing to build infrastructure themselves and only gave out allowances, such as for housing for their employees. Moreover, these farms started investing in projects in the settlements. As a consequence, schools, hospitals, and even partially the police offices are dependent on funding from the flower industry. For instance, according to Happ (2016, 87), the investments per school by one farm were equivalent to the Kenyan state's budget for the very same schools. In addition, four clinics at South Lake are fully funded (and hosted) by flower farms, and farm representatives make up the board of the only dispensary at North Lake (IV 7, Farm Manager, Grower). These philanthropic measures also fit in with the paternalistic attitude of managers towards their employees (see Chapter 6).

In the last years, the new market order has changed the attitude of the farms towards CSR. Measures did not necessarily vanish but are now not mainly done for instrumental reasons in order to stabilise the workforce's performance but as a reaction to external pressure. One farm manager describes this new attitude: 'I am here to produce and make a business, not only to help people. ... I built half the secondary school, but I can't take the whole burden of development on my shoulders' (IV 7, Farm Manager, Grower). Managers and also other stakeholders tend to blame either migrant labourers or the government for the conditions in the settlement. Both are accused of not investing in the settlements: labourers, as they perceive Naivasha mainly as a place of work and ultimately want to relocate back again to their region of origin; and the government, as they count on the flower industry's CSR measures. Moreover, the investments are impaired by the industry's financial precariousness that pressured farms to cut costs at all ends. This community worker describes the volatility of engaging farms in his organisation's projects: 'The financial support that can come in is, for instance, if we have an activity and the flower farm will chip in once or twice, but neither is it consistent

---

[8] Kuiper elaborates on the development of these settlements (2019, 185–96).

[9] See, for instance, the report about a typhoid outbreak in 1991 (Unknown Author 1991), or a dysentery outbreak in 1998 (Unknown Author 1998).

support nor is it reliable support, as we may sit, discuss, and agree; then later their finance department declines the request' (IV 67, Community Worker, Development Agency).

Yet, this does not mean that flower farms do not care about the development of settlements or do not invest in projects anymore. Their engagement is just framed differently and also takes new forms. Bair and Palpacuer (2015) conceive of CSR as a form of contested governance in GPNs. Drawing on Levy (2008), they define governance broadly as a form of control between internal ('industrial governance') and external ('global governance') actors. Here, CSR is understood as a tool to maintain the hegemonic position of firms within economic relations by absorbing criticism of actors external to these relations, such as NGOs. This is at least partly also the case in the Lake Naivasha cut flower industry. Here, CSR became more and more a form of absorbing criticism from NGOs and the media. CSR in the cut flower industry was economised, its role shifted from being a stabilising factor of labour input to a prerequisite of market linkages. Nowadays, managers value public promotion campaigns almost as much as the projects themselves (see Figure 14).

Corporate retailers require farms to fund CSR projects, as this farm manager describes:

> [A German supermarket] ordered now pretty well. It's a little bit more complicated. For instance: they do require us to have a demonstrable project ongoing which is socially related. So you are putting a school up, or a social, or a bus stop. We got big plans, but it depends on the money. (IV 22, Head of Production, Grower)

Certification schemes make this economisation even more explicit. Very similar to what Brown observed in her investigation of the production of Fairtrade bananas in Colombia (2013), labels fit well into the already existing framework of philanthropic measures and development practices. The labels thus allowed the cut flower industry to 'sell' these measures to buyers and customers. Here, Fairtrade stands out with its premium. The premium is especially used for social welfare projects in the communities surrounding the farms (see Table 4).

Social welfare projects in the cut flower industry were economised through their inclusion into market relations, the new market order 'commodified ethics' (Dolan 2007, 245). Bair and Palpacuer argue (2015, S9) that lead firms use this strategy to maintain their position in the GPN. Slightly diverging from this, in the cut flower industry, the economisation of CSR is stabilising a new market order in which corporate retailers are the new lead firms insisting on projects, whereas producers are the ones responsible for CSR projects.

Figure 14. Bus stop donated by a flower farm, Lake Naivasha, 2016 (Author).

This does not mean that social welfare projects do not benefit the communities around Lake Naivasha. In fact, they are a pillar of the health and educational systems and appreciated by stakeholders: 'I see quite a number of farms doing a lot for the local communities in Naivasha ... For example, on the issue of water supply, sanitation, health facilities, education sector; they are doing a remarkable job' (IV 52, Representative, Pastoralist Outreach Service). Moreover, as Raynolds observed for the Colombian flower industry (2012, 516), farm workers appreciate projects funded by the Fairtrade premium (see also Kuiper, Gemählich 2017, 43). Yet, at the same time, CSR became a central feature of the industry's competitive strategy while still being 'framed in terms of benevolence and voluntarism rather than as a fundamental responsibility' (Brown 2013, 2581). This way,

> [It] blunts civil society challenges that might otherwise entail a shift in the power ... and, consequently, a transfer of value from dominant towards

Table 4. Premium use in the cut flower industry (Author, Fairtrade Africa).

Services for workers and their families	**66%**
Education for workers and their families	18%
Investment in worker housing	18%
Financial and credit services for workers	12%
Other services for workers and their families	9%
Healthcare for workers and their families	7%
Payments to workers and their families	1%
Services for communities	**16%**
Education	8%
Social and economic services	4%
Healthcare	2%
Community infrastructure	1%
Environmental services	1%
Other services to communities	0%
Training and empowerment of workers	**16%**
Joint body and committee running costs	10%
Trainings for workers	5%
Support for Fairtrade Premium Committee or other workers' organisations	1%
Trainings for workers' representatives	1%
Other	**1.8%**

> weaker social actors in the form of increased participation, higher wages, improved working conditions and better environmental outcomes. (Bair, Palpacuer 2015, S15)

Or, to put it in the words of a local board committee of a Humanitarian NGO: 'Social responsibility: to cover their faces and throw a carrot and tell you, "You can eat on that while we are busy having a buffet of all sorts of meals"'. (IV 59, Board Committee, Humanitarian NGO).

Gaining control over apocalyptical headlines: Discourses about the Lake Naivasha cut flower industry

The Lake Naivasha cut flower industry is a highly contested field in public discourses in Kenya as well as in the countries where the flowers are marketed and consumed. Time and again the media in these countries have cast a damning light on the industry in Kenya, targeting in particular the Lake Naivasha area.[10] On a local level, however, the empirical data does not fully support the criticism. Instead of subscribing to overall negative stereotypes, local stakeholders take a rather more differentiated stance towards the flower industry.[11] These contested discourses play an important role in the Lake Naivasha cut flower industry. Studies of marketisation as well as GCC, GVC, and GPN studies have stressed that economic globalisation also has a discursive dynamic (Levy 2008, 944; Ouma 2015, 13). Markets are assemblages of heterogeneous elements with calculative agencies (Callon 2007b, 319). Discourses can have calculative agency, too, for instance by attaching value to the places of origins of certain commodities. In this section, I will analyse which role discourses play in the ongoing marketisation of the cut flower industry, how they attach or detach value to roses, and how different actors try to shape them.

There are several reasons why apocalyptical discourses about the cut flower industry spread in the first place. Many of these reports are based on a widely shared image of Lake Naivasha as an untouched, 'natural' paradise. This image can be traced back to the colonial settlers and is sustained by modern conservationists and the international media. These actors, for instance, often refer to Lake Naivasha as a Ramsar site. A local environmentalist sums up this perspective in a nutshell: 'I believe this should be a park. ... Push everyone out, keep birds and animals. The whole thing should be a big conservancy and they should move around and be happy and free' (IV 49, Project Coordinator, Environmental NGO). Moreover, tourist operators advertise its natural beauty. These reports promote a view of the cut flower industry as an intruder in an otherwise untouched natural setting. Take for example the description of Lake Naivasha in the *Rough Guide to Kenya* (Trillo et al. 2016): Lake Naivasha is introduced as a 'hauntingly atmospheric freshwater lake' (203) that is 'slightly forbidding – grey and placid one minute and suddenly green and choppy with whitecaps the next – but is hugely picturesque, with its purple mountain backdrop and floating islands of papyrus and water hyacinth' (206). The flower industry and their employees are then introduced as follows: 'But despite the development, and the ever-growing encroachment of farms and job seekers, Lake Naivasha is still a place of considerable natural beauty' (Trillo et al.

[10] See, for instance, the report by the German TV magazine *Panorama*, 18 August 2011, 'Billig-Rosen: Afrikaner zahlen mit ihrer Gesundheit (Cheap Roses: Africans pay with their health)'.

[11] This section focuses on stakeholder groups, national and international media, and NGOs and their perception of the cut flower industry. Perceptions from local communities, such as fishermen or those in the unplanned settlements, may differ from these views. For instance, in fisheries the flower industry is still often blamed in order to distract from policy failures (Dittmann 2018, 63–9).

2016, 206). So, first of all, the cut flower industry is criticised for simply existing at Lake Naivasha in a manner wholly independent from its economic activities. Scientific work on the lake's endangered ecological state (Mavuti, Harper 2006) has reinforced this image. Interestingly, most academic studies take a balanced stance towards the cut flower industry and view it as only one of many factors impacting on the ecology of the lake (see e.g., Harper et al. 2011).[12] Yet, what is often left out in reports or newspaper articles is the link between an endangered ecosystem and an unsustainable industry.[13]

In addition, as the KFC's CEO has previously put it, 'flowers have the best ingredients for a bad image and the big show' (IV 20). As one of the few non-food agricultural export products from Sub-Saharan Africa, roses are often framed by NGOs and the international media as a luxury good. The necessity of their production is often questioned by references to food security or nature conservation. See for instance how the Canadian NGO Food & Water Watch introduces its report on the Lake Naivasha cut flower industry:

> Isaac Ouma Oloo remembers Kenya's Lake Naivasha as pristine, its waters sustaining an abundance of fish, lions, antelope, leopards, hippopotamuses, and birds. But the overuse of water and environmental destruction caused by international flower farms have fouled his memories of the lake. 'Kenya is a begging country', he says. 'We're among the top on the list of the World Food Programme for food donations, even though in Naivasha we have a freshwater lake that would allow us to grow food to feed ourselves. Yet we take this water to grow flowers and then ship them 5,000 miles to Europe so that people can say 'I love you, darling' and then throw them away three days later. To me that is an immoral act'. (Food & Water Watch 2008, 1)

This image is fuelled by the high rate of unskilled labour in a capital-intensive agro-industry dominated by foreign shareholders. As a result, the flower industry at Lake Naivasha became a common target of criticism by NGOs and the international media, who are – according to LNGG's Executive Officer – in search for the 'four D's they need for Africa: disease, despair, disaster and death' (IV 89).

---

[12] They also put forward a nuanced perspective on the cut flower industry when interviewed as experts by various newspapers, see for example Harper in Kamadi 2011, and *The Guardian*, 14 February 2011, 'Growing Valentine's Day roses harming Kenya's ecological state'.

[13] See, for example, Kamadi 2011 quoting an Italian researcher: 'Observers say the benefits associated with the flower industry do not compare to environmental costs. Nic Pacini of the University of Calabria, Italy, says the sustainability of the flower industry and the jobs it creates should be evaluated in relation to the costs'.

The European media mostly puts a spotlight on the Kenyan cut flower industry around the peak days of cut flower sales – Valentine's and Mother's Day.[14] Most articles take particular farms as case studies and certain individuals as witnesses, for example NGO or stakeholder representatives.[15] These practices are criticised by the cut flower industry: 'Single people can do a lot of harm to the whole industry, especially interviews. Kenyans tend to tell everything the interviewer wants to hear in front of the camera' (IV 76, Sourcing Manager, Auction Services). Remarkably, almost all of these articles refer to Kenya and specifically the flower farms around Lake Naivasha. Here, the image of Lake Naivasha as a natural paradise is reflected.

The cut flower industry is of major interest to the Kenyan media as well. The Nations Archive contains almost 400 articles on the cut flower industry published by outlets of the Nation Media Group since the 1990s. These articles show some parallels to that of international media; for instance, they repeatedly depict the endangered ecological status of Lake Naivasha (Hunter 2009). Yet there are also some differences. Naturally, coverage is spread more evenly over the year. Moreover, the industry's role as a pillar of Kenya's economy and any threats to this status are often debated.[16] In these reports, either the Kenyan or the Lake Naivasha cut flower industry is usually referred to as a whole. Thus, interview partners are mostly industry representatives, such as KFC officials.[17]

The new cut flower market order is based on more direct connections between producers, retailers, and consumers. Certifications, such as Fairtrade, suggest traceability and transparency in these relations. In the process of framing Lake Naivasha as an important production site within this new market order, negative press reports produce overflows, in other words unexpected negative consequences of marketisation processes (Callon 1998a; see also Hale, Opondo 2005, 316). Or, as the KFC's president said, 'reputation is a business risk' (IV 43, Head of Flower Industry Groups). Negative reports by the international media are seen as a major threat, especially since they tend to generalise from negative examples, as one former farm shareholder and environmentalist reports: 'If we get one bad happening there, it will affect

---

[14] See, for example, *Mirror Online*, 13 February 2015, 'Valentine's Day roses: The real cost of your cheap flowers'.

[15] For instance, *BBC News*, 5 March 2017, 'No bed of roses: The Kenyan flower pickers fighting sexual harassment' extensively quotes the regional project manager of Hivos International.

[16] See for instance in the context of the negotiations about the EU-EAC EPA (Nation Reporters 2014).

[17] For instance, the above-mentioned article on trade negotiations features Jane Ngige, CEO of the KFC.

all of us, because overseas doesn't say it's [a Flower Farm] or Naivasha. No, it's Kenya and the industry's dead!' (IV 82, Former Shareholder, Grower).

These overflows created new agencies within the cut flower market, partly to contain them and partly utilising them. The cut flower industry applies several strategies to gain control over such discourses. For instance, the industry actively engages in lobbying and public relations. This is mainly done by the LNGG and the KFC, the self-declared 'national voice of the flower industry' (IV 11, Accountant, KFC), who counter negative press reports and rumours by publishing press releases or commentaries in newspapers.[18] Moreover, the industry made itself more accessible in order to create transparency: 'So, we are looking over everybody's shoulders to start, we had secrets but eventually we persuaded them that it is better they are open; go look at each other's innovations so that we as a whole have a good market' (IV 82, Former Shareholder, Grower). CSR projects and their advertisement are another strategy that has already been discussed above. Certifications did not only create the necessity to react to negative publicity, they can be used at the same time as an instrument to counter them. Labels claim to transmit information about supposedly sustainable production practices. Also, Fairtrade assists certified farms in their public relations, as this Flower Product Manager explains:

> With negative publicity, we try as much as possible through the communication department to be proactive enough to save farms. At times we have journalists who are out to make money with stories. That thing really affects farms, especially the fact that sometimes it's so timely like around Valentine's Day; it really hits the farms hard. So, we try as much as possible to make the farms more visible in terms of the activities they do, good practices and social compliance. (IV 75, Flower Product Manager, Fairtrade Africa)

The overflows in the form of negative publicity did not only create agencies in the flower industry, but also other stakeholders. For instance, campaigns by NGOs targeting the poor working conditions in the early 2000s were widely spread and contributed to the development of minimum standards and eventually the improvement of labour relations (Opondo 2006). For local stakeholders at Naivasha, new possibilities arose as well. Working on the reputation of the industry often translates into funding projects, as one employee of a development agency describes:

---

[18] See, for example, a commentary by Jane Ngige (2010), CEO of the KFC declaring 'We are innocent' in relation to fish dying at Lake Naivasha in 2010.

[It] is a matter of reputation. They want to be in the frontline doing something good. If you organise a clean-up exercise today for one of the settlements, the flower farms need to be there. They need to have their banners and even take photos and post on the website as part of what they are doing in conservation. So, they take up these initiatives; for their reputation and to increase their market share. (IV 50, Project Manager, Development Agency)

Some stakeholders also make use of the global attention on the cut flower industry to push their claims, although their interests are not directly impeded by flower farms. For instance, a pastoralist group claims land from a national research institute located in Lake Naivasha's riparian land. A leader of this group has been a major figure in many reports and debates on the cut flower industry.[19] He is well aware of his impact on these debates as he says:

I have gone several times to some of these international meetings like in the Netherlands, the UK, I have also been in Germany, and I came in with the support of a supermarket. I could hear in forums an ordinary German saying, 'Look, if you are doing A, B, C, D, we will not buy your flowers!' in front of the media. You can imagine the impact it will have, right from that supermarket to down here. ... Yes, there were conferences; there were serious talks and panels because you go there and some people don't know what happens here.

Interviewer: Did you have to wear Masai clothes?

Yes, I had to. I was in that attire in various conferences. ... I remember my first one was in 2011 in The Hague. The second one was 2012 in Amsterdam, and then [in] 2013, [in] January, I was in Cologne.

(IV 52, Representative, Pastoralist Outreach Service)

Due to this public attention and his experience in public relations, he was able to create awareness for the land claims of pastoralists.

As shown above, the new market order entails increased public attention on the cut flower industry. Discourses about the cut flower industry vary widely, and negative reports have created new agencies among stakeholders. These profit from publicity for the cut flower industry. At the same time, many of them have a very balanced and nuanced opinion about the industry, stressing its economic importance while asking for improvements in terms

---

[19] See, for example, *The Guardian*, 4 April 2011, 'The true cost of Mother's Day flowers'.

of the economic and social impact. Take, for example, this statement by an officer of an environmental NGO, which is typical of this position:

> First of all, when you look at the Flower Industry in Kenya, the heartbeat of the flower industry in Kenya is Naivasha. To a certain extent, it has been instrumental in contributing to the country's GDP, but in the initial years, not much focus was put on the welfare of the employees. However, with time, and with [the] adoption of employee welfare associations and the Fairtrade programme, currently the interests of the employees are slowly taken care of, but much needs to be done especially on remuneration. ... In relation to [the] environment, there is a big transformation, and the major farms are becoming more environmentally conscious, but this is largely because of the pressure from the market and the standardization and usage of products. To a certain aspect, it has helped in changing the consciousness of how to take care of the environment. However, small farms are still dragging [behind] the major farms. (IV 56, Monitoring Officer, Environmental NGO)

Conclusion: The contested sustainability of Lake Naivasha's SES

This chapter has shown that the cut flower industry is deeply entangled in the local SES. Its role in the cut flower market makes Lake Naivasha a profoundly global place with a multitude of cross-scalar relations. Due to these global linkages, the new cut flower market order has created new agencies at Lake Naivasha. Stakeholder competition over resources and its regulation are enmeshed in relations to cut flower markets; as well as social welfare projects that were economised and are now a stabilising factor of cut flower production. Lastly, the new market order implies increased public attention on the cut flower industry. The effort for higher transparency and traceability in cut flower value chains turns this attention into a business risk for flower growers. Hence, the cut flower industry actively engages in gaining control over discourses.

In conclusion, Lake Naivasha's sustainability is an important factor in the global cut flower market in two distinct ways. Firstly, its discursive contestation is a business risk for flower farmers. And secondly, the industry is dependent on the SES's stability due to the required inputs for production, such as water or labour.

Two examples illustrate this. Firstly, Lake Naivasha's water level is often taken as a reference point for its ecological status. Low lake levels often cause public outcries in both the national and international media. For instance, reports were especially rife in 2009 when the lake level was low (see Figure 15), condemning the flower industry for abstracting lake water and making it

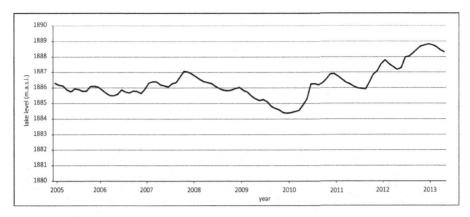

Figure 15. Lake levels at Lake Naivasha, 2005–13 (Author, KFC).

responsible for the low lake level (Riungu 2009). When I started my fieldwork in 2014, however, the lake level had just risen quickly by almost three metres. During this time, water abstraction was not made a topic of media reports. The fluctuating lake level affects the cut flower industry in two ways: the industry's reputation is harmed by media reports; moreover, low levels increase water abstraction costs and high lake levels cause flooding on some farms: due to its shallow water body, a change in just a few metres of water level may result in several kilometres of horizontal change (Mavuti, Harper 2006, 30).

Similarly, the lake's fish stock is often used as an indicator for its water quality and the adherence of flower farms to regulations on chemicals and water treatment. Fish mortalities have effects similar to low lake levels. Dead fish at Lake Naivasha are a popular cause of NGO and press reports, suggesting a causal relation between flower farms activities and the ecological demise. The cut flower industry publicly denies their responsibility and is supported by the Kenyan Marine and Fisheries Resource Institute:

> We tried to do some survey on that [fish mortality] and what we are finding out is that the oxygen level was quite low. So, we did not connect it to the flower farms. We tried to do some studies on the pesticides on the deal fish and the level was not high. So, we actually attributed that to low oxygen levels. (IV 66, Coordinating Officer, Public Research Institute)

Lake Naivasha's sustainability is a constitutive part of the new market order. Contestations about the SES's condition raise important questions about the 'real' and 'objective' impact of the cut flower industry. Most scientific studies on the lake's ecological state deemphasise its direct impact (OB 39, Stakeholder Conference). Fish stock is much more dependent on political decisions and the number of poachers (Dittmann 2018), and the eutrophication of the lake is to a large extent caused by smallholder farming in its catchment area (Harper et al. 2011). One might conclude that the overall attitude of farms towards their social-ecological environment has improved significantly. Yet, negative exceptions persist as shown by the case of the breakdown of Karuturi, one of the largest farms at South Lake between 2013 and 2016. In its last years, workers were not paid for several months and environmental measures were no longer funded.

This chapter has also shown that an analysis of the resilience of a spatially confined SES, as proposed by Anderies et al. (2004), is insufficient. The case of Lake Naivasha supports Hart's critique on the 'impact model' (2004, 91). The cut flower market is not an external, global force impacting on the Lake Naivasha SES in its 'baseline' (Cote, Nightingale 2012, 478) status. Rather, the new market order and the SES are mutually interdependent and create new agencies on both sides.

8

Conclusion: A New Market Order

The aim of this book was to explore the relationship between the agro-industry at Lake Naivasha and cut flower market orders in times of the growing importance of corporate retail chains and direct sales. Empirically, the analysis has shown that the market entry of retail chains and the reorganisation of the Lake Naivasha cut flower industry are mutually dependent, and that the reorganisation of global trade and retail of agricultural commodities has manifold and partly contradictory consequences for agricultures in the Global South and their sustaining social-ecological systems. Theoretically, the book favours a network-inspired approach over more classical approaches using the chain-metaphor (see Figure 16). Geographically, then, it questions all-too-linear and unidirectional representations of *global* market dynamics that result in *local* consequences for agro-industries in the Global South, and challenges macro-micro distinctions by showing how market orders are enacted in everyday practices.

To arrive at such conclusions, in this chapter I will first synthesise the empirical findings of this book along three lines which relate to the reorganisation of the cut flower industry: shifts in global trade and new market orders, the reorganisation of agro-industries, and the role of place and space in economic globalisation. On this basis, I will then consider what the empirical case at hand means for economic geography on a conceptual basis, before finally turning towards the political-economic repercussions of the reorganisation of the cut flower industry, and how current policy recommendations look and should look like at Lake Naivasha.

Shifts in global trade

A significant part of this book was dedicated to the question of how changes in the consumption and trade of cut flowers materialise at both the Dutch cut flower trade hub and the Lake Naivasha production cluster, or, more generally speaking, how shifts in global trade are brought about and how they materialise.

The cut flower industry has undergone a globalisation of production since the second half of the 20th century. Europe remains the most important export

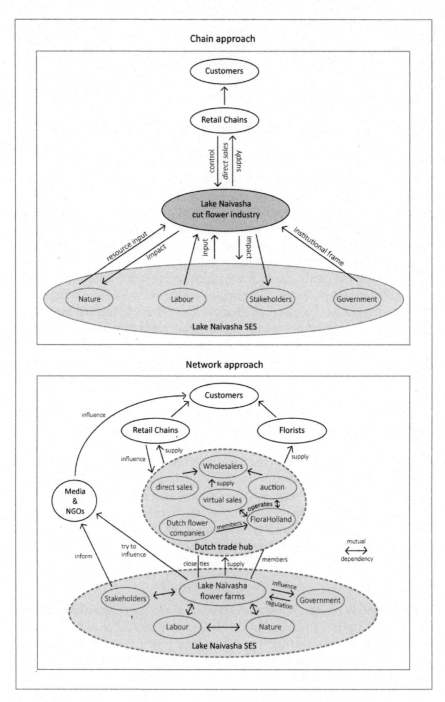

Figure 16. The cut flower industry as represented by chain and Actor-Network approaches (Author).

destination for Kenya. In the last 20 years, the European flower market has been characterised by the market entry of corporate supermarkets as part of the 'global retail revolution' (Selwyn 2016, 1776). Similar to many other non-traditional export products, such as grapes from Brazil (Selwyn 2016), wine from South Africa (Ponte, Ewert 2009), papayas from Jamaica (Cook 2004), or mangos from Ghana (Ouma 2015), Kenyan roses are an important part of the business strategies of large oligopolistic retail chains to increase their market-shares and exercise control over not only the consumption but also the trade and production of food and non-food commodities. In this way, cut flowers – although not a food commodity – can be seen as a part of a corporate regime as described by food regime theory. As my analysis shows, its main features, the 'reorganization of food supply chains, and centralization of agri-food relations, … the immanence of capital and its drive to deepen commodity relations' (McMichael 2005, 291), can clearly be observed in the cut flower industry. The strategies of corporate retailers often include contract farming or – as is the case in the cut flower industry – direct sourcing from producers. Although specialised florists still constitute a considerable part of the retail market, supermarkets have increased their shares in flower sales significantly over the last few years in all European countries.

But how does such a new market order come into being and expand geographically (see Berndt, Boeckler 2011, 1058)? As I have shown, it is not created unilaterally by lead firms, such as corporate retailers, and then pushed upstream via their supply chains by exerting control through direct sales or contracts – at least this is not the case in the flower industry. Rather, these changes are performed in everyday practices and slowly find their way through Actor-Networks in multiple ways. This observation does not neglect power asymmetries between producers in the Global South and corporate buyers in the Global North, it just goes beyond the classification of GCCs as buyer-driven and scrutinises 'the "janus-faced" nature of retailer power and asymmetries of power that are experienced along the supply chain' (Harvey 2007).

It is the Actor-Network at the Dutch cut flower hub that prevents the permanent and direct exercise of control of powerful buyers on Kenyan producers in the cut flower industry. Understanding this network also helps us to understand why, in the early days of the corporate food regime, the 'full vertical integration of the agri-food sector by food manufacturers did not eventuate' (Lawrence, Burch 2007, 8), at least not in the flower industry. The tight network of heterogeneous actors comprised of producers, growers' cooperatives, trade agents, and wholesalers has sustained its pivotal role in the global distribution of cut flowers despite the emergence of direct sales and the decline in Dutch flower production. Market encounters between producers and buyers – regardless of their origin – still rely to a large extent on these networks. As indicated in Figure 16, these encounters cannot be reduced to a direct link between European retailers and East African producers, but they have multiple forms and involve a variety of other actors: firstly, auctions have kept their pivotal role in linking (Kenyan) producers and (European) buyers. As a sociotechnical device within the Dutch cut flower industry, they do not only create linkages through actual transactions, but are also closely entangled in processes of valuation and price-making. Secondly, in the cut flower industry, direct sales are based on informality and usually involve sales agents or wholesalers, in addition to producers and buyers. Thirdly, emerging virtual market encounters, for example on online platforms, show that the market entry of retail chains has not led to simple buyer-driven value chains, but to even more complex market encounters, both in terms of volatility and quantity.

Kenyan flower producers make use of the whole range of market encounters to increase their flexibility and prevent dependency on single buyers. Nevertheless, there are still power asymmetries. As in the food industries within the corporate food regime, supermarkets use these asymmetries to 'strongly [influence] patterns of production and consumption' (Lawrence and Burch 2007, 9). These power asymmetries become effective in two processes that entail a high calculative agency for retail chains due to their knowledge about flower consumption. Firstly, retail chains dominate price-making processes which have led to a drop in cut flower prices and financial precariousness for Kenyan producers. Secondly, retail chains were able to impose their objectifications of flowers on breeders, growers, handlers, and traders all along the value chain. Indicators required by supermarkets for their ready-made bouquets, such as uniform quality and vase life, have become decisive factors for assessing cut flowers during market encounters, but also for breeding and planting new varieties on Kenyan farms and for packing and handling their produce. Furthermore, being a central part of the standardisation of flowers by supermarkets, certifications are the main restriction for market access and thus a tool of regulation and control in the cut flower industry.

By influencing price-setting mechanisms and objectifications of cut flowers in their interest, corporate retailers have managed to become dominant actors within the new market order. This new market order introduced formality (through certifications) and is based on low prices for consumers and producers. On the other hand, it requires flower growers to be able to cope with these conditions: plant, grow, and pack flowers according to these new objectifications and operate farms profitably despite low and volatile prices. In other words, the Lake Naivasha cut flower industry is a pillar of the new market order. This fits into Robinson's argument about non-traditional exports in Latin

America that 'utilize the region's comparative advantage in cheap labour as a basis for a "competitive" reinsertion into global markets' (Robinson 2008, 57). In the case of Latin American cut flowers, these dynamics – though different in detail – had already been observed in the 1980s (Korovkin 2003). As these cases show, cheap agricultural production in the Global South is not only the result of the global retail revolution, but also part of its fundamental conditions. It also shows that perspectives biased towards a 'local' perspective, as often taken in the case of the Kenyan cut flower industry (see e.g., Styles 2019), cannot sufficiently explain dynamics around Lake Naivasha.

The analysis of the cut flower industry also reveals that shifts in global trade and new market orders cannot simply be taken for granted and only analysed with regard to their consequences, but also have to be made objects of inquiry themselves. In order to understand their emergence, their materialisation, and their consequences, in all their complexity and diversity, new market orders have to be examined in detail, beyond simplifying categories, such as buyer-/ value-driven, or a narrow focus on single market encounters, such as direct sales. Facing rising polycentric trade systems with emerging South-South trade relations, the consideration of multiple value chains will become even more important in the future (see Horner, Nadvi 2018).

Reorganising agro-industries

The new market order is based on a reorganisation of the Lake Naivasha cut flower industry. New objectifications of cut flowers including certification schemes, low prices, complexified market encounters, and the traceability of commodities have resulted in fundamental internal changes for the cut flower industry at Lake Naivasha. I have shown that this results in financial precariousness for flower producers. Increased flexibility of production and sales channels and the expansion of farms are necessary requirements for most farms to cope with these new circumstances.

At the same time, Lake Naivasha flower farms have introduced innovations in production, packing, and handling in order to run themselves profitably. These innovations enable farms to decrease their production costs, raise productivity, and increase the value of their produce. Frequently, these innovations are technological, but they also involve new labour relations. With regard to technological changes, the cut flower industry is an extraordinary case compared to other agro-industries. The conditions of flower growing requires a great amount of spatially fixed investment into the technological infrastructure on a farm, which needs to be renewed regularly. Cut flower production and trade entails relatively high capital flows enabling profitable farms to trial new hardware. This reflects developments in non-agricultural sectors. According to

Goger's analysis (2013), when faced with new sourcing strategies from buyers, the Sri Lankan apparel industry 'has explicitly relied on upgrading and other strategic manoeuvres to survive in this volatile landscape' (Goger 2013, 2636).

With regard to labour relations, the cut flower industry is a remarkable case where a new market order dominated by corporate retail chains has led not only to a new system of labour management, but also to a stabilisation of employment. New agricultural market orders often require an experienced and trained workforce. As Selwyn has shown in the case of workers in Brazilian grape production (Selwyn 2012, 2013), this can lead to new agency for workers. In the cut flower industry, this has resulted in more stable forms of employment, but not in a significant improvement of remuneration.

Furthermore, I have demonstrated that the reorganisation of the cut flower industry is not limited to farms themselves, but also implies new relations to the surrounding SES at Lake Naivasha. This entails some partly conflicting consequences in terms of farms' resource use: the expansions of the last few years have made land scarce and increased water abstraction, whilst at the same time technological innovations have saved water and fertilisers and increased the productivity of growers. The new market order also brought with it increased public attention on the cut flower industry via NGOs and the media. Strategies to reduce reputational risks, such as CSR projects and interventions in public discourses, have become popular.

With regard to the reorganisation of agro-industries, the case of the Lake Naivasha cut flower industry is instructive in two ways: firstly, it reveals that reorganisation is a complex process with sometimes contradictory outcomes. It entails the forging and breaking of linkages, the exclusion and inclusion of actors, and economic and non-economic outcomes. Secondly, as shown in Figure 16, reorganisation goes beyond inter-firm or firm-internal relations; it is nested in the SES that sustains the agro-industries. These settings cannot only be seen as being affected by the consequences of dynamics in global trade or the origin of production inputs, but rather are part of the reorganisation itself. In order to analyse the relationship between the dynamics of global markets and the development of agro-industries, it is therefore necessary to exceed epistemological boundaries between 'the economy', politics, and ecology, and incorporate classical objects of inquiry from both economic geography, such as inter-firm coordination, and political ecology, such as environmental changes and resource exploitation (see Blaikie 1999).

Looking back from a mid-pandemic perspective, the time when most empirical data for this book was gathered now appears as a harbinger of what was to come during times of lockdown in the most important retail markets for Kenyan flowers. Many of the dynamics leading to a reorganisation of the cut flower industry outlined in this book have accelerated significantly over the past two years. The global Covid-19 pandemic has fuelled the shift to supermarket and online sales, has put farms under financial pressure, and made labour in the flower farms more precarious again. When florist shops were closed in Europe, consumers turned even more to supermarkets to buy flowers – increasing their market shares and simultaneously their importance. After a short slump in the early days of the pandemic in the spring of 2020, demand for Kenyan flowers was as high as ever. Yet, prices continued to be low or even dropped further (Quetsch 2021). On the other side, freight transport prices skyrocketed, increasing the financial pressure on flower growers. The reorganisation of the cut flower industry and its main features – more supermarket sales, high demand for large quantities of cheap and uniform roses, high flexibility in sales channels, and financial insecurity for growers – seems to have taken another leap forward.

Place and space in economic globalisation

By scrutinising the Dutch trade hub and the Lake Naivasha production cluster, this book has addressed the question of what role place plays in economic globalisation. The current role both of these places play in the cut flower industry is to a large extent the result of their specific historical development. The contemporary Dutch cut flower network originates from the country's history as a flower production hub. Although the focus shifted to the trade of flowers, the Actor-Network sustained its ability to create, enhance, and capture value by maintaining its stability despite being in flux and expanding beyond the country's borders and maintaining these distant linkages. Similarly, the foundations for the Lake Naivasha cut flower cluster were already laid long before the establishment of the first flower farms, through the coercive restructuring of land ownership, the creation of a wage labour market, and the first material infrastructures. But the cut flower industry is as much about history as it is about geography.

The idea of a 'global sense of place' is still instructive in this regard. Both the Dutch trade hub and the production cluster at Lake Naivasha are in no way confined to any singular spots on the map whatsoever, but are rather the locational expression of heterogeneous Actor-Networks that transgress territorial boundaries. The Dutch cut flower network includes companies with strong ties to Eastern African producers, breeders active all over the world, and, through virtual sales, buyers far away. Moreover, it is based on the informal and personal relationships of its actors that exceed the purely economic market encounters of the flower trade. These networks overlap with the Lake Naivasha production cluster, where Dutch and Indian actors dominate the management and ownership of flower farms. Here, the cut flower industry is deeply entangled within the non-floricultural Actor-Network. Through the cut flower industry, Lake Naivasha became a place of global interest with manifold translocal linkages. These connections do not only occur among floricultural management and firm networks, but also among many other stakeholders.

From this Actor-Network-inspired perspective, the empirical case at hand allows for some more general conclusions about place, space, and scale. Place and the relation of places do play an important role in economic globalisation. To some extent, this has been acknowledged by GPN scholars: 'The fortunes of regions are shaped not only by what is going on within them, but also through wider sets of relations of control and dependency, of competition and markets' (Coe et al. 2004, 469). However, these relations are still often conceptualised by some form of 'impact model' (Hart 2004, 91). This book suggests that places are not under the influence of globalisation, but are an integral and constitutional part of it.

Older concepts of political economy, such as World-System Theory (see Hopkins, Wallerstein 1986), have cautioned against the use of territorial units, such as the nation state, as *a priori* realities and view them as constituting parts of the respective world-system instead. In a similar vein, the Actor-Network approach utilised in this book considers the global, the national, the local, etc. as practical achievements. Thus, the case of the cut flower industry can be interpreted in a non-hierarchical way, or by way of using a flat ontology (see Marston et al. 2005). Despite its many criticisms, a flat ontology does not suggest the end of geography. On the contrary, it can be shown that the Dutch trade hub, for example, was much more successful in forging world-wide connections and in going global, while others such as the German or US-American cut flower industry were more and more confined to the short relations between retailers and consumers and thus lost shares in the production and trade of cut flowers.

In addition, place is never constituted only by the economic, the ecological, or the social. Still, many approaches of economic geography fall into the trap of 'purifying' the economic when analysing places: they conceive of place as mere 'background scenery' (Jones 2008, 72) into which economic processes are embedded, as an 'institutional framework' (Raikes et al. 2000, 393) that influences firms, or as a 'social context' (Palpacuer 2008) impacted by economic dynamics. As the case of Lake Naivasha has shown, dynamics in Actor-Networks and thus also in places are neither confined to one sphere nor can their origins be traced back monocausally to a single dimension. In fact, the success of the Dutch trade hub would not have been possible without the tight sociotechnical Actor-Network that entails non-economic personal relations between traders as well as devices such as the auction clock.

Dynamic chains or markets in the making?

Throughout this book, I have discussed the merits and limits of the GCC, GVC, and GPN frameworks and suggested a reading of cut flowers' economic geography that is inspired by marketisation studies. No doubt, the approaches that use the chain-metaphor offer a valuable methodology to trace and describe the linkages between sites of production, trade, and consumption. This heuristic enables expressive representations of global economic relations. With the concepts of governance and upgrading, it also offers useful analytical tools to describe inter-firm coordination and firm strategies to improve their position. Yet, at the same time, these representations bear the risk of simplification and superficiality and therefore may impede an accurate empirical analysis. Figure 16 illustrates these merits and limits. On the one hand, the illustration inspired by chain-approaches in the top half presents the general dynamics in the cut flower industry plain and simply: corporate retailers are depicted as powerful lead firms that control producers who are embedded in the Lake Naivasha SES. On the other hand, it overlooks the multitude of market encounters, translocal linkages between non-economic actors, and diverse outcomes of dynamics in economic relations. In doing so, the causes and consequences of complex economic relations may fall from view. The complexity of market encounters that characterises the new cut flower distribution system, however, is crucial to understand the reorganisation of the industry caused by the market entry of retail chains. Hence, the case of the cut flower industry supports Ouma's criticism that 'the existing chain literature often tells us little about how global economic connections come into being, how they are assembled practically by different actors, and what such chains look like "from below" or even "from within"' (Ouma 2015, 7).

I suggested that in order to fully understand how new market orders unfold, a marketisation perspective is a necessary complement to chain approaches. For this book, it offered the analytical concepts and notions to examine the complex cut flower market configuration: a focus on the forging of linkages in market encounters revealed the multitude of producer-buyer relationships and the flexibility of flower growers; the analysis of the objectification of cut flowers as well as of price-setting mechanisms showed how corporate retail chains are able to translate their knowledge about flower consumption into power over breeders, growers, and traders; and overall, a marketisation perspective reveals the incorporation of the non-economic sphere, such as its discursive, ecological, and social dimensions, in the making of markets that are more than a mere production input or institutional frame.

The cut flower industry and the focus on Lake Naivasha proved to be an instructive case for a study on marketisation. This is due to the specific configurations of the flower industry. The Dutch trade hub and the adjacent market encounters are largely based on personal relationships. Roses are a commodity highly contested in discourses surrounding the industry, which attracts the interest of NGOs as well as national and international media. Lake Naivasha is not only home to the cut flower industry, but also an ecological and tourist hotspot, and the bedrock of the livelihoods of 380,000 people. As shown, these dimensions play an important role in the making of the new cut flower order. Thus, the empirical case at hand requires an analytical approach that exceeds the economic dimensions of global economic entanglements and considers social, technical, ecological, and discursive aspects in the making and breaking of theses linkages. Similar claims have been made for the case of Ghanaian horticulture (Ouma 2015), the banana production in Colombia (Brown 2013), or the coffee crisis in Nicaragua (Wilson 2013).

However, the case of Lake Naivasha also differs from other studies on geographies of marketisation (see e.g., Ouma et al. 2013). The region is not newly incorporated into global markets nor has the industry recently emerged, rather it is an established cluster that has undergone internal reconfiguration ever since its inception. Hence, the cut flower industry is an instructive case as it reminds scholars to not narrowly focus on firms, industries, or regions newly enrolled into global markets. No matter how deeply entangled these Actor-Networks are within the global economy, their marketisation remains partial and imperfect. Moreover, new market orders do not only spread geographically in a Euclidean sense, but also in a topological sense, that is to say they incorporate Actor-Networks. Shifting the focus to internal dynamics and processes, reorganisation makes it possible to reveal the order and disorder of economic globalisation. It is thus necessary to take into account the fluidity of Actor-Networks and to incorporate 'the multiple, imperfect configurations of Actor-Networks back into the analysis allow[ing] us to rediscover those things that tend to become invisible and overlooked in a primary concern with stability' (Müller 2015, 79).

Governance for a fair future of the cut flower industry

New market orders bring along new beneficiaries and disadvantaged (see Ouma 2015, 41). Tracing value is one of the main concerns of GCC, GVC, and GPN studies, and 'even tentatively being able to systematically map the gains across a GPN' (Coe 2011, 397) continues to be a powerful tool. With regard to gains, European corporate retail chains are the biggest beneficiaries of the current cut flower market order. Despite low consumer prices, their margins are still remarkable. Supermarkets have reached this position mainly by making use of their knowledge in the objectifications of cut flowers and price-setting mechanisms. To a certain degree, European consumers can also be seen as beneficiaries, as the new market order guarantees them low prices for the uniform flower bouquets that they request (see FloraHolland 2015b).

Those mainly disadvantaged by this market order are the flower growers at Lake Naivasha, albeit to varying degrees. The case of the cut flower industry is thus a remarkable case that counters the idea of excessively lucrative investments into large-scale agro-industries. The 'gold rush' era of the Kenyan flower industry with profit margins of up to 50% is over. Large-scale farms in particular struggle with financial constraints due to the high amount of spatially fixed investments. In contrast, some middle-sized farms that realised the need for production innovation and flexibility are able to generate reasonable profits. For farm workers, the new market order has conflicting consequences. On the one hand, it led to more jobs and more stable employment conditions. Beyond that, the capital-labour relation between flower farms and their employees changed in favour of the latter. They receive a higher share of the revenues. Yet, on the other hand, this change is not primarily caused by higher remuneration, as real wages rose only moderately or even stagnated. It is rather due to lower revenues for the farms. Although it is quite remarkable that the drop in revenues for producers did not result in a drop in wages, the financial gains of workers when considering the cut flower value chain as a whole are unsatisfactory. In conclusion, regarding its financial outcomes, the new cut flower market order unilaterally benefits European corporate retail chains, does not significantly improve workers' situations, and disadvantages flower farmers.

The question of beneficiaries and those who are disadvantaged, however, must not only be approached financially. At this juncture, in particular, it becomes obvious that the debate on chains versus networks is not a mere academic exercise but highly relevant for policymaking. Currently, regulative tools based on the vertical logic of chain approaches are the predominant means to mitigate the negative impacts of the new market order on the Lake Naivasha SES and its stakeholders. Beyond some phytosanitary regulations that were imposed, public legislation struggles with finding appropriate responses to these impacts as they exceed legislative territories. Therefore, it is mainly industry- or NGO-based standards that dominate the governance of the market. As I have shown, these standards focus on actors involved in vertical trade relations such as producers and buyers. They largely neglect actors 'beyond the fences' of flower farms and the specific historical and geographical contexts of production regions. In Naivasha, for instance, this concerns the impact of flower farms on the SES that are not directly related to commodity production: the rapid growth of unplanned settlements without proper sanitary infrastructure, the importance of flower farms in social welfare systems, or the fencing of the riparian land with conflicting consequences for wildlife and pastoralists.

In order to sustainably regulate the environmental and social conditions of the cut flower trade and production, standards as well as public legislation need to find ways to incorporate the local and translocal Actor-Networks that the flower farms are part of. Hence, I suggest that a network approach is appropriate not only in academia but also in regulating policies. Regulations, both public and private, need to integrate actors and dimensions that are not part of the immediate economic transactions. Concerning public regulations, this means that policies concerning the cut flower industry require more consistency, both on a national and international level. As the case of the EU-EAC Economic Partnership Agreement has shown, regarding trade policies the EU strives for deregulation. At the same time, European (and other) public developmental agencies try to mitigate the effects of an unregulated industry on human-nature relations at Lake Naivasha. Concerning private regulations, this means that certification bodies need to engage more with local, regional, and national public regulations. So far, standards require only the compliance of the producers. Yet, as the case of the cut flower industry shows, these regulations are to a large extent ineffective. Certification bodies should help to strengthen them, for instance by building capacity for government bodies or tightening rules and controls.

These recommendations might lead to a fairer cut flower industry in terms of environmental and social conditions. Yet, one problem remains unsolved that will determine Lake Naivasha's future: the unequal distribution of financial gains. Lake Naivasha's future as a cut flower production hub will depend largely either on the ability of flower producers and the surrounding SES to cope with the financial precariousness caused by cheap roses, or on a more equal redistribution of revenues within the cut flower industry.

BIBLIOGRAPHY

Primary Sources

List of Interviews and Observations

No	Type	Position	Date	Place	Category	Category Organisation
1	Interview	General Manager	27.02.2014	Nairobi	Flower Farms	Breeder
2	Interview	Production Manager	05.03.2014	Naivasha	Flower Farms	Grower
3	Interview	Former Workers	06.03.2014	Naivasha	Flower Farms	Grower
4	Interview, Farm Tour	Production Manager	07.03.2014	Naivasha	Flower Farms	Grower
5	Interview	Former Leader	07.03.2014	Naivasha	Flower Industry	Union
6	Interview	Workers	08.03.2014	Naivasha	Flower Farms	Grower
7	Interview	Farm Manager	10.03.2014	Naivasha	Flower Farms	Grower
8	Interview	Head of Production	11.03.2014	Naivasha	Flower Farms	Grower
9	Interview	Former HR Manager	12.03.2014	Naivasha	Flower Farms	Grower
10	Farm Tour	Fairtrade Manager	18.03.2014	Naivasha	Flower Farms	Grower
11	Interview	Accountant	20.03.2014	Nairobi	Flower Industry	KFC
12	Interview	Head of Production	28.03.2014	Naivasha	Flower Farms	Grower
13	Farm Tour	Production Manager	28.03.2014	Naivasha	Flower Farms	Grower
14	Farm Tour	Farm Coordinator Head of Production	29.03.2014	Naivasha	Flower Farms	Grower

No	Type	Position	Date	Place	Category	Category Organisation
15	Interview	Fairtrade Manager	31.03.2014	Naivasha	Flower Farms	Grower
16	Interview	Production Manager	01.04.2014	Naivasha	Flower Farms	Grower
17	Interview	Farm Manager	03.04.2014	Naivasha	Flower Farms	Grower
18	Interview	Workers	03.04.2014	Naivasha	Flower Farms	Grower
19	Interview	Former General Manager	03.04.2014	Naivasha	Flower Farms	Grower
20	Interview	CEO	17.10.2014	Nairobi	Flower Industry	KFC
21	Interview	CEO	23.10.2014	Naivasha	Flower Industry	LNGG
22	Interview	Consultant & Head of production	24.10.2014	Naivasha	Flower Industry	Grower
23	Interview	Former Union Leader, NGO activist	25.10.2014	Naivasha	Flower Industry	Labour rights
24	Interview	CEO	29.10.2014	Naivasha	Stakeholders	Imarisha Naivasha
25	Interview	Head of Production	29.10.2014	Naivasha	Flower Farms	Grower
26	Farm Tour	Assistant Production Manager Packhouse Manager Supervisor Propagation	04.11.2014	Naivasha	Flower Farms	Grower
27	Interview	Director	04.11.2014	Naivasha	Stakeholders	WRMA
28	Interview	Farm Manager	06.11.2014	Naivasha	Flower Farms	Grower
29	Interview	Sales Manager	07.11.2014	Naivasha	Flower Industry	Supplier
30	Interview	General Manager	11.11.2014	Naivasha	Flower Farms	Grower
31	Farm Tour	Research Data Analyst	12.11.2014	Naivasha	Flower Farms	Breeder
32	Interview	Sales Manager General Manager Breeding	12.11.2014	Naivasha	Flower Farms	Breeder

No	Type	Position	Date	Place	Category	Category Organisation
33	Farm Tour	Sales Manager	12.11.2014	Naivasha	Flower Farms	Breeder
34	Interview	Managing Director	19.11.2014	Naivasha	Flower Farms	Breeder
35	Farm Tour	Managing Director	19.11.2014	Naivasha	Flower Farms	Breeder
36	Interview	General Manager	22.11.2014	Naivasha	Flower Farms	Breeder
37	Interview	Managing Director	22.11.2014	Naivasha	Flower Farms	Breeder
38	Farm Tour	Managing Director	22.11.2014	Naivasha	Flower Farms	Breeder
39	Stakeholder Conference	Miscellaneous	26.11.2014	Naivasha	Stakeholders	
40	Interview	Managing Director	28.11.2014	Naivasha	Flower Farms	Breeder
41	Interview	Managing Director	02.12.2014	Naivasha	Flower Farms	Grower
42	Interview	Managing Director	03.12.2014	Naivasha	Flower Industry	Consultancy
43	Interview	Managing Director, Head of Several Flower Industry Groups	11.12.2014	Nairobi	Flower Farms Flower Industry	Grower Flower Industry Groups
44	Interview	Production Manager	18.05.2015	Nanyuki	Flower Farms	Grower
45	Interview	General Manager	23.05.2015	Naivasha	Flower Farms	Grower
46	Interview	CEO	25.05.2015	Naivasha	Flower Industry	LNGG
47	Interview	CEO	26.05.2015	Naivasha	Stakeholders	Imarisha Naivasha
48	Interview	Chairman	28.05.2015	Naivasha	Stakeholders	Environmental NGO
49	Interview	Project Coordinator	29.05.2015	Naivasha	Stakeholders	Environmental NGO
50	Interview	Project Manager	29.05.2015	Naivasha	Stakeholders	Development Project/ Agency

No	Type	Position	Date	Place	Category	Category Organisation
51	Interview	Chairman	30.05.2015	Naivasha	Stakeholders	Environmental NGO
52	Interview	Chairman, Representative	01.06.2015	Naivasha	Stakeholders	LaNaWRUA, Pastoralist Outreach Service
53	Interview	Product Manager	03.06.2015	Nairobi	Flower Industry	Cargo Airline
54	Trade Fair	Miscellaneous	03.06.2015	Nairobi	Flower Industry	Miscellaneous
55	Interview	Project Coordinator	04.06.2015	Nairobi	Stakeholders	Development Agency
56	Interview	Monitoring Officer	05.06.2015	Naivasha	Stakeholders	Environmental NGO
57	Interview	General Manager	08.06.2015	Naivasha	Flower Farms	Grower
58	Farm Tour	General Manager	08.06.2015	Naivasha	Flower Farms	Grower
59	Interview	Board Committee	09.06.2015	Naivasha	Stakeholders	Humanitarian NGO
60	Interview	Senior Warden	10.06.2015	Naivasha	Stakeholders	Conservancy State Corporation
61	Interview	General Manager	11.06.2015	Nairobi	Flower Industry	Service Provider
62	Interview	Sales Executive	11.06.2015	Nairobi	Flower Industry	Freight Forwarder
63	Interview	Agronomist	12.06.2015	Nairobi	Flower Industry	Supplier
64	Interview	Officer	15.06.2015	Naivasha	Stakeholders	WRMA
65	Interview	General Manager Exports	16.06.2015	Nairobi	Flower Industry	Freight Forwarder
66	Interview	Coordinating Officer	17.06.2015	Naivasha	Stakeholders	Public Research Institute
67	Interview	Community Worker	18.06.2015	Naivasha	Stakeholders	Development Agency
68	Interview	Sales Manager	18.06.2015	Naivasha	Flower Industry	Supplier

No	Type	Position	Date	Place	Category	Category Organisation
69	Interview	Officer	19.06.2015	Naivasha	Stakeholders	Government Organisation
70	Interview	Researcher	20.06.2015	Kinangop	Stakeholders	National Research Institution
71	Interview	Executive Officer	22.06.2015	Nakuru	Stakeholders	Policy NGO
72	Interview	Packhouse Manager, Assistant HR Manager	23.06.2015	Naivasha	Flower Farms	Grower
73	Farm Tour	Packhouse Manager, Assistant HR Manager	23.06.2015	Naivasha	Flower Farms	Grower
74	Interview	Member	24.06.2015	Naivasha	Stakeholders	Self Help Group
75	Interview	Flower Product Manager	26.06.2015	Nairobi	Flower Industry	Fairtrade Africa
76	Interview	Sourcing Manager	01.07.2015	Nairobi	Flower Industry	Auction Services
77	Interview	Production Manager	06.07.2015	Naivasha	Flower Farms	Grower
78	Interview	Shareholder	21.07.2015	Nairobi	Flower Farms	Flower Business Park, Grower
79	Interview	Technical Officer	22.07.2015	Nairobi	Flower Industry	Government Organisation
80	Interview	Deputy County Commissioner	28.07.2015	Naivasha	Stakeholders	Government
81	Farm Tour	Financial Director	29.07.2015	Naivasha	Flower Farms	Grower
82	Interview	Honorary Secretary, Former Shareholder	03.08.2015	Naivasha	Stakeholders, Flower Farms	Environmental NGO, Grower
83	Interview	Officer	03.08.2015	Naivasha	Stakeholders	Development Project
84	Interview and Tour	Sales and Marketing	15.09.2015	Aalsmeer	Flower Industry	Flower Company

No	Type	Position	Date	Place	Category	Category Organisation
85	Auction Visit	Miscellaneous	16.09.2015	Aalsmeer	Flower Industry	Flower Auction
86	Interview	Flower Trader	17.09.2015	Aalsmeer	Flower Industry	Flower Wholesaler
87	Interview	Sales Manager	18.09.2015	Aalsmeer	Flower Industry	Import/Export
88	Trade Fair	Miscellaneous	09.06.2016	Nairobi	Flower Industry	
89	Interview	Executive Officer	14.06.2016	Naivasha	Flower Industry	LNGG
90	Interview	CEO	15.06.2016	Naivasha	Stakeholders	Imarisha Naivasha
91	Interview	Director	16.06.2016	Naivasha	Flower Farms	Grower
92	Interview	CEO	17.06.2016	Nairobi	Flower Industry	KFC
93	Group Discussion	Miscellaneous	22.02.2017	Cologne	Flower Industry	Transfair, Certifier

Archive Sources

Kenya National Archives

Annual Reports, Naivasha Division.
Annual Reports, Nakuru Division.
BV/64/50: Horticultural Development Plan, 1970.

Kenya National Archive, Provincial Deposit Nakuru (KNN Nakuru)

GU/1/7: The Divisional Development Committee 1984–9.

Nations Archive, Nairobi

Gibendi, R., 'Now EAC partners abandon', *Daily Nation*, 7 October 2014.
Hunter, N., 'The tragedy that is Lake Naivasha', *Business Daily,* 5 October 2009.
Kamadi, G., 'Team identifies programme to restore Naivasha', *Business Daily*, 3 October 2011.
Kenya Today Reporters, 'Ethiopia Woos Kenya's Leading Flower Farmers', *Kenya Today*, 25–31 October 2010.
Mayoyo, P., 'Rogue firms deny Kenya Sh130bn in tax', *Daily Nation*, 12 May 2014.
Mutambo, A., 'Relief as Dar signs EAC pact with EU to bail out Kenya', *Saturday Nation*, 18 October 2014.

Nation Reporters, 'Alarm as East Africa fails to strike export deal with EU on fresh produce', *Daily Nation*, 24 April 2014.

Ngige, J., 'Why fish are dying in L. Naivasha', *Daily Nation*, 26 February 2010.

Omondi, G., 'Dutch firm's grip on flower exports to loosen as Kenya rejoins Eurozone free trade', *Daily Nation*, 17 December 2014.

Otieno, J., 'Kenya regains preferential access to EU markets in time for Valentine's', *The EastAfrican*, 27 December 2014–2 January 2015.

Redfern, P., 'Kenya loses Sh42bn annually to flower sector tax evasion', *Business Daily*, 6 April 2011.

Riungu, C., 'Lake Naivasha is dying', *The East African*, 20–26 July 2009.

Sambu, Z., 'Kenya "ready" to soften stance on EU trade pact', *Sunday Nation*, 11 May 2014.

Unknown Author, 'Jabs Campaign', *Daily Nation*, 6 July 1991.

Unknown Author, 'Dysentery "controlled"', *Daily Nation*, 28 July 1998.

Xinhua, 'Sign trade deal with EU, flower lobby urges bloc', *Daily Nation*, 2 July 2013.

Secondary Sources

Alba, R. (1982). 'Taking Stock of Network Analysis: A Decade's Results', *Research in the Sociology of Organizations*, 1, 39–74.

Altmann, M. (2016). 'Developments and trends in the flower and plant market for 2015/2016. Edited by IPM Essen. Essen'. Available at: http://www.intracen.org/uploadedFiles/intracen.org/Content/Exporters/Market_Data_and_Information/Market_information/Market_Insider/Floriculture/Developments%20and%20trends%20in%20the%20flower%20and%20plant%20market%20for%202015%20-%202016.pdf [Accessed 7 January 2019].

Amin, A. (2002). 'Spatialities of Globalisation', *Environment and Planning A*, 34(3), 385–99.

Anderies, J. M.; Janssen, M. A.; Ostrom, E. (2004). 'A Framework to Analyze the Robustness of Social-ecological Systems from an Institutional Perspective', *Ecology and Society*, 9(1), 18.

Anderson, B.; McFarlane, C. (2011). 'Assemblage and geography', *Area*, 43(2), 124–7.

Anker, R.; Anker, M. (2014). *Living Wage for Kenya with Focus on Fresh Flower Farm Area near Lake Naivasha*. Edited by Fairtrade International, Sustainable Agriculture Network/Rainforest Alliance, UTZ Certified.

Appelbaum, R.; Smith, D.; Christerson, B. (1994). 'Commodity Chains and Industrial Restructuring in the Pacific Rim: Garment Trade and Manufacturing', in: G. Gereffi, M. Korzeniewicz (eds), *Commodity chains and global capitalism* (Westport: Praeger Publishers), 187–204.

Ase, L. -E. (1987). 'A Note on the Water Budget of Lake Naivasha, Kenya. Especially the Role of Salvinia Molesta Mitch and Cyperus papyrus L.', *Geografiska Annaler. Series A, Physical Geography*, 69(3/4), 415–29.

Aufhauser, E.; Reiner, C. (2010). 'Die Macht der Supermarktketten. Steuerung globaler Produktionsnetze durch den Einzelhandel', in: C. Staritz, C. Reiner,

K. Fischer (eds), *Globale Güterketten. Weltweite Arbeitsteilung und ungleiche Entwicklung* (Wien: Promedia; Südwind), 246–71.

Awange, J. L.; Forootan, E.; Kusche, J.; Kiema, J. B. K.; Omondi, P. A.; Heck, B. et al. (2013). 'Understanding the Decline of Water Storage across the Ramser-Lake Naivasha using Satellite-Based Methods', *Advances in Water Resources*, 60, 7–23.

Bair, J. (2005). 'Global Capitalism and Commodity Chains: Looking Back, Going Forward', *Competition & Change*, 9(2), 153–80.

Bair, J. (2008). 'Analysing global economic organization: embedded networks and global chains compared', *Economy and Society*, 37(3), 339–64.

Bair, J. (ed.) (2009a). *Frontiers of Commodity Chain Research* (Stanford: Stanford University Press).

Bair, J. (2009b). 'Global Commodity Chains: Genealogy and Review', in: J. Bair (ed.), *Frontiers of Commodity Chain Research* (Stanford: Stanford University Press), 1–34.

Bair, J. (2014). 'Editor's Introduction. Commodity Chains in and of the World System', *Journal of World-Systems Research*, 20(1), 1–10.

Bair, J. (2017). 'Contextualising compliance: hybrid governance in global value chains', *New Political Economy*, 22(2), 169–85.

Bair, J.; Berndt, C.; Boeckler, M.; Werner, M. (2013). 'Guest Editorial. Dis/articulating Producers, Markets, and Regions: New Directions in Critical Studies of Commodity Chains', *Environment and Planning A*, 45(11), 2544–52.

Bair, J.; Palpacuer, F. (2015). 'CSR beyond the corporation: contested governance in global value chains', *Global Networks*, 15(s1), S1–19.

Bair, J.; Werner, M. (2011). 'Commodity Chains and the Uneven Geographies of Global Capitalism. A Disarticulations Perspective', *Environment and Planning A*, 43(5), 988–97.

Barnes, T. J. (2008). 'Making Space for the Economy. Live Performances, Dead Objects, and Economic Geography', *Geography Compass*, 2(5), 1432–48.

Barrett, H.; Browne, A.; Ilbery, B. (2004). 'From farm to supermarket. The trade in Fresh Horticultural Produce from Sub-Saharan Africa to the United Kingdom', in: A. Hughes, S. Reimer (eds), *Geographies of Commodity Chains* (New York: Routledge), 19–38.

Barrientos, S.; Dolan, C.; Tallontire, A. (2003). 'A Gendered Value Chain Approach to Codes of Conduct in African Horticulture', *World Development*, 31(9), 1511–26.

Barrientos, S.; Gereffi, G.; Rossi, A. (2011). 'Economic and social upgrading in global production networks. A new paradigm for a changing world', *International Labour Review*, 150(3–4), 319–40.

Barrientos, S.; Kritzinger, A. (2004). 'Squaring the Circle. Global Production and the Informalization of Work in South African Fruit Exports', *Journal of International Development*, 16(1), 81–92.

Bathelt, H.; Glückler, J. (2012). *Wirtschaftsgeographie. Ökonomische Beziehungen in räumlicher Perspektive* (Stuttgart: Ulmer).

Bathelt, H.; Zakrzewski, G. (2007). 'Messeveranstaltungen als fokale Schnittstellen der globalen Ökonomie', *Zeitschrift für Wirtschaftsgeographie*, 51(1), 14–30.

Becht, R. (2007). *Environmental Effects of the Floricultural Industry on the Lake Naivasha Basin* (Enschede: ITC International Institute for Geo-Information Science and Earth Observation).

Becht, R.; Harper, D. (2002). 'Towards an understanding of human impact upon the hydrology of Lake Naivasha, Kenya', *Hydrobiologia*, 488, 1–11.

Berndt, C.; Boeckler, M. (2009). 'Geographies of circulation and exchange. Constructions of markets', *Progress in Human Geography*, 33(4), 535–51.

Berndt, C.; Boeckler, M. (2010). 'Geographies of markets. Materials, morals and monsters in motion', *Progress in Human Geography*, 35(4), 559–67.

Berndt, C.; Boeckler, M. (2011). 'Performative Regional (dis)Integration. Transnational Markets, Mobile Commodities, and Bordered North–South Differences', *Environment and Planning A*, 43(5), 1057–78.

Berndt, C.; Boeckler, M. (2012). 'Geographies of Marketization', in: T. J. Barnes, J. Peck, E. S. Sheppard (eds), *The Wiley-Blackwell Companion to Economic Geography* (Chichester, Malden: Wiley-Blackwell), 199–212.

Bernstein, H. (2016). 'Agrarian political economy and modern world capitalism. The contributions of food regime analysis', *Journal of Peasant Studies*, 43(3), 611–47.

Besky, S. (2008). 'Can a Plantation be Fair? Paradoxes and Possibilities in Fair Trade Darjeeling Tea Certification', *Anthropology of Work Review*, 29(1), 1–9.

Blaikie, P. (1999). 'A Review of Political Ecology. Issues, Epistemology and Analytical Narratives', *Zeitschrift für Wirtschaftsgeographie*, 43(3–4), 131–47.

Boeckler, M.; Berndt, C. (2013). 'Geographies of circulation and exchange III. The great crisis and marketization "after markets"', *Progress in Human Geography*, 37(3), 424–32.

Bolo, M. O. (2008). 'The Lake Naivasha Cut Flower Cluster in Kenya', in: D. Zhihua Zeng (ed.), *Knowledge, Technology, and Cluster-Based Growth in Africa* (Washington, DC: The World Bank), 37–51.

Bosco, F. J. (2008). 'Actor-Network Theory, Networks, and Relational Approaches in Human Geography', in: S. Aitken, G. Valentine (eds), *Approaches to Human Geography* (London: SAGE), 136–46.

Brown, S. (2013). 'One Hundred Years of Labor Control. Violence, Militancy, and the Fairtrade Banana Commodity Chain in Colombia', *Environment and Planning A*, 45(11), 2572–91.

Burch, D.; Dixon, J.; Lawrence, G. (2013). 'Introduction to symposium on the changing role of supermarkets in global supply chains: from seedling to supermarket: agri-food supply chains in transition', *Agriculture and Human Values*, 30(2), 215–24.

Calas, B. (2013). 'Mondialisation, Clusterisation et recyclage colonial. Naivasha, laboratoire d'une Afrique émergente', *EchoGéo*, 26, 1–25.

Çalışkan, K.; Callon, M. (2009). 'Economization, Part 1. Shifting Attention from the Economy towards Processes of Economization', *Economy and Society*, 38(3), 369–98.

Çalışkan, K.; Callon, M. (2010). 'Economization, Part 2. A Research Programme for the Study of Markets', *Economy and Society*, 39(1), 1–32.

Callon, M. (1998a). 'An essay on framing and overflowing: economic externalities revisited by sociology', in: M. Callon (ed.), *The laws of the markets* (Oxford, Malden: Blackwell Publishers), 244–69.

Callon, M. (1998b). 'Introduction: the embeddedness of economic markets in economics', in: M. Callon (ed.), *The laws of the markets* (Oxford, Malden: Blackwell Publishers), 1–57.

Callon, M. (ed.) (1998c). *The laws of the markets* (Oxford, Malden: Blackwell Publishers).

Callon, M. (2007a). 'An Essay on the Growing Contribution of Economic Markets to the Proliferation of the Social', *Theory, Culture & Society*, 24(7–8), 139–63.

Callon, M. (2007b). 'What Does it Mean to Say That Economics Is Performative?', in: D. MacKenzie, F. Muniesa, L. Siu (eds), *Do Economists Make Markets? On the Performativity of Economics* (Princeton: Princeton University Press), 311–57.

Callon, M.; Muniesa, F. (2005). 'Peripheral Vision. Economic Markets as Calculative Collective Devices', *Organization Studies*, 26(8), 1229–50.

Cannon, T.; Müller-Mahn, D. (2010). 'Vulnerability, resilience and development discourses in Context of climate change', *Natural Hazards*, 55(3), 621–35.

Cattaneo, O.; Gereffi, G.; Staritz, C. (eds) (2010). *Global Value Chains in a Postcrisis World. A Development Perspective* (Washington, DC: World Bank).

CBI (2016). 'CBI Trade Statistics: Cut Flowers and Foliage' (The Hague: Centre for the Promotion of Imports from developing countries). Available at: https://www.cbi.eu/sites/default/files/market_information/researches/trade-statistics-cut-flowers-foliage-2016.pdf [Accessed 12 November 2018].

CBI (2017a). 'Exporting Roses to Europe' (The Hague: Centre for the Promotion of Imports from developing countries). Available at: https://www.cbi.eu/node/2034/pdf/ [Accessed 1 March 2018].

CBI (2017b). 'Exporting Roses to Germany' (The Hague: Centre for the Promotion of Imports from developing countries). Available at: https://www.cbi.eu/node/1846/pdf/ [Accessed 1 March 2018].

CBI (2017c). 'Through what Channels can you get Cut Flowers or Foliage onto the European Market?' (The Hague: Centre for the Promotion of Imports from developing countries). Available at: https://www.cbi.eu/node/1843/pdf/ [Accessed 1 March 2019].

CBI (2017d). 'What Competition do you Face on the European Cut Flowers and Foliage Market?' (The Hague: Centre for the Promotion of Imports from developing countries). Available at: https://www.cbi.eu/node/1844/pdf/ [Accessed 22 March 2019].

Clelland, D. (2014). 'Unpaid Labour as Dark Value in Global Commodity Chains', in: W. A. Dunaway (ed.), *Gendered commodity chains. Seeing women's work and households in global production* (Stanford: Stanford University Press), 72–87.

Cloke, P.; Cook, I.; Crang, P.; Goodwin, M.; Painter, J.; Philo, C. (2004). *Practising human geography* (London, Thousand Oaks, New Delhi: SAGE).

Coase, R. H. (1937). 'The Nature of the Firm', *Economica*, 4(16), 386–405.

Coe, N.; Dicken, P.; Hess, M.; Yeung, H. W. -C. (2010). 'Making connections. Global Production Networks and World City Networks', *Global Networks*, 10(1), 138–49.

Coe, N. M. (2011). 'Geographies of production II. A global production network A-Z', *Progress in Human Geography*, 36(3), 389–402.

Coe, N. M.; Dicken, P.; Hess, M. (2008). 'Global production networks: realizing the potential', *Journal of Economic Geography*, 8(3), 271–95.

Coe, N. M.; Hess, M.; Yeung, H. W. -C.; Dicken, P.; Henderson, J. (2004). '"Globalizing" regional development: a global production networks perspective', *Transactions of the Institute of British Geographers*, 29(4), 468–84.

Coe, N. M.; Yeung, H. W. -C. (2015). *Global production networks: theorizing economic development in an interconnected world* (Oxford: Oxford University Press).

Collins, J. (2014). 'A Feminist Approach to Overcoming the Closed Boxes of the Commodity Chain', in: W. A. Dunaway (ed.), *Gendered commodity chains. Seeing women's work and households in global production* (Stanford: Stanford University Press), 27–37.

Cook, I. (2004). 'Follow the Thing. Papaya', *Antipode*, 36(4), 642–64.

Cote, M.; Nightingale, A. J. (2012). 'Resilience thinking meets social theory. Situating social change in socio-ecological systems (SES) research', *Progress in Human Geography*, 36(4), 475–89.

Crang, M.; Cook, I. (2007). *Doing ethnographies* (Los Angeles, London: SAGE).

Dannenberg, P. (2012). *Standards in internationalen Wertschöpfungsketten. Akteure, Ziele und Governance in der Obst- und Gemüse-Wertekette Kenia-EU* (Berlin: Lit-Verlag).

Dannenberg, P.; Kulke, E. (2014). 'Dynamics in agricultural value chains', *Die Erde*, 145(3), 121–6.

Dannenberg, P.; Revilla Diez, J. (2016). 'Socio-economic networks and value chains in the Global South – an institutional perspective', *Die Erde*, 147(3), 169–72.

Deleuze, G.; Guattari, F. (1988). *A thousand plateaus. Capitalism and schizophrenia* (London, New York: Continuum).

Derudder, B.; Witlox, F. (eds) (2010). *Commodity chains and world cities* (Chichester: Wiley-Blackwell).

Destatis (2017). *Land- und Forstwirtschaft, Fischerei. Landwirtschaftliche Bodennutzung: Anbau von Zierpflanzen* (Statistisches Bundesamt: Wiesbaden).

Dicken, P.; Kelly, P. F.; Olds, K.; Wai-Chung Yeung, H. (2001). *Chains and networks, territories and scales: towards a relational framework for analysing the global economy*, Global Networks, 1(2), 89–112.

Dittmann, J. (2018). '"Sometimes the lake misbehaves". Zur Politischen Ökologie der Fischerei im Naivasha-See, Kenia' (Berlin: wvb).

Dolan, C. S. (2007). 'Market Affections. Moral Encounters with Kenyan Fairtrade Flowers', *Ethnos*, 72(2), 239–61.

Dolan, C. S.; Tewari, M. (2001). 'From What We Wear to What We Eat Upgrading in Global Value Chains', *IDS Bulletin*, 32(3), 94–104.

Dörry, S. (2017). 'A review of Global Production Networks. Theorizing Economic Development in an Interconnected World By Neil M. Coe and Henry Wai-Chung Yeung', *Economic Geography*, 93(2), 209–11.

Dunaway, W. A. (2014a). 'Bringing Commodity Chain Analysis Back to Its

World-Systems Roots. Rediscovering Women's Work and Households', *Journal of World-Systems Research*, 20(1), 64–81.

Dunaway, W. A. (ed.) (2014b). *Gendered commodity chains. Seeing women's work and households in global production* (Stanford: Stanford University Press).

Dunaway, W. A. (2014c). 'Introduction', in: W. A. Dunaway (ed.), *Gendered commodity chains. Seeing women's work and households in global production* (Stanford: Stanford University Press), 1–24.

Ermann, U. (2005). *Regionalprodukte. Vernetzungen und Grenzziehungen bei der Regionalisierung von Nahrungsmitteln* (Stuttgart: Steiner).

Ettlinger, N. (2008). 'The predicament of firms in the new and old economies. A critical inquiry into traditional binaries in the study of the space-economy', *Progress in Human Geography*, 32(1), 45–69.

Everard, M.; Harper, D. (2002). 'Towards the sustainability of the Lake Naivasha Ramsar site and its catchment', *Hydrobiologia*, 488, 191–203.

Everard, M.; Vale, J. A.; Harper, D.; Tarras-Wahlberg, H. (2002). 'The physical attributes of the Lake Naivasha catchment rivers', *Hydrobiologia*, 488, 13–25.

Fairtrade Africa (2019). 'What is Fairtrade?'. Available at: https://www.fairtradeafrica.net/about-us/about-fairtrade/what-is-fairtrade/ [Accessed 30 May 2019].

Fairtrade International (2014). 'Fairtrade Standard for Hired Labour. Version 15.01.2014_v1.5'. Available at: https://www.fairtrade.net/fileadmin/user_upload/content/2009/standards/documents/generic-standards/HL_EN.pdf [Accessed 30 May 2019].

Fleury, A.; Fleury, M. T. (2001). 'Alternatives for Industrial Upgrading in Global Value Chains: The Case of the Plastics Industry in Brazil', *IDS Bulletin*, 32(3), 116–26.

FloraHolland (2015a). *Annual Report 2015* (Royal FloraHolland. Aalsmeer).

FloraHolland (2015b). *Consumer Study Rose 2015* (Royal FloraHolland: Aalsmeer).

FloraHolland (2017). *Annual Report 2017* (Royal FloraHolland. Aalsmeer).

FloraHolland (2020). *Annual Report 2020* (Royal FloraHolland. Aalsmeer).

Food & Water Watch (2008). 'Lake Naivasha. Withering Under the Assault of International Flower Vendors' (Washington, Ottawa: The Council of Canadians). Available at: http://www.foodandwatereurope.org/wp-content/uploads/2009/11/FoodandWaterEuropeLakeNavaisha.pdf [Accessed 1 July 2019].

Freidberg, S. (2001). 'On the trail of the global green bean. Methodological considerations in multi-site ethnography', *Global Networks*, 1(4), 353–68.

FSI (Floriculture Sustainability Initiative) (2015). 'FSI Equivalency Tool'. Available at: http://www.standardsmap.org/fsi/ [Accessed 22 March 2019].

Gereffi, G. (1994). 'The Organization of Buyer-Driven Global Commodity Chains: How U.S. Retailers Shape Overseas Production Networks', in: G. Gereffi, M. Korzeniewicz (eds), *Commodity chains and global capitalism* (Westport: Praeger Publishers), 95–122.

Gereffi, G. (1999). 'International trade and industrial upgrading in the apparel commodity chain', *Journal of International Economics*, 48(1), 37–70.

Gereffi, G. (2014). 'A Global Value Chain Perspective on Industrial Policy and Development in Emerging Markets', *Duke Journal of Comparative and International Law*, 24(3), 433–58.

Gereffi, G.; Humphrey, J.; Kaplinsky, R.; Sturgeon, T. (2001). 'Introduction: Globalisation, Value Chains and Development', *IDS Bulletin*, 32(3), 1–8.

Gereffi, G.; Humphrey, J.; Sturgeon, T. (2005). 'The governance of global value chains', *Review of International Political Economy*, 12(1), 78–104.

Gereffi, G.; Kaplinsky, R. (eds) (2001). 'The Value of Value Chains. Spreading the Gains from Globalisation', *IDS Bulletin*, 32(3).

Gereffi, G.; Korzeniewicz, M. (eds) (1994). *Commodity chains and global capitalism* (Westport: Praeger Publishers).

Gereffi, G.; Korzeniewicz, M.; Korzeniewicz, R. (1994). 'Introduction: Global Commodity Chains', in: G. Gereffi, M. Korzeniewicz (eds), *Commodity chains and global capitalism* (Westport: Praeger Publishers), 1–14.

Gerring, J. (2017). *Case study research. Principles and practices* (Cambridge: Cambridge University Press).

Gibbon, P. (2001). 'Agro-Commodity Chains. An Introduction', *IDS Bulletin*, 32(3), 60–8.

Gibbon, P.; Bair, J.; Ponte, S. (2008). 'Governing global value chains. An introduction', *Economy and Society*, 37(3), 315–38.

Gibbon, P.; Riisgaard, L. (2014). 'A New System of Labour Management in African Large-Scale Agriculture?', *Journal of Agrarian Change*, 14(1), 94–128.

Global Value Chains Initiative (2016). 'Concepts & Tools'. Available at: https://globalvaluechains.org/concept-tools [Accessed 28 February 2018].

Goffman, E. (1976). *Frame analysis. An essay on the organization of experience* (Cambridge, Mass.: Harvard University Press).

Goger, A. (2013). 'From Disposable to Empowered. Rearticulating Labor in Sri Lankan Apparel Factories', *Environment and Planning A*, 45(11), 2628–45.

Goody, J. (1993). *The culture of flowers* (Cambridge: Cambridge University Press).

Grabher, G. (1994). *The embedded firm. On the socioeconomics of industrial networks* (London: Routledge).

Grabher, G. (2006). 'Trading routes, bypasses, and risky intersections. Mapping the travels of "networks" between economic sociology and economic geography', *Progress in Human Geography*, 30(2), 163–89.

Granovetter, M. (1985). 'Economic Action and Social Structure. The Problem of Embeddedness', *American Journal of Sociology*, 91(3), 481–510.

Hale, A.; Opondo, M. (2005). 'Humanising the Cut Flower Chain: Confronting the Realities of Flower Production for Workers in Kenya', *Antipode*, 37(2), 301–23.

Hall, S. (1996). 'Race, articulation and societies structured in dominance', in: H. A. Baker, M. Diawara, R. H. Lindeborg (eds), *Black British cultural studies. A reader* (Chicago: University of Chicago Press), 16–60.

Happ, J. (2016). *Auswirkungen der Fairtrade-Zertifizierung auf den afrikanischen Blumenanbau. Das Beispiel Naivasha, Kenia* (Norderstedt: Books on Demand).

Harper, D. M.; Morrison, E. H. J.; Macharia, M. M.; Mavuti, K. M.; Upton, C. (2011). 'Lake Naivasha, Kenya: Ecology, Society and Future', *Freshwater Reviews*, 4(2), 89–114.

Hart, G. (2004). 'Geography and development. Critical ethnographies', *Progress in Human Geography*, 28(1), 91–100.

Harvey, D. (1990). 'Between space and time: Reflections in the geographical imagination', *Annals of the Association of American Geographers*, 80(3), 418–34.

Harvey, D. (2001). 'Gloablization and the "Spatial Fix"', *Geographische Revue*, 3(2), 23–30.

Harvey, D. (2005). *A Brief History of Neoliberalism* (Oxford: Oxford University Press).

Harvey, M. (2007). 'The Rise of Supermarkets and Asymmetries of Economic Power', in: G. Lawrence, D. Burch (eds), *Supermarkets and agri-food supply chains. Transformations in the production and consumption of foods* (Cheltenham, Northampton: E. Elgar), 51–73.

Havice, E.; Campling, L. (2013). 'Articulating Upgrading. Island Developing States and Canned Tuna Production', *Environment and Planning A*, 45(11), 2610–27.

Hayes, C. F. (1997). *Oserian. Place of Peace* (Nairobi: Rima Publications).

Henderson, J.; Dicken, P.; Hess, M.; Coe, N.; Yeung, H. W. -C. (2002). 'Global production networks and the analysis of economic development', *Review of International Political Economy*, 9(3), 436–64.

Hess, M. (2004). '"Spatial" relationships? Towards a reconceptualization of embeddedness', *Progress in Human Geography*, 28(2), 165–86.

Hinchliffe, S. (2007). *Geographies of nature. Societies, environments, ecologies* (Los Angeles, London: SAGE).

Hinchliffe, S.; Woodward, K. (eds) (2004). *The natural and the social. Uncertainty, risk and change* (London: Routledge).

Hopkins, T.; Wallerstein, I. (1977). 'Patterns of Development of the Modern World-System. Research Proposal', *Review (Fernand Braudel Center)*, 1(2), 111–45.

Hopkins, T.; Wallerstein, I. (1986). 'Commodity Chains in the World-Economy Prior to 1800', *Review (Fernand Braudel Center)*, 10(1), 157–70.

Hopkins, T.; Wallerstein, I. (1994a). 'Commodity Chains: Construct and Research', in: G. Gereffi, M. Korzeniewicz (eds), *Commodity chains and global capitalism* (Westport: Praeger Publishers), 17–20.

Hopkins, T.; Wallerstein, I. (1994b). 'Conclusions About Commodity Chains', in: G. Gereffi, M. Korzeniewicz (eds), *Commodity chains and global capitalism* (Westport: Praeger Publishers), 48–50.

Horner, R.; Nadvi, K. (2018). 'Global value chains and the rise of the Global South. Unpacking twenty-first century polycentric trade', *Global Networks*, 18(2), 207–37.

Hughes, A. (2000). 'Retailers, knowledges and changing commodity networks: the case of the cut flower trade', *Geoforum*, 31(2), 175–90.

Hughes, A. (2001). 'Global commodity networks, ethical trade and governmentality: organizing business responsibility in the Kenyan cut flower industry', *Transactions of the Institute of British Geographers*, 26(4), 390–406.

Hughes, A.; Reimer, S. (eds) (2004a). *Geographies of Commodity Chains* (New York: Routledge).

Hughes, A.; Reimer, S. (2004b). 'Introduction', in: A. Hughes, S. Reimer (eds), *Geographies of Commodity Chains* (New York: Routledge), 1–16.

Humphrey, J.; Schmitz, H. (2000). *Governance and upgrading. Linking industrial cluster and global value chain research* (Brighton: Institute of Development Studies).

Humphrey, J.; Schmitz, H. (2002). 'How does insertion in global value chains affect upgrading in industrial clusters?', *Regional Studies*, 36(9), 1017–27.

Hurt, S. R. (2003). 'Co-operation and coercion? The Cotonou Agreement between the European Union and acp states and the end of the Lomé Convention', *Third World Quarterly*, 24(1), 161–76.

Jackson, P. (2002). 'Commercial cultures: transcending the cultural and the economic', *Progress in Human Geography*, 26(1), 3–18.

Jones, A. (2008). 'Beyond embeddedness. Economic practices and the invisible dimensions of transnational business activity', *Progress in Human Geography*, 32(1), 71–88.

Jong, T. de (2011). *Water Abstraction Survey in Lake Naivasha Basin, Kenya* (Wageningen University: Wageningen).

Kaplinsky, R.; Morris, M. (2001). *A Handbook for Value Chain Research* (IDRC).

Kenya Human Rights Commission (2012). 'Wilting in bloom. The irony of women labour rights in the cut-flower sector in Kenya'. Available at: https://www.khrc.or.ke/publications/63-wilting-in-bloom-the-irony-of-women-s-labour-rights-in-the-cut-flower-sector-in-kenya/file.html [Accessed 3 June 2019].

Ketter, N. C.; Kariuki, W.; Wesonga, J. M.; Elings, A.; Hoogerwerf, F. (2015a). 'Vegetative growth of rose flower in cocopeat and soil in Naivasha, Kenya', *ISHS Acta Horticulturae*, 1104, 95–102.

Ketter, N. C.; Wesonga, J. M.; Wariara, K.; Elings, A.; Hoogerwerf, F. (2015b). 'Evaluation of a cocopeat-based substrate system for rose production in Naivasha, Kenya', *ISHS Acta Horticulturae*, 1077, 111–19.

Kim, H.; Lee, S. -H. (1994). 'Commodity Chains and the Korean Automobile Industry', in: G. Gereffi, M. Korzeniewicz (eds), *Commodity chains and global capitalism* (Westport: Praeger Publishers), 281–96.

Kimani, R.; Mwangi, B.; Gichuki, C. (2012). 'Treatment of flower farm wastewater effluents using constructed wetlands in Lake Naivasha, Kenya', *Indian Journal of Science and Technology*, 5(1), 1870–8.

KNBS (1969). *Kenya Population Census. Volume I* (Kenya National Bureau of Statistics. Nairobi).

KNBS (2010). *Kenya Population Census 2009* (Kenya National Bureau of Statistics. Nairobi).

KNBS (2018). 'Economic Survey 2018. Kenya National Bureau of Statistics'. Available at: https://www.knbs.or.ke/download/economic-survey-2018/ [Accessed 19 March 2019].

Kogut, B. (1985). 'Designing Global Strategies: Comparative and Competitive Value-Added Chains', *Sloan Management Review*, 26(4), 15–28.

Korovkin, T. (2003). 'Cut-Flower Exports, Female Labor, and Community Participation in Highland Ecuador', *Latin American Perspectives*, 30(4), 18–42.

Korzeniewicz, M. (1994). 'Commodity Chains and Marketing Strategies: Nike and the Global Athletic Footwear Industry', in: G. Gereffi, M. Korzeniewicz (eds), *Commodity chains and global capitalism* (Westport: Praeger Publishers), 247–65.

Kuhn, A.; Britz, W.; Willy, D. K.; van Oel, P. (2016). 'Simulating the viability of water institutions under volatile rainfall conditions – The case of the Lake Naivasha Basin', *Environmental Modelling & Software*, 75, 373–87.

Kuiper, G. (2019). *Agro-industrial Labour in Kenya. Cut Flower Farms and Migrant Workers' Settlements* (Cham: Palgrave Macmillan).

Kuiper, G.; Gemählich, A. (2017). 'Sustainability and Depoliticisation. Certifications in the Cut-Flower Industry at Lake Naivasha, Kenya', *Africa Spectrum*, 52(3), 31–53.

Kulke, E. (2008). 'Agrarian Clusters and Chains in Rural Areas of Germany and Poland', in: C. Stringer, R. Le Heron (eds), *Agri-food commodity chains and globalising networks* (Aldershot: Ashgate), 137–45.

Kwa, A.; Lunenborg, P.; Musonge, W. (2014). *African, Caribbean and Pacific (ACP) countries' position on Economic Partnership Agreements (EPAs)* (Luxembourg: EU Publications Office).

Lang, B.; Sakdapolrak, P. (2014). 'Belonging and recognition after the post-election violence: a case study on labour migrants in Naivasha, Kenya', *Erdkunde*, 68(3), 185–96.

Lang, B.; Sakdapolrak, P. (2015). 'Violent place-making. How Kenya's post-election violence transforms a workers' settlement at Lake Naivasha', *Political Geography*, 45, 67–78.

Latour, B. (1987). *Science in action. How to follow scientists and engineers through society* (Cambridge, Mass.: Harvard University Press).

Latour, B. (1993). *The pasteurization of France* (Cambridge, Mass., London: Harvard University Press).

Latour, B. (2001). *Das Parlament der Dinge. Für eine politische Ökologie* (Frankfurt am Main: Suhrkamp).

Latour, B. (2002). *We have never been modern* (Cambridge, Mass.: Harvard University Press).

Latour, B. (2009). *Reassembling the social. An introduction to actor-network-theory* (Oxford: Oxford University Press).

Latour, B. (2010). *Eine neue Soziologie für eine neue Gesellschaft. Einführung in die Akteur-Netzwerk-Theorie* (Frankfurt am Main: Suhrkamp).

Latour, B.; Woolgar, S. (1981). *Laboratory life. The social construction of scientific facts* (Beverly Hills: SAGE).

Law, J. (1999). 'After ANT: complexity, naming and topology', in: J. Law, J. Hassard (eds), *Actor Network Theory and After* (Oxford: Blackwell), 1–14.

Law, J.; Mol, A. (2001). 'Situating technoscience: an inquiry into spatialities', *Environment and Planning D*, 19(5), 609–21.

Lawrence, G.; Burch, D. (2007). 'Understanding Supermarkets and Agri-food Supply Chains', in: G. Lawrence, D. Burch (eds), *Supermarkets and agri-food supply chains. Transformations in the production and consumption of foods* (Cheltenham, Northampton: E. Elgar), 1–26.

Lee, N.; Cason, J. (1994). 'Automobile Commodity Chains in the NICs: A Comparison of South Korea, Mexico, and Brazil', in: G. Gereffi, M. Korzeniewicz (eds), *Commodity chains and global capitalism* (Westport: Praeger Publishers), 223–43.

Leslie, D.; Reimer, S. (1999). 'Spatializing commodity chains', *Progress in Human Geography*, 23(3), 401–20.

Levelt, M. (2010). *Global trade & the Dutch hub. Understanding variegated forms of embeddedness of international trade in the Netherlands: clothing, flowers, and high-tech products* (Oisterwijk: BOXPress).

Levy, D. L. (2008). 'Political Contestation in Global Production Networks', *Academy of Management Review*, 33(4), 943–63.

Lowery, R. S.; Mendes, A. J. (1977). 'Procambarus clarkii in Lake Naivasha, Kenya, and its effects on established and potential fisheries', *Aquaculture*, 11(2), 111–21..

Luetchford, P. (2011). 'Falling Foul of Fair: The Politics of Supply Chains', in: M. Warrier (ed.), *The politics of fair trade. A survey* (London, New York: Routledge), 53–67.

MacKenzie, D.; Muniesa, F.; Siu, L. (eds) (2007). *Do Economists Make Markets? On the Performativity of Economics* (Princeton: Princeton University Press).

Marcus, G. E. (1995). 'Ethnography in/of the World System. The Emergence of Multi-Sited Ethnography', *Annual Review of Anthropology*, 24 (1), 95–117.

Marshall, J. P.; Goodman, J. (2013). 'Disordering network theory. An introduction', *Global Networks*, 13(3), 279–89.

Marston, S. A.; Jones, J. P.; Woodward, K. (2005). 'Human geography without scale', *Transactions of the Institute of British Geographers*, 30(4), 416–32.

Massey, D. (1991). 'A Global Sense of Place', *Marxism Today*, June 1991, 24–9.

Mavuti, K. M.; Harper, D. (2006). 'The ecological state of Lake Naivasha, Kenya, 2005: Turning 25 years research into an effective Ramsar monitoring programme', in: E. Odada, D. Olago (eds), *Proceedings of the 11th World Lakes Conference* (Nairobi), 30–4McCormick, D. (2001). 'Value Chains and the Business System. Applying a Simplified Model to Kenya's Garment Industry', *IDS Bulletin*, 32(3), 105–15.

McMichael, P. (2005). 'Global Development and The Corporate Food Regime', *Research in rural sociology and development*, 11, 265–99.

McMichael, P. (2009). 'A food regime genealogy', *Journal of Peasant Studies*, 36(1), 139–69.

Mekonnen, M. M.; Hoekstra, A. Y.; Becht, R. (2012). 'Mitigating the Water Footprint of Export Cut Flowers from the Lake Naivasha Basin, Kenya', *Water Resources Management*, 26(13), 3725–42.

Moberg, M.; Lyon, S. M. (2010). 'What's Fair? The Paradox of Seeking Justice through Markets', in: S. M. Lyon, M. Moberg (eds), *Fair trade and Social justice. Global ethnographies* (New York: New York University Press), 1–24.

Müller, M. (2015). 'A half-hearted romance? A diagnosis and agenda for the relationship between economic geography and actor-network theory (ANT)', *Progress in Human Geography*, 39(1), 65–86.

Muniesa, F.; Millo, Y.; Callon, M. (2007). 'An introduction into market devices', in: M. Callon, Y. Millo, F. Muniesa (eds), *Market devices* (Malden: Blackwell), 1–12.

Murdoch, J. (1998). 'The Spaces of Actor-Network Theory', *Geoforum*, 29(4), 357–74.

Nadvi, K. (2008). 'Global standards, global governance and the organization of global value chains', *Journal of Economic Geography*, 8(3), 323–43.

Neilson, J. (2014). 'Value chains, neoliberalism and development practice. The

Indonesian experience', *Review of International Political Economy*, 21(1), 38–69.

Nevins, J.; Peluso, N. L. (2008). 'Commoditization in Southeast Asia', in: J. Nevins, N. L. Peluso (eds), *Taking Southeast Asia to market. Commodities, nature, and people in the neoliberal age* (Ithaca: Cornell University Press), 1–26.

Niebuhr, D. (2016). *Making Global Value Chains* (Wiesbaden: Springer Fachmedien).

Njogu, P.; Kitetu, J.; Keriko, J. (2010). 'Sustainable Ecosystem Management versus Economic Exploitation: A Case Study of Lake Naivasha Basin, Kenya', *Journal of Environmental Science and Engineering*, 4(7), 50–5.

Ogola, G. (2011). 'The Political Economy of the Media in Kenya. From Kenyatta's Nation-Building Press to Kibaki's Local-Language FM Radio', *Africa Today*, 57(3), 77–95.

Opondo, M. (2006). *Emerging Corporate Social Responsibility in Kenya's Cut Flower Industry* (University of Nairobi. Nairobi).

Otiang'a-Owiti, G. E.; Oswe, I. A. (2010). 'Human impact on lake ecosystems: the case of Lake Naivasha, Kenya', *African Journal of Aquatic Science*, 32(1), 79–88.

Ouma, S. (2010). 'Global Standards, Local Realities: Private Agrifood Governance and the Restructuring of the Kenyan Horticulture Industry', *Economic Geography*, 86(2), 197–222.

Ouma, S. (2015). *Assembling export markets. The making and unmaking of global food connections in West Africa* (Chichester, Malden: Wiley-Blackwell).

Ouma, S.; Boeckler, M.; Lindner, P. (2013). 'Extending the margins of marketization. Frontier regions and the making of agro-export markets in northern Ghana', *Geoforum*, 48, 225–35.

Oxford Dictionary (2018). 'Stakeholder'. Available at: www.en.oxforddictionaries.com/definition/stakeholder [Accessed 12 September 2018].

Oya, C.; Schaefer, F.; Skalidou, D.; McCosker, C.; Langer, L. (2017). *Effects of certification schemes for agricultural production on socio-economic outcomes in low- and middle-income countries. A systematic review* (London: The Campbell Collaboration).

Oyugi, D. O.; Mavuti, K. M.; Aloo, P. A.; Ojuok, J. E.; Britton, J. R. (2014). 'Fish habitat suitability and community structure in the equatorial Lake Naivasha, Kenya', *Hydrobiologia*, 727, 51–63.

Özveren, E. (1994). 'The Shipbuilding Commodity Chain, 1590-1790', in: G. Gereffi, M. Korzeniewicz (eds), *Commodity chains and global capitalism* (Westport: Praeger Publishers), 20–34.

Palpacuer, F. (2008). 'Bringing the social context back in: governance and wealth distribution in global commodity chains', *Economy and Society*, 37(3), 393–419.

Patel-Campillo, A. (2011). 'Transforming Global Commodity Chains. Actor Strategies, Regulation, and Competitive Relations in the Dutch Cut Flower Sector', *Economic Geography*, 87(1), 79–99.

Peters, E. D. (2008). 'GCCs and Development. A Conceptual and Empirical Review', *Competition & Change*, 12(1), 11–27.

Piore, M. J.; Sabel, C. F. (1984). *The second industrial divide. Possibilities for prosperity* (New York: Basic Books).

Polanyi, K. (1978). 'The great transformation. Politische und ökonomische Ursprünge von Gesellschaften und Wirtschaftssystemen' (Frankfurt am Main: Suhrkamp).

Ponte, S.; Ewert, J. (2009). 'Which Way is "Up" in Upgrading? Trajectories of Change in the Value Chain for South African Wine', *World Development*, 37(10), 1637–50.

Ponte, S.; Gibbon, P. (2005). 'Quality standards, conventions and the governance of global value chains', *Economy and Society*, 34(1), 1–31.

Porter, M. E. (1998). *The competitive advantage of nations* (London: Macmillan Business).

Quetsch, J. (2021). 'The market for flowers and ornamental plants grew in 2020 – despite pandemic', *BGI – Close to Green*, 1, 4–20. Available at: https://bgi-ev.de/data/2021/02/BGI-Magazin_Fr%C3%BChjahr_2021-f%C3%BCr-WEbsite.pdf [Accessed 16 October 2021].

Raikes, P.; Friis Jensen, M.; Ponte, S. (2000). 'Global commodity chain analysis and the French filière approach: comparison and critique', *Economy and Society*, 29(3), 390–417.

Raynólds, L. (1994). 'Institutionalizing Flexibility: A Comparative Analysis of Fordist and Post-Fordist Models of Third World Agro-Export Production', in: G. Gereffi, M. Korzeniewicz (eds), *Commodity chains and global capitalism* (Westport: Praeger Publishers), 143–61.

Raynolds, L. (2012). 'Fair Trade Flowers. Global Certification, Environmental Sustainability, and Labor Standards', *Rural Sociology*, 77(4), 493–519.

Riisgaard, L. (2007). 'What's in it for labour? Private Social Standards in the Cut flower industries of Kenya and Tanzania'. Available at: https://www.econstor.eu/bitstream/10419/84538/1/DIIS2007-16.pdf [Accessed 21 October 2021].

Riisgaard, L. (2009a). 'Global Value Chains, Labor Organization and Private Social Standards: Lessons from East African Cut Flower Industries', *World Development*, 37(2), 326–40.

Riisgaard, L. (2009b). *How the market for standards shapes competition in the market for goods. Sustainability standards in the cut flower industry* (Copenhagen: DIIS Working Paper, 2009/7).

Riisgaard, L. (2010). 'The political economy of private social standards in the cut flower industry', in: P. Gibbon, S. Ponte, E. Lazaro (eds), *Global Agro-Food Trade and Standards* (London: Palgrave Macmillan), 136–61.

Riisgaard, L. (2011). 'Towards more stringent sustainability standards? Trends in the cut flower industry', *Review of African Political Economy*, 38(129), 435–53.

Riisgaard, L.; Gibbon, P. (2014). 'Labour Management on Contemporary Kenyan Cut Flower Farms. Foundations of an Industrial-Civic Compromise', *Journal of Agrarian Change*, 14(2), 260–85.

Rikken, M. (2012). 'Kenya Flower Industry Global Competitiveness Report'. Available at: http://proverde.nl/wp-content/uploads/2015/04/ProVerde-Kenya-Flower-Industry-Global-Competiveness-Report.pdf?289be7 [Accessed 23 March 2019].

Robbins, P.; Marks, B. (2010). 'Assemblage Geographies', in: S. Smith, R. Pain,

S. Marston, J. P. Jones, III (eds), *The SAGE handbook of social geography* (London: SAGE), 176–94.

Robinson, W. I. (2008). *Latin America and Global Capitalism. A Critical Globalization Perspective* (Baltimore: Johns Hopkins University Press).

Rockoff, T. E.; Groves, M. (1995). 'Design of an Internet-based system for remote Dutch auctions', *Internet Research*, 5(4), 10–16.

Rose, G. (1997). 'Situating knowledges. Positionality, reflexivities and other tactics', *Progress in Human Geography*, 21(3), 305–20.

Rouillé, G.; Blanchon, D.; Calas, B.; Temple-Boyer, É. (2015). 'Environnement, écologisation du politique et territorialisations. Les nouvelles politiques de l'eau (gire et pse) au Kenya', *Espace géographique*, 44(2), 131–46.

Ruming, K. (2009). 'Following the Actors. Mobilising an actor-network theory methodology in geography', *Australian Geographer*, 40(4), 451–69.

Sassen, S. (2010). 'Global inter-city networks and commodity chains. Any intersections?', *Global Networks*, 10(1), 150–63.

Savelli, E.; Schwartz, K.; Ahlers, R. (2019). 'The Dutch aid and trade policy. Policy discourses versus development practices in the Kenyan water and sanitation sector', *Environment and Planning C*, 37(6), 1126–47.

Schmitz, H.; Nadvi, K. (1999). 'Clustering and Industrialization. Introduction', *World Development*, 27(9), 1503–14.

Scholvin, S.; Revilla Diez, J.; Breul, M. (2017). 'Neil M. Coe and Henry W. Yeung: Global Production Networks. Theorizing Economic Development in an Interconnected World', *Zeitschrift für Wirtschaftsgeographie*, 61(2). 117-8

Seal, M. (2011). *Wildflower. The Extraordinary Life and Mysterious Murder of Joan Root* (London: Orion Books).

Selwyn, B. (2012). 'Beyond firm-centrism: re-integrating labour and capitalism into global commodity chain analysis', *Journal of Economic Geography*, 12(1), 205–26.

Selwyn, B. (2013). 'Social Upgrading and Labour in Global Production Networks. A Critique and an Alternative Conception', *Competition & Change*, 17(1), 75–90.

Selwyn, B. (2015). 'Commodity chains, creative destruction and global inequality: a class analysis', *Journal of Economic Geography*, 15(2), 253–74.

Selwyn, B. (2016). 'Global value chains and human development. A class-relational framework', *Third World Quarterly*, 37(10), 1768–86.

Singh, P. (2013). 'No Roses Without Thorns: Global Consumers of Cut Flowers as Political Actors', *Kentucky Journal of Equine, Agriculture & Natural Resources Law*, 6(1), 23–57.

Smith, S.; Barrientos, S. (2005). 'Fair Trade and Ethical Trade. Are There Moves Towards Convergence?', *Sustainable Development*, 13(3), 190–8.

Starosta, G. (2010). 'Global Commodity Chains and the Marxian Law of Value', *Antipode*, 42(2), 433–65.

Sturgeon, T. (2009). 'From Commodity Chains to Value Chains: Interdisciplinary Theory Building in an Age of Globalization', in: J. Bair (ed.), *Frontiers of Commodity Chain Research* (Stanford: Stanford University Press), 110–35.

Sturgeon, T. J. (2001). 'How Do We Define Value Chains and Production Networks?', *IDS Bulletin*, 32(3), 9–18.

Styles, M. A. (2019). *Roses from Kenya. Labor, environment, and the global trade in cut flowers* (Seattle: University of Washington Press).

Swyngedouw, E. (2014). 'Where is the political? Insurgent mobilisations and the incipient "return of the political"', *Space and Polity*, 18(2), 122–36.

Taglioni, D.; Winkler, D. (2016). *Making Global Value Chains Work for Development* (Washington, DC: World Bank Group).

Tallontire, A.; Opondo, M.; Nelson, V.; Martin, A. (2011). 'Beyond the vertical? Using value chains and governance as a framework to analyse private standards initiatives in agri-food chains', *Agriculture and Human Values*, 28(3), 427–41.

Tarafdar, S.; Harper, D. (2008). 'Anti-persistence in levels of Lake Naivasha: Assessing effect of human intervention through time-series analysis', *Physica A: Statistical Mechanics and its Applications*, 387(1), 296–302.

Thrift, N.; Olds, K. (1996). 'Refiguring the economic in economic geography', *Progress in Human Geography*, 20(3), 311–37.

Topik, S. (2009). 'Historizing Commodity Chains. Five Hundred Years of the Global Coffee Commodity Chain', in: J. Bair (ed.), *Frontiers of Commodity Chain Research* (Stanford: Stanford University Press), 37–62.

TransFair (2017). 'Blumen und Pflanzen. Fact Sheet' (Köln: Fairtrade Deutschland). Available at: https://www.fairtrade-deutschland.de/fileadmin/DE/mediathek/pdf/fairtrade_blumen_und_pflanzen_factsheet.pdf [Accessed 15 April 2019].

Trillo, R.; Constable, H.; Heuler, H.; Williams, L. (2016). *The Rough Guide to Kenya* (London: Rough Guides).

UNESCO (1971). 'Convention on Wetlands of International Importance especially as Waterfowl Habitat, Ramsar, Iran, revised Amendments of 5/28/1987'. Available at: https://www.ramsar.org/sites/default/files/documents/library/current_convention_text_e.pdf [Accessed 19 April 2019].

van Heck, E.; Ribbers, P. (1997). 'Experiences With Electronic Auctions in the Dutch Flower Industry', *Electronic Markets*, 7(4), 29–34.

van Horen, L. (2017a). 'Chain organisation in European floriculture' (Utrecht: Rabobank). Available at: https://services.rabobank.com/publicationservice/download/publication/token/7bNkYlmZa49Jeg9izwhY [Accessed 1 July 2019].

van Horen, L. (2017b). 'Changes in consumer behaviour' (Utrecht: Rabobank). Available at: https://services.rabobank.com/publicationservice/download/publication/token/dVcwM0nZtDWE7TsIhSz2 [Accessed 1 July 2019].

van Horen, L. (2017c). 'Internationalisation strategy' (Utrecht: Rabobank). Available at: https://services.rabobank.com/publicationservice/download/publication/token/fxYlyPNidbT0XFlsYZG8 [Accessed 1 July 2019].

van Liemt, G. (1999). *The world cut flower industry. Trends and prospect* (Geneva: International Labor Organization).

Verschuren, D.; Laird, K. R.; Cumming, B. F. (2000). 'Rainfall and drought in equatorial east Africa during the past 1,100 years', *Nature*, 403, 410–14.

Verstoep, J. (2015). 'Challenges in water management in the Lake Naivasha Basin. Analysis on the effects and performance of IWRAP for different irrigation water user groups in the Lake Naivasha Basin, Kenya' (Wageningen: Wageningen University). Available at: http://edepot.wur.nl/345816 [Accessed 24 April 2019].

Wallerstein, I. (1974). *The Modern World-System I. Capitalist Agriculture and the Origins of the European World-Economy in the Sixteenth Century* (New York: Academic Press).

Wallerstein, I. (1980). *The Modern World-System II. Mercantilism and the Consolidation of the European World-Econmy, 1600–1750* (New York: Academic).

Wallerstein, I. (2001). *The modern World-System III. The second era of great expansion of the capitalist world-economy 1730–1840s* (New York: Academic Press).

Werner, M.; Bair, J.; Fernández, V. R. (2014). 'Linking Up to Development? Global Value Chains and the Making of a Post-Washington Consensus', *Development and Change*, 45(6), 1219–47.

Whatmore, S. (2002). *Hybrid Geographies. Natures Cultures Spaces* (London: SAGE).

Whatmore, S. (2005). 'Hybrid Geographies. Author's Responses and Reflections', *Antipode*, 37(4), 842–5.

White, H. C. (2004). *Markets from networks. Socioeconomic models of production* (Princeton, Woodstock: Princeton University Press).

Williamson, O. E. (1985). 'The economic institutions of capitalism. Firms, markets, relational contracting' (New York: Free Press).

Wilson, B. R. (2013). 'Breaking the Chains. Coffee, Crisis, and Farmworker Struggle in Nicaragua', *Environment and Planning A*, 45(11), 2592–609.

World Bank (2018). 'Global Value Chains' (Washington: The World Bank Group). Available at: http://www.worldbank.org/en/topic/global-value-chains [Accessed 6 March 2018].

Yeung, H. W. -C.; Coe, N. M. (2015). 'Toward a Dynamic Theory of Global Production Networks', *Economic Geography*, 91(1), 29–58.

Ziegler, C. (2007). *Favored flowers. Culture and economy in a global system* (Durham: Duke University Press).

Zierhofer, W. (1999). 'Geographie der Hybriden', *Erdkunde*, 53(1), 1–13.

Other Media Sources

Kelly, N., 'No bed of roses: The Kenyan flower pickers fighting sexual harassment', *BBC News*, 5 March 2017. Available at: https://www.bbc.com/news/business-39103419 [Accessed 24 October 2021].

Killelea, A., 'Valentine's Day roses: The real cost of your cheap flowers', *Mirror Online*, 13 February 2015. Available at: https://www.mirror.co.uk/money/valentines-day-roses-reviewed-how-7345790 [Accessed 24 October 2021].

Lawrence, F., 'The true cost of Mother's Day flowers', *The Guardian*, 4 April 2011. Available at: https://www.youtube.com/watch?v=cdcqg4CroYo [Accessed 24 October 2021].

Richter, M., 'Billig-Rosen: Afrikaner zahlen mit ihrer Gesundheit (Cheap Roses: Africans pay with their health)', *Panorama*, 18 August 2011. Available at: https://daserste.ndr.de/panorama/archiv/2011/-,panorama13474.html [Accessed 24 October 2021].

Smithers, R., 'Growing Valentine's Day roses harming Kenya's ecological state', *The Guardian*, 14 February 2011. Available at: https://www.theguardian.com/environment/2011/feb/14/valentines-day-roses-kenya [Accessed 24 October 2021].

INDEX

Future Rural Africa

Printed in the United States
by Baker & Taylor Publisher Services